LIBRARY OF NEW TESTAM

605

formerly the Journal for the Study of the New Testament Supplement series

Editor
Chris Keith

Editorial Board
Dale C. Allison, John M.G. Barclay, Lynn H. Cohick,
R. Alan Culpepper, Craig A. Evans, Robert Fowler,
Simon J. Gathercole, Juan Hernandez Jr., John S. Kloppenborg,
Michael Labahn, Love L. Sechrest, Robert Wall, Steve Walton,
Catrin H. Williams

THE FEAR OF GOD IN 2 CORINTHIANS 7:1

Its Meaning, Function, and Eschatological Context

Euichang Kim

LONDON • NEW YORK • OXFORD • NEW DELHI • SYDNEY

T&T CLARK
Bloomsbury Publishing Plc
50 Bedford Square, London, WC1B 3DP, UK
1385 Broadway, New York, NY 10018, USA

BLOOMSBURY, T&T CLARK and the T&T Clark logo are trademarks of
Bloomsbury Publishing Plc

First published in Great Britain 2019
Paperback edition published 2020

Copyright © Euichang Kim, 2019

Euichang Kim has asserted his right under the Copyright, Designs and Patents Act, 1988,
to be identified as Author of this work.

For legal purposes the Acknowledgements on p. xi constitute
an extension of this copyright page.

All rights reserved. No part of this publication may be reproduced or transmitted
in any form or by any means, electronic or mechanical, including photocopying,
recording, or any information storage or retrieval system, without prior permission
in writing from the publishers.

Bloomsbury Publishing Plc does not have any control over, or responsibility for, any
third-party websites referred to or in this book. All internet addresses given in this
book were correct at the time of going to press. The author and publisher regret
any inconvenience caused if addresses have changed or sites have ceased to exist,
but can accept no responsibility for any such changes.

A catalogue record for this book is available from the British Library.

A catalogue record for this book is available from the Library of Congress.

Library of Congress Cataloging-in-Publication Data

ISBN: HB: 978-0-5676-8493-6
        PB: 978-0-5676-9613-7
        ePDF: 978-0-5676-8494-3
        ePUB: 978-0-5676-8496-7

Series: Library of New Testament Studies, 2345678X, volume 605

Typeset by RefineCatch Limited, Bungay, Suffolk

To find out more about our authors and books visit www.bloomsbury.com
and sign up for our newsletters.

CONTENTS

List of Abbreviations	viii
Acknowledgements	xi

Chapter 1
INTRODUCTION — 1
- I. Status Quaestionis — 3
- II. The Problem Raised by Lexicography — 5
  1. The Meaning of the Fear of God in the OT — 6
  2. The Meaning of the Fear of God in the NT — 8
- III. Methodology — 10
- IV. Summary of Thesis — 19
- V. Outline of the Thesis — 20

Chapter 2
THE FEAR OF GOD WITHIN THE CONTEXT OF 2 CORINTHIANS — 23
- I. The Fear of God within the Immediate Context of 2 Cor 7:1 — 23
  1. The Literary Structure of 2 Cor 6:14–7:1 — 23
  2. The Semantic Relationship between 2 Cor 7:1 and the Catena of Scripture — 26
- II. The Fear of God within the Larger Context of 2 Corinthians — 30
  1. The Fear of the Lord in 2 Cor 5:11 — 30
  2. The Judgment Seat of Christ in 2 Cor 5:10 — 33
     1) Who Will Judge? — 35
     2) Who Will Be Judged? — 38
  3. The Content of Paul's Fear in 2 Cor 6:1 — 40
  4. Who Is the Lord in 2 Cor 5:11? — 44
     1) The Context — 46
     2) The Solitary Use of Κύριος — 46
     3) The OT Background — 50
- III. The Isaianic Context of 2 Cor 4–6 and the Fear of God — 53

Chapter 3
THE FEAR OF GOD WITHIN THE CONTEXT OF THE CATENA OF SCRIPTURE — 57
- I. The Fear of God within Its Isaianic Context — 57
  1. The Isaiah Text — 59
  2. The Fear of God as a Response to God's Deliverance — 61

II.	The Fear of God in the Context of Isa 50:4–52:11	64
1.	The Literary Structure of Isa 50:4–51:8	64
2.	The Immediate Context of the Fear of God	67
3.	The Significance of the Fear of God in Isa 50:10–11	71
4.	The Fear of God and God's Commands in Isa 52:11	74
III.	The Fear of God in The Context of Lev 26:11–12	77
1.	Fear in Leviticus	78
2.	The Structure of Lev 26	80
3.	The Covenant Formula	82
IV.	The Fear of God in the Context of the New Covenant	84
1.	Ezekiel	85
2.	Jeremiah	90
V.	Conclusion	92

Chapter 4
THE FEAR OF GOD WITHIN THE CONTEXT OF SECOND TEMPLE JUDAISM

		95
I.	2 Cor 6:14–7:1 Within the Context of Second Temple Judaism	95
II.	The Psalms of Solomon	98
1.	The Fear of God and the Theme of Judgment in the Psalms	98
2.	The Fear of God in Ps. Sol. 17	100
3.	The Psalms as Background for the Fear of God in 2 Cor 7:1	102
III.	The Book of Jubilees	102
1.	The Similarities between Jubilees and 2 Cor 6:14–7:1	103
2.	The Theme of Judgment in Jubilees	107
3.	The Fear of God in Jubilees	109
4.	Jubilees as Background for the Fear of God in 2 Cor 7:1	111
IV.	4 Ezra and 6 Ezra	112
1.	4 Ezra and 6 Ezra	113
2.	The Fear of God and the Theme of Judgment in 4 Ezra	114
3.	4 Ezra as Background for the Fear of God in 2 Cor 7:1	118
V.	The Testaments of the Twelve Patriarchs	118
1.	The Jewish and Christian Backgrounds of the Testaments	119
2.	Ethics and the Fear of God in the Testaments	121
3.	The Fear of God in the Testament of Benjamin	125
4.	The Testaments as Background for the Fear of God in 2 Cor 7:1	127
VI.	The Fear of God within the Spectrum of Second Temple Judaism	128

Chapter 5
THE FEAR OF GOD WITHIN PAUL'S ESCHATOLOGY

		131
I.	The Fear of God and the Integrity of 2 Cor 7:1	131
1.	Interpolation Theories	132
2.	The Salvation-Historical Hermeneutic	136

		3. The Fear of God and the Past Approaches to 2 Cor 6:14–7:1	138
	II.	The Argument of 2 Cor 7: 1	139
		1. Having These Promises	140
		2. Let Us Cleanse Ourselves from Every Defilement of Flesh and Spirit	143
		3. Completing Holiness	145
		4. In the Fear of God	150
	III.	Paul's Eschatology and the Fear of God	151
		1. Temple Purity	154
		2. The Command to Separate	157

Chapter 6
CONCLUSION 161
   I. Overview 161
   II. Implications for Reading Second Corinthians 163
      1. 2 Cor 7:5, 11, 15 163
      2. 2 Cor 11:3; 12:20–1 166

Bibliography of Works Cited 169
Biblical Citations Index 181
General Index 183

LIST OF ABBREVIATIONS

AB	Anchor Bible
ABD	*Anchor Bible Dictionary*. Edited by David Noel Freedman. 6 vols. New York: Doubleday, 1992
AnBib	Analecta Biblica
AOTC	Abingdon Old Testament Commentaries
AVTRW	Aufsätze und Vorträge zur Theologie und Religionswissenschaft
BDAG	Danker, Frederick W., Walter Bauer, William F. Arndt, and F. Wilbur Gingrich. *Greek–English Lexicon of the New Testament and Other Early Christian Literature*. 3rd ed. Chicago: University of Chicago Press, 2000 (Danker-Bauer-Arndt-Gingrich)
BECNT	Baker Exegetical Commentary on the New Testament
BETL	Bibliotheca Ephemeridum Theologicarum Lovaniensium
BFT	Biblical Foundations in Theology
BHT	Beiträge zur historischen Theologie
BNTC	Black's New Testament Commentaries
BTAS	Biblical Tools and Studies
BTCB	Brazos Theological Commentary on the Bible
BZAW	Beihefte zur Zeitschrift für die alttestamentliche Wissenschaft
BZNW	Beihefte zur Zeitschrift für die neutestamentliche Wissenschaft
CB	Century Bible
CBET	Contributions to Biblical Exegesis and Theology
CBQ	*Catholic Biblical Quarterly*
CRINT	Compendia Rerum Iudaicarum ad Novum Testamentum
COQG	Christian Origins and the Question of God
CSCO	Corpus Scriptorum Christianorum Orientalium. Edited by Jean Baptiste Chabot et al. Paris, 1903
CurBR	*Currents in Biblical Research* (formerly *Currents in Research: Biblical Studies*)
DBIM	*Dictionary of Biblical Imagery*. Edited by Leland Ryken, James C. Wilhoit, and Tremper Longman III. Downers Grove, IL: InterVarsity Press, 1998
DLNT	*Dictionary of the Later New Testament and Its Developments*. Edited by Ralph P. Martin and Peter H. Davids. Downers Grove, IL: InterVarsity Press, 1997
DPL	*Dictionary of Paul and His Letters*. Edited by Gerald F. Hawthorne and Ralph P. Martin. Downers Grove, IL: InterVarsity Press, 1993
EBib	Etudes bibliques
EC	Epworth Commentary
ECC	Eerdmans Critical Commentary
EDEJ	*The Eerdmans Dictionary of Early Judaism*. Edited by John Joseph Collins and Daniel C. Harlow. Grand Rapids; Cambridge: Eerdmans, 2010

EDSS	*Encyclopedia of the Dead Sea Scrolls*. Edited by Lawrence H. Schiffman and James C. VanderKam. 2 vols. New York: Oxford University Press, 2000
EKK	Evangelisch-Katholischer Kommentar zum Neuen Testament
FAT	Forschungen zum Alten Testament
FRLANT	Forschungen zur Religion und Literatur des Alten und Neuen Testaments
GAP	Guides to Apocrypha and Pseudepigrapha
HAR	*Hebrew Annual Review*
HCOT	Historical Commentary on the Old Testament
HTS	Harvard Theological Studies
ICC	International Critical Commentary
Int	*Interpretation*
ISCO	International Studies on Christian Origins
ITC	International Theological Commentary
IVPNTC	The IVP New Testament Commentary Series
JAARSup	Journal of the American Academy of Religion Supplements
JBL	*Journal of Biblical Literature*
JCTCRS	Jewish and Christian Texts in Contexts and Related Studies
JSHRZ	*Jüdische Schriften aus hellenistisch-römischer Zeit*
JSJSup	Supplements to the Journal for the Study of Judaism
JSNT	*Journal for the Study of the New Testament*
JSNTSup	Journal for the Study of the New Testament Supplement Series
JSOT	*Journal for the Study of the Old Testament*
LCL	Loeb Classical Library
LNTS	The Library of New Testament Studies
NAC	New American Commentary
NCBC	New Cambridge Bible Commentary
NDBT	*New Dictionary of Biblical Theology*. Edited by T. Desmond Alexander and Brian S. Rosner. Downers Grove, IL: InterVarsity Press, 2000
NETS	*A New English Translation of the Septuagint*. Edited by Albert Pietersma and Benjamin G. Wright. New York: Oxford University Press, 2007
NIBCNT	New International Biblical Commentary on the New Testament
NIBCOT	New International Biblical Commentary on the Old Testament
NICNT	New International Commentary on the New Testament
NICOT	New International Commentary on the Old Testament
NIDTTE	*New International Dictionary of New Testament Theology and Exegesis*. Edited by Moisés Silva. 5 vols. Grand Rapids: Zondervan, 2014
NIGTC	New International Greek Testament Commentary
NIVAC	NIV Application Commentary
NovT	*Novum Testamentum*
NovTSup	Supplements to Novum Testamentum
NSBT	New Studies in Biblical Theology
NTAbh	Neutestamentliche Abhandlungen
NTL	New Testament Library
NTS	*New Testament Studies*
OTG	Old Testament Guide
OTL	Old Testament Library

OTS	Old Testament Studies
OtSt	*Oudtestamentische Studiën*
PNTC	Pillar New Testament Commentary
RRA	Rhetoric of Religious Antiquity
RB	*Revue biblique*
RTR	*Reformed Theological Review*
SBLEJL	SBL Early Judaism and Its Literature
SBLSymS	SBL Symposium Series
SNTSMS	Society for New Testament Studies Monograph Series
SP	Sacra Pagina
STDJ	Studies on the Texts of the Desert of Judah
SUNT	Studien zur Umwelt des Neuen Testaments
SVTG	Septuaginta Vetus Testamentum Graecum
SVTP	Studia in Veteris Testamenti Pseudepigrapha
TDNT	*Theological Dictionary of the New Testament*. Edited by Gerhard Kittel and Gerhard Friedrich. Translated by Geoffrey W. Bromiley. 10 vols. Grand Rapids: Eerdmans, 1964–1976
TDOT	*Theological Dictionary of the Old Testament*. Edited by G. Johannes Botterweck and Helmer Ringgren. Translated by John T. Willis et al. 8 vols. Grand Rapids: Eerdmans, 1974–2006
THKNT	Theologischer Handkommentar zum Neuen Testament
TLOT	*Theological Lexicon of the Old Testament*. Edited by Ernst Jenni, with assistance from Claus Westermann. Translated by Mark E. Biddle. 3 vols. Peabody, MA: Hendrickson, 1997
TNTC	Tyndale New Testament Commentaries
VT	*Vetus Testamentum*
VTSup	Supplements to Vetus Testamentum
WBC	Word Biblical Commentary
WTJ	*Westminster Theological Journal*
WUNT	Wissenschaftliche Untersuchungen zum Neuen Testament
ZAW	*Zeitschrift für die alttestamentliche Wissenschaft*
ZNW	*Zeitschrift für die neutestamentliche Wissenschaft*

ACKNOWLEDGEMENTS

This study is a revised version of my doctoral dissertation completed in 2017 at the University of St. Andrews. First and foremost, I want to give thanks to God. It was only for Him I started my studies and it is only by Him I could complete this project. God has shown His great faithfulness to me through the many people who have helped to make this book possible in one way or another.

Special acknowledgment is due to my mentor and *Doktorvater*, Dr. Scott Hafemann, who has been a model of scholarship for me. His excellence in scholarship and exegetical skills, and also his passion and sincerity regarding the Bible, have made a great impact upon me throughout my studies. They will continue to have an influence upon my development as a student and scholar of the Bible. I also want to give thanks to my *Doktormutter*, Debara Hafemann, whose hearty encouragement and love have supported me and my family throughout the program. I would also like to thank Dr. David Moffitt and Dr. David Starling for their helpful comments as internal and external examiners of my original thesis.

Gratitude must also be expressed to my parents Sung-Bong Kim and Sun-Sook Joo, from whom I inherited and learned my faith in Christ and the Bible. Their constant encouragement, support, and love have carried me through the journey. I am also grateful to my extended family, Helen, Yousu, Libby, and Marc for their unwavering support.

Writing a doctoral dissertation cannot be done in solitude, but requires constant support and encouragement from a community. Thus, my gratitude goes to my colleagues at the University of St. Andrews and at Westminster Theological Seminary, in particular Janghoon Park, Jihye Lee, Minsu Lee, Tim Fox, Jen Gilbertson, Isaac Blois, Kai Akagi, and Steven Jo, who provided many helpful comments, insights, and encouragement along the way.

I also want to thank many churches and church members around the world (in Korea, the US, the UK, Germany, etc.) who have supported and prayed for our family. Special thanks to Mr. B. Sohn and Mrs. N. Kim, Mr. D. Han and Mrs. Y. Lee, Mr. T. Kim, Mr. J. Lee and Mrs. J. Cho, and Mr. S. Kim for their generous support in more ways than can be counted.

Last, but definitely not least, I am overflowing with thankfulness for my wife Durum, who is my better half. Her constant love, help, and sacrifice are invaluable gifts, as is our son, Joshua. I thank and praise God for my family, who have been the most wonderful partners in this endeavor. As such, it is to them I lovingly dedicate this book.

Soli Deo Gloria
Euichang Kim
Seoul, South Korea, July 2018

Chapter 1

INTRODUCTION

The purpose of this study is to set forth a hypothesis regarding the meaning and function of "the fear of God" in Paul's theology by examining its role in 2 Cor 7:1 within its literary context and salvation-history.[1] Although "the fear of God" is a significant theme in the OT, from which Paul derived the main lines of his thought, his use of the motif has seldom been studied. This is striking given the fact that Paul mentions "fear" repeatedly in his letters, employing a range of terminology.[2] Moreover, 2 Cor 7:1, as the climax of the argument of 6:14–7:1, is arguably the most significant place to begin in understanding Paul's use of the fear of God because it is the only place, where, in one setting, Paul: (1) uses fear with explicit reference to God (φόβος θεοῦ), (2) requires it of believers,[3] and (3) relates it to an OT source.[4]

---

1. By "salvation-history" I am working on a "fulfillment" model of the relationship between the Scriptural texts and Paul's perspective in which the fulfillment is viewed to be a "salvific" in its implications. I will discuss this more in detail in Chapter Five.

2. Terms related to fear (φοβέω, φοβέομαι, φόβος, ἀφόβως) appear a total of twenty-six times in the Pauline corpus: "fear" (φόβος) in Rom 8:15; 13:3 (2x), 7 (2x); 2 Cor 7:5, 11; 1 Tim 5:20; "to fear" (φοβέω, φοβέομαι) in Rom 11:20; 13:4; 2 Cor 11:3; 12:20; Gal 2:12; 4:11; Eph 5:33; Col 3:22; "without fear" (ἀφόβως) in 1 Cor 16:10; Phil 1:14; "fear of God" (φόβος θεοῦ) in Rom 3:18; 2 Cor 7:1; "fear of the Lord" (φόβος τοῦ κυρίου) in 2 Cor 5:11; "fear of Christ" (φόβος Χριστοῦ) in Eph 5:21; and "fear and trembling" (φόβος καὶ τρόμος) in 1 Cor 2:3; 2 Cor 7:15; Phil 2:12; Eph 6:5.

3. In Rom 3:18, the other place where the fear of God appears, it describes the unbelievers, "who do not have the fear of God in their eyes."

4. In the present work, I am following those scholars who have argued for the Pauline authorship and/or integrity of 2 Cor 6:14–7:1 in its present location within 2 Corinthians, e.g., William J. Webb, *Returning Home: New Covenant and Second Exodus as the Context for 2 Corinthians 6.14–7.1*, JSNTSup 85 (Sheffield: JSOT Press, 1993); Reimund Bieringer, "2 Korinther 6,14–7,1 im Kontext des 2. Korintherbriefes. Forschungsüberblick und Versuch eines eigenes Zugangs," in *Studies on 2 Corinthians*, ed. Reimund Bieringer and Jan Lambrecht, BETL 122 (Leuven: Leuven University Press; Peeters, 1994), 551–70; G. K. Beale, "The Old Testament Background of Reconciliation in 2 Corinthians 5–7 and

Because of its uncommon vocabulary,[5] its unique catena of OT citations,[6] and its exclusive instructions concerning unbelievers,[7] 2 Cor 6:14–7:1 has of course formed the center of much scholarly discussion. These debates have focused largely on the identification of the Scriptural citations in 6:16c–18, the connection to other contemporary Jewish documents, and its authenticity and/or integrity in 2 Corinthians. At the same time, however, scholarly treatments of 6:14–7:1 have paid comparatively little attention to 7:1, where Paul summarizes his previous arguments with a concluding exhortation:

> Therefore (οὖν), beloved ones, since we have these promises, let us cleanse ourselves from every defilement regarding flesh and spirit, thus completing holiness, which is brought about by the fear of God.[8]

Moreover, it has seldom been noticed that, even though this verse picks up all of the other central aspects in the catena of OT citations in 6:16c–18 (cf. its reference to "these promises," "cleansing from defilement," and "completing

---

Its Bearing on the Literary Problem of 2 Corinthians 6:14–7:1," in *The Right Doctrine from the Wrong Texts? Essays on the Use of the Old Testament in the New* (Grand Rapids: Baker Books, 1994), 217–47; James M. Scott, "The Use of Scripture in 2 Corinthians 6.16c–18 and Paul's Restoration Theology," *JSNT* 56 (1994): 73–99; Scott J. Hafemann, "Paul's Use of the Old Testament in 2 Corinthians," *Int* 52 (1998): 246–57; David I. Starling, *Not My People: Gentiles as Exiles in Pauline Hermeneutics*, BZNW 184 (Berlin; New York: de Gruyter, 2011), 61–106; Emmanuel Nathan, "Fragmented Theology in 2 Corinthians: The Unsolved Puzzle of 6:14–7:1," in *Theologizing in the Corinthian Conflict: Studies in the Exegesis and Theology of 2 Corinthians*, ed. Bieringer, Reimund et al., BTAS 16 (Leuven: Peeters, 2013), 211–28. I will take up this issue more directly in Chapter Five.

5. The passage of 2 Cor 6:14–7:1 contains six NT *hapax legomena* (ἑτεροζυγέω, μετοχή, συμφώνησις, Βελιάρ, συγκατάθεσις, μολυσμός) and three Pauline *hapax legomena* (ἐμπεριπατέω, εἰσδέξομαι, παντοκράτωρ).

6. Scholars argue 2 Cor 6:16c–18 to be an example of "composite citation (Zitatkomibination)." Christopher D. Stanley, *Paul and the Language of Scripture*, SNTSMS 74 (Cambridge: Cambridge University Press, 1992), 217–30; idem, "Composite Citations: Retrospect and Prospect," in *Composite Citations in Antiquity. Vol. 1*, eds. Sean A. Adams and Seth M. Ehorn, LNTS 525 (London: T&T Clark, 2016), 204n3; Paul Han, *Swimming in the Sea of Scripture: Paul's Use of the Old Testament in 2 Corinthians 4.7–13.13*, LNTS 519 (London: Bloomsbury, 2014), 90–97. In his survey of composite citations, Dietrich-Alex Koch (*Die Schrift als Zeuge des Evangeliums: Untersuchungen zur Verwendung und zum Verständnis der Schrift bei Paulus*, BHT 69 [Tübingen: Mohr Siebeck, 1986], 172–90) does not include 2 Cor 6:16c–18 because he regards it as a non-Pauline interpolation (24n43, 45), but nevertheless acknowledges that 2 Cor 6:16c–18 belongs to the form of citation combination (172n1).

7. For example, Hans Dieter Betz ("2 Cor 6:14–7:1: An Anti-Pauline Fragment?" *JBL* 92 [1973]: 88–108) sees this to be problematic. Cf. 1 Cor 5:10.

8. My translation. I will defend this rendering at greater length in Chapter Five.

holiness"), the motif of "the fear of God" seems to appear without introduction or preceding reference. Both arguing for and against Pauline authorship of 6:14–7:1, scholars have not pointed out this surprising feature of 7:1, nor have they provided a satisfactory answer regarding *why* the fear of God is referenced in 7:1, *what* it means, and hence *how* it functions in the argument.

This present study, therefore, takes as its starting point the following questions: "What motivates the reference to the fear of God in 2 Cor 7:1?" "What, in view of the answer to this question, does this motif actually mean in 2 Cor 7:1?" and finally, "What role does this motif play in 2 Cor 7:1 and, furthermore, in 2 Cor 6:14–7:1?" This present study seeks to answer these questions by first exploring this motif in the various OT passages explicitly cited in 6:16c–18, which lead up to the climactic assertion about the fear of God in 7:1, and then by comparing the understanding of this OT motif with the use of the same motif in representative Second Temple Jewish documents. The premise of the study is that these traditional Jewish understandings of the fear of God, especially those found in an eschatological context, will shed light on Paul's understanding and use of the fear of God in 2 Cor 7:1.

I. Status Quaestionis

Compared with the vast swathe of studies on 2 Cor 6:14–7:1, scholarly discussions about the fear of God in 7:1 are scarce in number and divergent in their interpretations. On the one hand, scholars who do not accept the Pauline authorship of 2 Cor 6:14–7:1 argue that the fear of God in 7:1 is a Christian "stylistic modification" of an interpolated fragment (probably from Essene material)[9] or "a non-Pauline phrase, pointing, as in Judaism, to the eschatological judgment."[10] On the other hand, scholars who accept Pauline authorship of the passage mostly acknowledge the connection between "the fear of God" in 7:1 and "the fear of the Lord" in 5:11, and interpret the fear of God as a response to God's final judgment.[11] However, these scholars differ in their understanding not only of the nature of "the

---

9. Joachim Gnilka, "2 Cor 6:14–7:1 in the Light of the Qumran Texts and the Testaments of the Twelve Patriarchs," in *Paul and Qumran: Studies in New Testament Exegesis*, ed. Jerome Murphy-O'Connor (London: G. Chapman, 1968), 66–7.

10. Betz, "2 Cor 6:14–7:1," 99n78.

11. E.g., Victor Paul Furnish, *II Corinthians*, AB 32A (Garden City, NY: Doubleday, 1984), 366; Christian Wolff, *Zweite Brief des Paulus an die Korinther*, THKNT 8 (Berlin: Evangelische Verlagsanstalt, 1989), 8; Jan Lambrecht, *Second Corinthians*, SP 8 (Collegeville, MN: Liturgical Press, 1999), 119: "implicitly refers to the judgment and thus adds an eschatological connotation"; Scott J. Hafemann, *2 Corinthians*, NIVAC (Grand Rapids: Zondervan, 2000), 289: "as its allusion back to 5:10–11 indicates, it refers to God's judgment between believers and unbelievers," also 295; Frank J. Matera, *II Corinthians: A Commentary*, NTL (Louisville; London: Westminster John Knox, 2003), 168; Murray J. Harris, *The Second*

fear of God,"[12] but also of its origin in this context.[13] The reason for this variance is twofold: first, as I will discuss below, the traditional "dual understanding" of the fear of God that distinguishes two kinds of fear (negative/positive) fails to explain the fear of God in 7:1. Here, both negative and positive features of fear seem to join— the fear of God alludes to the final judgment as in 5:10-11 (negative fear), *and* at the same time promotes the holiness of believers (positive fear).[14] Thus, in order to understand the fear of God in 7:1, a different explanation is required that can include both features.[15] Second, as with the other referents of 7:1, one should seek to understand the fear of God in 7:1 against the OT background of 6:16c-18. Although scholars have often referred to the OT context in general as the background for the motif of the fear of God in 7:1, such as the common appeal to

Epistle to the Corinthians: A Commentary on the Greek Text, NIGTC (Grand Rapids; Milton Keynes: Eerdmans; Paternoster, 2005), 514-15; Craig S. Keener, *1-2 Corinthians*, NCBC (Cambridge: Cambridge University Press, 2005), 198: "in view of the day of judgment"; Thomas Schmeller, *Der Zweite Brief an die Korinther*, EKKNT 8 (Neukirchen-Vluyn: Ostfildern: Neukirchener Theologie; Patmos-Verlag, 2010), 378: "im Blick auf den göttlichen Richter"; Ralph P. Martin, *2 Corinthians*, 2nd rev., WBC 40 (Grand Rapids: Zondervan, 2014), 376; Mark A. Seifrid, *The Second Letter to the Corinthians*, PNTC (Grand Rapids; Nottingham, England: Eerdmans; Apollos, 2014), 302; George H. Guthrie, *2 Corinthians*, BECNT (Grand Rapids: Baker Academic, 2015), 361.

12. Harris, *Second Corinthians*, 514-15: "a reverential awe and holy dread before God"; Matera, *II Corinthians*, 168: "reverential awe"; Guthrie, *2 Corinthians*, 361: an "emotional state in which one reflects upon the awesome dimensions of God's power and is appropriately sobered…[it is a] reverent reflection on the devastating gravity of being out of step with God's will"; Wolff, *Zweite Brief*, 153: "im Bewusstsein um die Verantwortung vor Gott"; Martin, *2 Corinthians*, 376 and Seifrid, *Second Corinthians*, 302: "reverence"; Yulin Liu (*Temple Purity in 1-2 Corinthians*, WUNT 2/343 [Tübingen: Mohr Siebeck, 2013], 230) argues that the fear of God indicates one's appropriate response to God's providential acts.

13. For example, Paul Barnett (*The Second Epistle to the Corinthians*, NICNT [Grand Rapids: Eerdmans, 1997], 357n77) and Martin (*2 Corinthians*, 376) argue that this motif is influenced by wisdom literature in the OT (cf. Hafemann, *2 Corinthians*, 289: "'the fear of the Lord' is the distinguishing mark of the wise [Ps. 2:11; 5:7; Prov. 1:7, 29; 8:13]"), while Keener (*1-2 Corinthians*, 198) highlights its (contemporary) Jewish tradition.

14. Matera, *II Corinthians*, 168: "The Corinthians will accomplish this [life of holiness] if they live with the same reverential awe ('the fear of God') that guides Paul's moral conduct (5:11)." Likewise, Harris, *Second Corinthians*, 514-15.

15. Few scholars have attempted to explain the fear of God with anything other than the dual approach, simply repeating its main tenets without adding new arguments. E.g., Hafemann, *2 Corinthians*, 289: "[The fear of God] is therefore not simply a desire to gain rewards or an attitude of 'reverence for God.'" Also Guthrie, *2 Corinthians*, 361: "Neither mere caution nor a debilitating terror, the term communicates an emotional state in which one reflects upon the awesome dimensions of God's power and is appropriately sobered. Holiness of life stems from reverent reflection on the devastating gravity of being out of step with God's will."

the role of the fear of the Lord in wisdom literature, few have attempted to explain the motif against the backdrop of the specific OT citations of 6:16c–18.[16]

In sum, despite the acknowledgment of the eschatological weight that the fear of God carries in 7:1 (especially in light of 5:10–11), there has not been a detailed analysis of its function within the immediate argument of 6:14–7:1. However, by neglecting the backdrop of the specific OT passages cited in 6:16c–18 against which Paul understands the fear of God in 7:1, as well as the wider context in 2 Corinthians of Paul's discussion of his "new covenant" ministry and his corresponding exhortations to the Corinthians as "the temple of the living God" (6:16), one fails to see the significant role and function that the fear of God takes up in Paul's thought. Therefore, a study of the fear of God is needed that illumines both the narrow relationship between 6:14–18 and 7:1, and the broad relationship between 7:1 and 2 Corinthians. Moreover, despite the numerous attempts to explain the other aspects in 7:1 against a Second Temple Jewish background, none of these attempts traces the treatment of the motif of the fear of God in the literature of Second Temple Judaism in order to establish the context in which this aspect of Paul's argument stands. Hence, a closer examination of the understanding of the fear of God in the Second Temple period will help us to see how Paul's understanding of the fear of God corresponds to and deviates from his contemporary setting.

II. The Problem Raised by Lexicography

There have been several significant lexicographical studies of the motif of "the fear of God" in the OT and NT, all of which have argued that the latter is almost exclusively dependent upon the former.[17] Thus, it is important to start our examination of the fear of God first in the OT, where this motif appears more prominently than in the NT itself.[18]

---

16. E.g., Webb (*Returning Home*, 66) connects the fear of God to the new covenant context, but he does not examine the background of the fear of God in the previous section of 2 Cor 6:16c–18: "[T]he fear of the Lord (within the heart) develops those things which the new covenant was intended to produce" (cf. Isa 59:19, 21; Jer 32:39–40; 33:9). Likewise, in his recent commentary, B. J. Oropeza (*Exploring Second Corinthians: Death and Life, Hardship and Rivalry*, RRA 3 [Atlanta: SBL Press, 2016], 439, 442–3) refers to the connection between the fear of God in 2 Cor 7:1 and Jer 32:36–41.

17. Siegfried Plath, *Furcht Gottes: Der Begriff yārʾā im Alten Testament* (Stuttgart: Calwer Verlag, 1963); Joachim Becker, *Gottesfurcht im Altem Testament*, AnBib 25 (Rome: Pontificio Instituto Biblico, 1965); H. P. Stähli, "ירא," *TLOT* 2:568–78; H. F. Fuhs, "יָרֵא," *TDOT* 6:290–315; H. Balz, G. Wanke, "φοβέω, φοβέομαι, φόβος, δέος," *TDNT* 9:189–219; Moisés Silva, "φόβος," *NIDNTTE* 4:609–14.

18. Leland Ryken, "Fear," *DBIM* 277: "It is important to note, however, that the preponderance of references [to the fear of God] occur in the OT." Likewise, Stanley E. Porter, "Fear, Reverence," *DPL* 291.

1. The Meaning of the Fear of God in the OT

According to *TLOT*, the vast majority of occurrences of "fear" (יראה) in the OT (about 80 percent) exhibit a theological usage, i.e., "the fear of God."[19] For example, the adjectival form, "frightful" (נורא), is used as an attribute of God,[20] of his name,[21] of his deeds,[22] and of his eschatological day of judgment,[23] while the verb, "to fear" (ירא), appears in relation to the experience of God's theophanic presence,[24] in relation to God's deeds as a historical activity and demonstration of power,[25] such as the creation,[26] the Exodus,[27] or the punishment of the evil ones,[28] and in relation to the sanctuary[29] or to an individual man/the people of God.[30] In sum, in the OT God is to be feared not through his dreadful works alone, but also in response to his majesty and holiness.[31]

According to this, "fear" carries also a positive and active aspect, since God's acts as well as his power, holiness, and majesty not only elicit "fear" from those who are in rebellion against God, but also demand a positive acknowledgment of fear from his faithful people. In other words, "fear" in OT contexts results not only from the threat itself, but also in response to the author of the threat, so that "fear" also becomes a "reverence" that leads people to submissive recognition.[32] In this regard, this aspect of the fear of God identifies itself with the people's obedience to God, expressed in their observance of moral laws and cultic demands. With this development, the fear of God loses its original emotional character of fearing God's punishment or judgment altogether.[33] Miklós Pálfy thus contends that this

---

19. Fuhs, *TDOT* 6:296. Also Stähli, *TLOT* 2:570-73. For detailed examination of each use of ירא, see Stähli's chart on 570.

20. E.g., Exod 15:11; Deut 7:21; 10:17; 1 Chr 16:25; Neh 1:5; 4:8; 9:32; Job 37:22; Pss 47:3; 68:36; 76:8, 13; 89:8; 96:4; Dan 9:4; Zeph 2:11.

21. E.g., Deut 28:58; Pss 99:3; 111:9; Mal 1:14.

22. E.g., Exod 34:10; Deut 10:21; 2 Sam 7:23 (= 1 Chr 17:21); Pss 65:6; 66:3; 106:22; 145:6; Isa 64:2.

23. E.g., Joel 2:11; 3:4; Mal 3:23.

24. E.g., Exod 20:18, 20; Deut 5:5. For a more detailed survey on fear before God's theophany, see Fuhs, *TDOT* 6:301-2.

25. E.g., Job 6:21; Pss 65:9; 76:9; Isa 25:3; 41:5; Jer 10:7; Hab 3:2; Zech 9:5.

26. E.g., Pss 33:8; 65:9; Jer 5:22, 24.

27. E.g., Exod 14:31; Mic 7:17.

28. E.g., Pss 40:4; 52:8; 64:10.

29. E.g., Lev 19:30; 26:2; 2 Sam 6:9 (= 1 Chr 13:12).

30. E.g., Exod 34:30; Deut 28:10; Josh 4:14; 1 Sam 12:18; 31:4 (= 1 Chr 10:4); 2 Sam 1:14.

31. Wanke, *TDNT* 9:201.

32. Ibid.

33. Thus, Wanke, *TDNT* 9:201-2. Likewise, Fuhs (*TDOT* 6:296) comments that the verb "fear" appears in the OT in parallel not only with other verbs meaning "fear," but also

positive aspect of fear is related to the "pious attitude" in the OT for which God constantly exhorts his people to strive:

> Da jedoch der hebräische Mensch der Unsicherheit und Relativität der "Furcht vor der Gottheit" bewußt war, verwendet er den Begriff *jir'at jahwe* sehr oft zur Bezeichnung des Verhältnisses von Gott und Mensch bzw. der Frömmigkeit im Alten Testament.[34]

Scholars argue that this positive and active aspect of fear, which appears at various places throughout the OT, is to be distinguished from its negative sense of "terror," and denotes a human attitude of submission that expresses itself in human conduct that is orientated to the will of God. For example, in Deuteronomy and the Deuteronomistic literature, the fear of God appears "in a series of formulae which demand piety oriented to the Deuteronomist Law."[35] In these passages, fearing God functions positively and describes the corresponding result of obedience to God's word and commandments.[36] This entails obedience to the demand to hear his voice or serve him,[37] so that God exhorts his people to learn it as a statute or commandment.[38] A similar sentiment is found in the wisdom literature, where the fear of God plays as a key concept and expresses an essential characteristic of the covenant people, so that the concept of the fear of God "has left the emotional realm here and become an object of reflection."[39] Here too, the fear of God describes

---

with such expressions as "love" (Deut 10:12); "cleave to" (Deut 10:20; 13:5); "serve" (Deut 6:13; 10:12, 20; 13:5; Josh 24:14; 1 Sam 12:14); "keep commandments" (Deut 5:29; 6:2; 8:6; 13:5; 17:19; 31:12); "walk in his ways" (Deut 8:6; 10:12); "follow" (Deut 13:5); "hearken to his voice" (Deut 13:5; 1 Sam 12:14); "do the commandments" (Deut 6:24).

34. Miklós Pálfy, "Allgemein-Menschliche Beziehungen der Furcht im Alten Testament," in *Schalom: Studien zu Glaube und Geschichte Israels: Alfred Jepsen zum 70sten Geburtstag*, ed. Karl-Heinz Bernhardt, AVTRW (Stuttgart: Calwer Verlag, 1971), 23. According to Pálfy, 26, the fear of God is a gift of the love of God, i.e., a gift of salvation that corresponds to the godly demand for a sincere service to God, and appears in relation to three themes in the OT: the fear of God as fear in front of God (*Gottesfurcht als Furcht vor Gott*), the fear of God as fearing and trusting God (*Gottesfurcht als Furcht und Vertrauen*), and the fear of God in regard to the resolution of the tension between fear and trust (*die Auflösung der Spannung zwischen Furcht und Vertrauen*).

35. Wanke, *TDNT* 9:201. Fearing God therefore appears in a close interrelationship with observing the law, which is further defined and understood on the basis of the covenant formula. Thus, Stähli, *TLOT* 2:575.

36. Deut 4:10; 8:6.

37. Deut 6:13; 8:6; 10:12, 20; 13:5.

38. Deut 14:22.

39. Wanke, *TDNT* 9:202. Also similarly, Stähli, *TLOT* 2:576–77; Fuhs, *TDOT* 6:311–13.

the moral attitude of the righteous in the community or of various groups of pious participants in the cult.[40]

2. The Meaning of the Fear of God in the NT

In the majority of instances where the φόβος word-group appears in the NT, its meaning lies within the traditional framework laid out in the OT.[41] In general, it describes a reaction to man's encounter with force and its scale of reactions ranges from spontaneous terror and anxiety to honour and respect.[42] At variance with other extra-biblical Greek uses of the φόβος word-group, however, where the terms are used negatively to frighten people, so that the experience of it is often to be suppressed or banished by enlightenment and instruction, "fear" in the NT, as in the OT, can represent a positive aspect, i.e., the expression of faith.[43] Moisés Silva thus argues that the connection with the OT is especially clear in the religious use of φόβος, which he interprets as "awe" or "reverence."[44] In this context, fear is defined in terms of the Christian life, so that, in contrast to other fears that are to be rejected,[45] this fear "cannot be separated from faith as a basic attitude of the man who depends wholly and utterly on God."[46] Christians know the presence of Christ in the Spirit, possess confidence in the face of suffering, and do not need to fear death anymore. Nevertheless, they are to fear God in both his grace and wrath and be dependent on his saving work.

As part of this NT perspective, Stanley E. Porter argues that for Paul, too, "fear" refers to two distinct realities. In the first place, it refers to "the appropriate level of respect and honor to be shown to another, often in light of fulfilling one's service

---

40. Wanke, *TDNT* 9:203. Thus, Becker (*Gottesfurcht*, 187) argues that the fear of God in wisdom texts indicates "a fixed term for just, ethical behavior." Also, Plath, *Furcht Gottes*, 78. In contrast, it is noteworthy that these wisdom and hortatory elements of the fear of God are less prominent in the Qumran literature and apocalyptic writings. Stähli, *TLOT* 2:578; Balz, *TDNT* 9:206; Fuhs, *TDOT* 6:314–15.

41. According to Balz (*TDNT* 9:208), "In the NT the word group φοβ- is represented by φοβέομαι 95 times, φόβος 47, ἔμφοβος 5, ἀφόβως 4, φοβερός 3, ἔκφοβος 2 and ἐκφοβέω and φόβητρον once each, a sum total of 158 times. The main use is in the Gospels and Acts: only the noun is rather more common in Paul." For a more detailed survey, see pp. 208–17; *NIDTTE* 4:612–13. For its specific Pauline uses, see above note 2.

42. Balz, *TDNT* 9:192. In comparison, in LXX φόβος occurs almost 200 times and it is often used as a religious reverence.

43. Ibid., 195–6. Similarly, Silva, *NIDTTE* 4:610–11; Wanke, *TDNT* 9:199.

44. Silva, *NIDTTE* 4:612. E.g., Acts 9:31; 2 Cor 7:1; Col 3:22; Eph 5:21; 1 Pet 2:17; Rev 11:18.

45. E.g., "fear of man" in Matt 10:28; Luke 12:4; "fear of death" in Heb 2:15; "fear of rulers" in Rom 13:3. Cf. "fear of the wicked at the eschaton" in Luke 21:26; Heb 10:27, 31; Rev 18:10, 15.

46. Balz, *TDNT* 9:209.

to God. It also implies terror at the prospect of failing to fulfill one's obligation."[47] Porter thus argues that, for Paul, this concept of fear or reverence is grounded in the OT idea, and is distinguished from terror that stems from being subjected to an angry deity.[48] Instead, this positive fear, which Porter refers to as "healthy fear or reverence,"[49] reflects in the Pauline corpus an appropriate response of the covenant people to their God, while the negative fear, in the sense of "terror," derives from disobedience or not showing due respect.[50] Porter claims that this positive fear "motivates appropriate behavior in relation to God or Christ, to the state or to other humans."[51] According to Porter, therefore, the fear of God in the NT can sometimes refer to fear before the God who judges (cf. 1 Pet 1:17), but it is more often the reverence or awe before God's overpowering presence that motivates the appropriate response and behavior of believers.[52]

These studies above provide a helpful survey of the semantic landscape and various contexts in which the fear of God appears throughout the Scriptures. As such, they are foundational for our present study. However, in defining the meaning of the fear of God in both the OT and NT, scholars have argued that there are two kinds of fear represented by the same set of terms: a negative fear that derives from God's judgment, i.e., a "terror" or "dread," and a positive fear that expresses itself in obedience to the Law and holiness in life, i.e., an "awe" or "reverence."

The present study will call into question this consensus regarding such a dual approach to the fear of God with respect to Paul's understanding of the fear of God in 2 Cor 7:1 and the OT backdrop from which he draws it in 6:16c–18, as well as in the broader context of the Second Temple Judaism in which his thought takes place. It will seek to show that, in these key contexts, the traditional two categories of "fear" seem to collapse. This work will thus argue that the fear of God—at least for Paul and the OT texts he cites, if not for the rest of the OT and NT—does not denote two kinds of fear, but only one: that is, *one's feeling of alarm or trepidation in regard to God that is brought about by the realization of the reality of God's eschatological judgment.* The distinctions in the function of the fear of God

---

47. Porter, *DPL* 291.

48. Ibid. Likewise, in idem, "Fear," *DLNT* 370–1, Porter argues for a two-sided approach to fear: "On the one hand there is suitable fear of God, other people and things, fear that in some contexts appropriately represents respect and provides a suitable basis for Christian conduct. On the other hand there is admonition not to have a craven fear of God, humans or things such as suffering in the light of God's larger plan and purpose." Porter, 372–3, further argues that there are two sides to the fear of God in the NT writings more generally. Repeated in idem, "Fear," *NDBT* 497.

49. Porter, *DPL* 291.

50. Ibid. Porter, 292, supports his argument based on Rom 3:18 and 11:20: "The link between fear and reverence as an appropriate response to God and fear or terror for disobedience is well illustrated by these passages." Likewise, Ryken, *DBIM* 277.

51. Porter, *DPL* 293. Likewise, Ryken, *DBIM* 277.

52. Porter, *DLNT* 371–2.

observed by these past studies are better explained not by positing *two types of fear*, but by recognizing that this *single fear* functions differently in relationship to *two types of persons and times* in which this fear is experienced. In other words, "believers," who as members of the covenant have already experienced God's salvation, possess the fear of God "in the present" that motivates them to pursue a holy life in anticipation of the judgment to come in the future, while "unbelievers," who are outside God's salvation "in the present," do not fear God and thus continue to live wickedly (cf. 2 Cor 5:11; 7:1 with Rom 3:18 and its corresponding way of life in 3:10–17). Conversely, those who "fear God" in the present will not fear God in the eschatological judgment, but those who have not "feared God" in the present will fear God on that future day when his wrath comes upon them. It is this distinction in person and time—not a distinction between two kinds of fear—that explains the contours of Paul's argument in 2 Cor 7:1 against its OT background.

Thus, while the dual understanding of the fear of God distinguishes between the fear one has in anticipation of the eschatological judgment and the fear that expresses itself in and motivates believers' holy life, we will argue that the relationship between 2 Cor 5:10–11 and 7:1 makes it clear that it is the very same "fear of the Lord" deriving from "the judgment seat of Christ" that "motivates" Paul in his ministry of persuading others to pursue holiness. Hence, the understanding of the single nature of the fear of God as one's feeling of alarm or trepidation in regard to God that is brought about by the realization of the reality of God's eschatological judgment explains how in both 5:11 and 7:1 the "fear" deriving from the reality of God's judgment functions similarly both for Paul and for the Corinthians, with whom Paul shares a new identity of believer (6:16).[53] For, as will be argued below, the fear of God in Paul's exhortation in 7:1 refers to the "positive fear" that promotes holy life in the present precisely because it is at the same time the "negative fear" related to the judgment to come. The experience of "the fear of God" in the present thus functions as an essential mark of the believer, not the unbeliever.

III. Methodology

This study will examine Paul's reference to "the fear of God" in 2 Cor 7:1 by placing it within the larger literary context of 2 Corinthians and then, within its own context, by following the OT texts that Paul cites in 6:16c–18 back to their own larger contexts in order to show how these broader contextual themes are picked up and summarized in 7:1, including Paul's reference to the fear of God.[54] This

---

53. This work will deal with the connection between 2 Cor 7:1 and 5:11 in the next chapter.

54. Cf. N. T. Wright, *Paul and the Faithfulness of God*, COQG 4 (London: SPCK, 2013), 176–7: "Even when it often seems obscure to a present-day reader, the context of a scriptural allusion or echo is again and again very important. Whole passages, whole themes, can be

study will thus argue that the motif of the fear of God in 7:1 forms an inclusion with 5:11, framing the intervening argument, and that the broader scriptural contexts of the citations in 6:16c–18 shed considerable additional light on the apostle's understanding of the meaning and rhetorical function of the fear of God in 7:1.

Since in this study we will deal only with the OT passages that appear explicitly in citations in 6:16c–18, we will build our argument on the basis of the OT citations recognized by nearly all scholars.[55] These texts are indicated as well in the margins of Nestle-Aland, *Novum Testamentum Graece*, 28th ed. (NA[28]) which are a good indicator of the scholarly consensus. NA[28] lists the OT citations in 2 Cor 6:16c–18 as follows: Lev 26:11 and Ezek 37:27 for 2 Cor 6:16de; Isa 52:11 for 2 Cor 6:17ac; Ezek 20:34 for 2 Cor 6:17d; 2 Sam 7:14 for 2 Cor 6:18a; and 2 Sam 7:8 LXX for 2 Cor 6:18b.[56] Moreover, scholars have long recognized that 2 Cor 6:16c–18 is not a mere catalogue of varied OT passages but is rather comprised of "composite citations" of multiple Scriptural texts seen by the author to be mutually related.[57] After examining

---

called to mind with a single reference." Also, J. Ross Wagner, *Heralds of the Good News: Isaiah and Paul "in Concert" in the Letters of Romans*, NovTSup 101 (Leiden: Brill, 2002), 356: "Paul's citations and allusions to Isaiah are not plunder from random raids on Israel's sacred texts. Rather, they are the product of sustained and careful attention to the rhythms and cadences of individual passages as well as to larger themes and motifs that run throughout the prophet's oracles." Cf. indeed, as Beale ("Reconciliation," 235) observed: "The inability of commentators to account for how verses 16–18 [in 2 Cor 6] fit into the logical flow of the epistle may be due to the lack of any serious attempt to study the Old Testament quotes in their original contexts."

55. Especially helpful for this task are the works of Beale ("Reconciliation," 217–47), Scott ("Use of Scripture," 73–99), and Webb (*Returning Home*, 31–58).

56. For the same reason, this work will not discuss the motif of the fear of God in the wisdom literature in the OT, but limit the discussion to those OT passages that are explicitly cited. For a detailed discussion regarding the relationship between the fear of God and wisdom literature, see Tremper Longman III, *The Fear of the Lord Is Wisdom: A Theological Introduction to Wisdom in Israel* (Grand Rapids: Baker Academic, 2017), 1–62. Longman briefly mentions 2 Cor 5:11 and 7:15 in his book: "Paul ascribes his motivation to spread the gospel to his fear of God" (p. 251). Longman rightly argues that the Christian faith is characterized by the fear of God and that this fear causes the believers to pursue an obedient life, but he falls short in explaining the relationship between the fear of God and the judgment of God.

57. For the definition of a "composite citation" as "a text where literary borrowing occurs in a manner that includes two or more passages from the same or different authors fused together and conveyed as though they are only one," see now Sean A. Adams and Seth M. Ehorn, "What Is a Composite Citation? An Introduction," in *Composite Citations in Antiquity. Vol. 1*, eds. Sean A. Adams and Seth M. Ehorn, LNTS 525 (London: T&T Clark, 2016), 4. In using the term "citation/quotation" instead of "allusion" to describe Paul's use of OT passages in 2 Cor 6:16c–18, I do not intend to draw a distinction between those

the practices of such citations in the Pauline corpus, Dietrich-Alex Koch categorizes the examples into "mixed citations," in which a part of Scripture is reshaped by incorporating within it a different scriptural text,[58] and "composite citations," in which two or more texts of scripture are directly merged together but are not thrust into each other.[59] Koch acknowledges the citations in 2 Cor 6:16c–18 as belonging to the latter category, but does not further examine the passage since he doubts its authenticity.[60] Building on Koch's study, Christopher D. Stanley defines a "composite citation" as "fusing together verses from two or more texts and presenting them as if they were a single citation," and further distinguishes within the composite citations in the Pauline corpus between a "combined citation," where multiple excerpts are joined back-to-back under a single citation formula, and a "conflated citation," where a word or phrase from a passage is inserted into another passage and creates a new text.[61] Stanley argues that the citations in 2 Cor 6:16c–18 are knitted together into "a tightly woven rhetorical unit rather than being thrown together haphazardly in the moment of dictation" and that they include both combined citations (vv. 16c–18) and a conflated citation (v. 18).[62] Our study of the structure will confirm Stanley's more precise distinction within the composite citation in 6:16c–18.

In a recent volume, Sean A. Adams and Sean M. Ehorn have supported these categories and distinctions of Stanley by examining the formal characteristics of composite citations, arguing that composite citations must exhibit two defining structural aspects. First, a "citation" consists of the following factors:

two categories, neither do I propose criteria to do so. In fact, not only is the line blurry between citation and allusion in biblical studies, but also the attempt to distinguish them goes beyond the scope of this study since it would require an investigation in its own right. On this point, see William A. Tooman, *Gog of Magog: Reuse of Scripture and Compositional Technique in Ezekiel 38–39*, FAT 2/52 (Tübingen: Mohr Siebeck, 2011), 4–5: "There is no standard for how many borrowed words are required to qualify an allusion as a quotation. Nor do biblical scholars agree on whether identical morphology and order of elements are required in a quotation" (quoted from p. 5). In the same context, Richard B. Hays (*Echoes of Scripture in the Letters of Paul* [New Haven: Yale University Press, 1989], 23) argues that "quotation," "allusion," and "echo" indicate a spectrum of intertextual reference, moving from the explicit to the subliminal, so that, according to Wagner, *Heralds*, 10n38, Hays has shown that a sharp distinction between quotation (citation) and allusion does not apply in many cases where Paul quotes scriptures.

58. "Mischzitaten," "bei denen ein Teil eines Schriftwortes unter Verwendung einer anderen Schriftstelle umgeformt worden ist." Koch, *Schrift*, 160.

59. "Zitatkombinationen," "in denen zwei [oder mehrere] Schriftworte unmittelbar zusammengefügt, jedoch nicht ineinandergeschoben sind." Ibid., 172.

60. Ibid., 172n1.

61. Stanley, "Composite Citations," 204. Cf. idem, *Language*, 258–9.

62. Ibid., 217–30, (quoted from p. 217). Stanley later regards 2 Cor 6:14–7:1 as a later interpolation. Idem, *Arguing with Scripture: The Rhetoric of Quotations in the Letters of Paul* (New York: T&T Clark, 2004), 98n1.

The text must be marked as a citation in some manner, either with: (1) an explicit attribution to an author or speaker; (2) the use of an introductory formula; (3) a noticeable break in syntax between the citation and its new literary context; or, (4) if the citation is well-known in antiquity or cited elsewhere by the same author it can reasonably be considered a citation.[63]

Second, a "composite" nature of a citation means that:

Within the citation, two or more texts must be fused together. This fusing together must not include conjunctions that break between the two fused texts (e.g., καί, καὶ πάλιν, etc.). In some instances, the presence of a conjunction within a citation will need to be examined more closely in order to determine if the syntax is broken. Prior or following a list of citations, if the citing author refers to a plurality of sources, the citation should not be considered composite.[64]

Thus, 2 Cor 6:16c–18 fits to the category of a "composite citation" that consists of both "combined" and "conflated" citations since: (1) the passage starts with an introductory formula in v. 16c, καθὼς εἶπεν ὁ θεὸς ὅτι, and it also ends with a quotation formula in v. 18b, λέγει κύριος παντοκράτωρ,[65] and (2) even though the passage includes conjunctions that connect citations from different scripture texts, such as διό in v. 17a and καί (from κἀγώ) in v. 17d, it will become clear in our study that the Scriptural texts all function as a unified rhetorical unit supporting and advancing the author's argument.[66] As such, they also support and provide the context for understanding the summary statement in 7:1, including its reference to the fear of God.[67]

---

63. Adams and Ehorn, "Composite Citation," 3.
64. Ibid., 4.
65. I will discuss this in more detail in Chapter Two. Both Koch (*Schrift*, 11–23) and Stanley (*Language*, 33–4) argue that a clear introductory formula indicates a citation.
66. In their most recent volume, Adams and Ehorn introduce "condensed citations" as the third type of composite citation, which "work with a single text and shorten or summarize it." Sean A. Adams and Seth M. Ehorn, "Introduction," in *Composite Citations in Antiquity. Vol. 2*, eds. Sean A. Adams and Seth M. Ehorn, LNTS 593 (London: T&T Clark, 2018), 4. However, since this type does not match with 2 Cor 6:16c–18, this work will not discuss it. In the same volume, Ciampa discusses the composite citations in 1–2 Corinthians in depth in his article, including 2 Cor 6:16–18. Ciampa's argument mostly overlaps with that of this work, but despite his acknowledgment of the link between the OT catena and 7:1, he does not further his argument regarding the different motifs in 7:1, including the fear of God. Roy E. Ciampa, "Composite Citations in 1–2 Corinthians and Galatians," in *Composite Citations in Antiquity. Vol. 2*, eds. Sean A. Adams and Seth M. Ehorn, LNTS 593 (London: T&T Clark, 2018), 160–74.
67. Tooman (*Gog*, 5n13) argues that an author may alter the words of the original source as long as the readers can identify the points at which the quoted material begins and ends in the targeted text.

To make this case, this study will acknowledge and pursue the "allusive effect" of the broader Scriptural contexts of the composite citation in 6:16c–18. Ever since the work of C. H. Dodd, scholars have recognized that in citing OT texts Paul often has their wider contexts in view.[68] In this regard, Richard B. Hays has argued programmatically that:

> *citations allude* to their original contexts, and the most significant elements of intertextual correspondence between old context and new can be implicit rather than voiced, perceptible only within the silent space framed by the juncture of two texts.[69]

Moreover, according to Hays, such a correspondence between contexts can be established by an "allusive echo," also known as an "intertextual echo," "transumption,"

---

68. C. H. Dodd, *According to the Scripture: The Sub-Structure of New Testament Theology* (London: Nisbet, 1953), 132: "the governing intention [of the treatment of the Scripture in the NT] is to exploit *whole contexts* selected as the varying expression of certain fundamental and permanent elements in the biblical revelation" (emphasis added). Also Florian Wilk, who examines Paul's use of Isaianic texts in 1 and 2 Corinthians, argues that "The relevance of [Paul's] quotations from and allusions to Isaiah is reinforced by the fact that in each case [in 1 Cor 1:18–3:4; 15; 2 Cor 2:14–7:3], the respective Isaianic context is mirrored at various points in his exposition. In several cases it must be conceded that the context taken into account includes only a few verses or shows up through conceptual rather than verbal links.... In every instance it is evident that Paul did not isolate the oracle quoted or alluded to from its original context but has interpreted it in accordance with that context." Florian Wilk, "Isaiah in 1 and 2 Corinthians," in *Isaiah in the New Testament* (London: T&T Clark, 2005), 157. Scott J. Hafemann makes a similar observation after examining Paul's understanding of the ministry of the new covenant in 2 Cor 3 against the backdrop of Exod 32–34, "[I]t must be recognized that for Paul, Exodus 32–34 is not simply a story, but a *biblical* narrative. This means, above all, that the interpreter must be alert to the theological intention and significance of the story." Scott J. Hafemann, *Paul, Moses, and the History of Israel: The Letter/Spirit Contrast and the Argument from Scripture in 2 Corinthians 3*, WUNT 2/81 (Tübingen: J. C. B. Mohr, 1995), 194, original emphasis. As such, the present study is an exegetical contribution to the broad study of biblical "intertextuality," or more specifically, to Paul's use and understanding of Scripture. The literature on this flourishing field of study is immense and beyond the focus of this work. Useful is the summary of the various approaches to Paul's use of the OT in Mark Gignilliat, *Paul and Isaiah's Servants: Paul's Theological Reading of Isaiah 40–66 in 2 Corinthians 5:14–6:10*, LNTS 330 (London: T&T Clark, 2007), 1–16. Also for more discussion, see Hays, *Echoes*, 1–33; Wagner, *Heralds*, 9–13; Tooman, *Gog*, 4–35. For dissenting opinion, see Stanley, *Arguing*, 171–83; Steve Moyise, "Quotations" in Stanley E. Porter and Christopher D. Stanley, eds., *As It Is Written: Studying Paul's Use of Scripture*, SBLSymS 50 (Atlanta: SBL Press, 2008), 15–28.

69. Hays, *Echoes*, 155, emphasis added.

or "metalepsis," which appears when a literary echo links the text in which it occurs to an earlier text, thus evokes the unstated or suppressed (transumed) points of resonance between the two texts.[70]

Following Hays' argument, J. Ross Wagner comments that in the case of Paul, "intertextual echo nearly always functions in tandem with more obvious references to scripture, including citations marked by introductory formulas and more explicit modes of allusions."[71] Hence, not only can the composite *citations* in 6:16c–18 be seen to *allude* to their original contexts, but also the reference to "the fear of God" in 7:1 can be understood to be an "allusive echo" to these same contexts.

Two objections can be anticipated regarding this project. First, it can be questioned whether there is in fact an "allusion" in 2 Cor 7:1 back to the OT texts and contexts cited in 6:16c–18. Second, it can be questioned whether the competency of the audience to discern such an allusion, or even a (composite) citation, plays a determinative role in the nature and/or complexity of Paul's argument.[72] Contrary to those who argue that Paul's exhortation in 2 Cor 7:1 does not necessarily evoke the OT texts of 6:16c–18 or their broader contexts of the OT texts cited in 6:16c–18, the following observations may be made: first, since 7:1 concludes (οὖν) the former argument of 6:14–18, the most natural assumption is that 7:1 refers back to the OT texts cited in 6:16c–18; second, as my thesis will demonstrate, the content of 7:1 meets Hays' widely accepted seven criteria for determining the existence of an intertextual echo in a text—availability, volume, recurrence, thematic coherence, historical plausibility, history of interpretation, and satisfaction.[73] Moreover, though my own work is breaking new ground, scholars such as Steve Moyise have also recognized the echoes in 7:1 to the context of the previous Scriptural citation (cf. Hays' criterion of "history of interpretation").[74] Ultimately, the evidence for the legitimacy of my approach will be seen in the

---

70. Ibid., 20.

71. Wagner, *Heralds*, 10.

72. Cf. Christopher D. Stanley, *Arguing with Scripture: The Rhetoric of Quotations in the Letters of Paul* (New York: T&T Clark, 2004), 38–61; idem, "Paul's 'Use' of Scripture: Why the Audience Matters," in *As It Is Written*, 125–55.

73. Hays, *Echoes*, 29–33. Cf. Stanley E. Porter ("Allusions and Echoes," in *As It Is Written*, 29–40), who proposes using the following criteria for determining an allusion: reference to a prior literary work; indirect reference; intentionality on the part of the author; a focus upon the author making the allusion rather than the readers recognizing it; and shared common knowledge.

74. According to Moyise (*Paul and Scripture: Studying the New Testament Use of the Old Testament* [Grand Rapids: Baker Academic, 2010], 92), even though none of the OT texts cited in 6:16c–18 specifically mention the temple, they are contextually all related to God's making his dwelling place with his people and their context thus supports the exhortation in 2 Cor 7:1 to be separate. The present study, regarding "the fear of God" in 7:1, may thus be seen as a corollary to Moyise's work on the theme of the temple.

results it produces for explaining the meaning and significance of 7:1 within its immediate context and within Paul's thought in the larger context of 2 Corinthians (cf. Hays' criterion of "satisfaction").

The issue regarding the competency of the audience not only goes beyond the scope of this study, but also is difficult to resolve, being an argument from silence—all that we have, in fact, is what Paul actually does in his writing.[75] Nevertheless, focusing on Paul's *intention* in his use of the fear of God in 2 Cor 7:1 through examining its literary context within 2 Corinthians, especially Cor 5:11–7:1, can help us to resolve this issue in part because, as Stanley himself argues, "By framing his quotations in such a way that their 'meaning' could be determined from *the context of his letter*, Paul did his best to insure that his quotations would be understood in the manner in which *he intended them*."[76] William A. Tooman argues that a literary allusion between texts is only intentional and presupposes that readers have access to the evoked texts (physically or through memory) so that the readers' recognition of the allusion will influence their understanding of both the evoked and alluding texts and their recognition of the source text would be absolutely central to the success of an allusion.[77] Therefore, even if we suppose the Corinthians to be, as Stanley argues, "the minimal audience" that had little specific knowledge about the content of the Jewish Scriptures,[78] we are justified in arguing that Paul's essential point regarding the fear of God in 2 Cor 7:1 would be understood by the audience, based on our examination of the antecedent passage

---

75. See Stanley's remarks on this issue in "What We Learned—and What We Didn't," in *Paul and Scripture: Extending the Conversation*, ed. Christopher D. Stanley (Atlanta: SBL Press, 2012), 321–30, especially 325–7: "In fact, one of the chief points that the seminar failed to resolve was how much of Paul's biblical language he expected his audience to recognize and how much was the unconscious product of his own deep roots in the Jewish Scriptures" (quoted from p. 323).

76. Stanley, *Arguing*, 176, emphasis added. Stanley ("Composite Citations," 207) also argues that the purposes of "composite citations," as in 2 Cor 6:16c–18, are: (1) to recall a well-known text to the reader's mind, (2) to demonstrate the quoting author's literary prowess, and (3) to support or advance the quoting author's argument. According to Stanley, the third purpose is the most common reason for creating composite citations. Stanley (*Paul and the Language of Scripture,* 34) also argues that the explicit introductory formulae indicate to the reader that a quotation is indeed present.

77. Tooman, *Gog*, 7.

78. Stanley, *Arguing*, 69. In the later work, Stanley (ibid., 98n1) does not examine the quotations in 2 Cor 6:16c–18 because he regards them (along with the whole of 2 Cor 6:14–7:1) as a later interpolation. However, in his earlier monograph, *Paul and the Language of Scripture*, 217–30, Stanley examines 2 Cor 6:16–18 and regards the catena as "combined citations" of Lev 26:11–12; Isa 52:11; Ezek 20:34; 2 Kgdms 7:8, 14. Moreover, Stanley, 217n127, argues that 2 Cor 6:16b supplies a biblical foundation for v. 16a, "while the thought of vv. 17–18 is *picked up and applied in 7.1*" (emphasis added).

regarding "the fear of the Lord" in 5:11 and the subsequent passages in which "fear" is mentioned in 7:5, 11, 15; 11:3 and 12:20-21.[79]

Therefore, within the immediate literary context of 2 Cor 5:11-7:1 in particular, the main contribution of this work will be its examination of "the fear of God" in 7:1 against the background of the OT texts cited in the catena of 6:16c-18, taking these citations to be "footnotes" to their wider contexts. In so doing, this study takes a similar approach to that of Mark Gignilliat, who examines the Isaianic backdrop to 2 Cor 5:14-6:10 by focusing on the presence of the Isaianic "direct quotation" in 2 Cor 6:2 as evidence for and a pointer to the "allusions" to Isaiah which he observes in its surrounding context.[80] The works of G. K. Beale,[81] David I. Starling,[82] and William J. Webb[83] are beneficial for this study as well in that these scholars elucidate the eschatological elements of 2 Cor 6:14-7:1 on

---

79. In addition, for convincing counterarguments against Stanley's position that on the whole Paul's diverse first century audiences could not have understood his scriptural allusions, and therefore the original contexts of the rhetoric quotations are not important for Paul's arguments (*Arguing*, 60-61, 171-83), see Wagner (*Heralds*, 33-9), who posits that it was possible that the listeners of Paul's letter became interpreters capable of hearing the multitude of scripture voices in that Paul's letter was most likely copied, discussed, and even studied. As evidence for this view, Wagner, 37, argues that "the Corinthian assembly discussed Paul's 'prior letter' at some length; when they could not agree on the meaning of Paul's instructions or desired further clarification of some things he had said, they sent him a letter of their own (1 Cor 7:1; cf. 5:9-11)"; Steve Moyise ("Does Paul Respect the Context of His Quotations?" in *Paul and Scripture*, 105) argues that the weakness of Stanley's argument is that "it implies both a strong authoritarian streak in Paul's rhetoric and a lack of curiosity in his readers"; Richard F. Ward ("Pauline Voice and Presence as Strategic Communication," in *Orality and Textuality in Early Christian Literature*, Semeia 65 [Atlanta: Scholars, 1995], 95-107) argues that Paul's emissary to Corinth would not only recite but interpret the contents of the letter to the Corinthians, so that "the oral rendering and interpretation of the letters completes the apostle's *logos* for the church" (quoted from p. 103); Gordon D. Fee (*Pauline Christology: An Exegetical-Theological Study* [Peabody, MA: Hendrickson, 2007], 23-5), who argues that Stanley fails to take into serious consideration the capacity for remembering the spoken word in an oral/aural culture; and Sean A. Adams and Seth M. Ehorn ("Conclusion," in *Composite Citations in Antiquity. Vol. 2*, eds. Sean A. Adams and Seth M. Ehorn, LNTS 593 [London: T&T Clark, 2018], 230) who argue that there is evidence that some readers spent energy on composite citations, specifically in attempting to "correct" the author's attribution.

80. Gignilliat, *Servants*, 1-30. Gignilliat, 4, distinguishes "allusion" from "direct quotation" and argues: "Allusion, as distinct from direct quotation, does not have the formal aspects of a direct quotation and is therefore a 'nonformal invocation by an author of a text (or person, event, etc.) that the reader could reasonably have been expected to know.'"

81. Beale, "Reconciliation," 217-47.

82. Starling, *Not My People*, especially 61-106.

83. Webb, *Returning Home*, especially 31-158.

the basis of the OT contexts of the texts cited in 6:16c–18. In addition to these studies, particularly significant is the work of Rolf Rendtorff, whose examination of the covenant formulae in the OT, including that of Lev 26:11 cited in 2 Cor 6:16e, provides an important foundation for understanding the framework of Paul's thinking in 6:16-7:1.[84]

Finally, in addition to interpreting the fear of God in 2 Cor 7:1 within the immediate context of 6:14–7:1 and the wider literary context of 2 Corinthians, we will also place Paul's understanding of "the fear of God" alongside selected Second Temple Jewish texts in order to compare how others within Paul's tradition understood the fear of God, particularly in light of an eschatological context. The Second Temple Jewish context of the fear of God is particularly significant for our study because most scholars, whether accepting Pauline authorship of 2 Cor 6:14–7:1 or not, agree on the similarities between this passage and Second Temple Jewish documents.[85] An exploration of the motif of the fear of God in a variety of texts and genres, such as the Psalms of Solomon, Jubilees, 4 Ezra (in comparison to 6 Ezra), and the Testaments of the Twelve Patriarchs, will thus help to establish the spectrum of the Second Temple Jewish understanding of the motif that continued to influence first century Jewish beliefs. The Second Temple Jewish texts examined were therefore representatively chosen to show the spectrum of understanding that was available to Paul and his contemporaries.

More specifically, the examination of the motif of the fear of God in the Second Temple Jewish milieu will show that many other Jews, like Paul, also tried to explain the role the fear of God among God's people would play in their eschatological salvation.[86] Moreover, an examination of the fear of God in these

---

84. Rolf Rendtorff, *The Covenant Formula: An Exegetical and Theological Investigation* (Edinburgh: T&T Clark, 1998), especially 11–28; 57–92.

85. E.g., Joseph A. Fitzmyer, "Qumrân and the Interpolated Paragraph in 2 Cor 6,14–7,1," *CBQ* 23 (1961): 271–80; William O. Walker Jr., *Interpolations in the Pauline Letters*, JSNTSup 213 (London: Sheffield Academic Press, 2001); Gnilka, "2 Cor 6:14–7:1"; Albert L. A. Hogeterp, *Paul and God's Temple: A Historical Interpretation of Cultic Imagery in the Corinthian Correspondence*, BTAS 2 (Leuven; Dudley, MA: Peeters, 2006), 365–78; Liu, *Temple Purity*, 196–233; Peter J. Tomson, "Christ, Belial, and Women: 2 Cor 6:14–7:1 Compared with Ancient Judaism and with the Pauline Corpus," in *Second Corinthians in the Perspective of Late Second Temple Judaism*, ed. Reimund Bieringer, CRINT 14 (Leiden; Boston: Brill, 2014), 79–131; George J. Brooke, "2 Corinthians 6:14–7:1 Again: A Change in Perspective," in *The Dead Sea Scrolls and Pauline Literature*, STDJ 102 (Leiden: Brill, 2014), 1–16.

86. In this regard, we follow the approach exemplified by Rodrigo Jose Morales, who argues that, "The Second Temple literature shows which of these texts still influenced eschatological expectations among Jews of the period, as well as which themes tended to appear together, and so provide a helpful body of literature to compare with Paul's use of OT imagery." Rodrigo Jose Morales, *The Spirit and the Restoration of Israel: New Exodus and New Creation Motifs in Galatians*, WUNT 2/282 (Tübingen: Mohr Siebeck, 2010), 8.

Second Temple Jewish texts will further justify understanding Paul's own treatment of this motif against the OT background set forth in 6:16c–18, both by its parallel and contrast with his Jewish contemporaries' treatments of the same OT motif.[87]

In sum, this study focuses on the meaning and eschatological function of the motif of the fear of God in 2 Cor 7:1 in view of the scriptural contexts of 6:16c–18, with an eye towards its role within the letter's larger apologetic argument, which itself depends on Paul's reading of Israel's Scripture. The foundation for our work thus entails a close, syntactical reading of the internal argument of 6:14–7:1 within its own literary context and within the OT contexts of the Scriptures cited in 6:16c–18, which to help clarify Paul's own thought can then be compared and contrasted with representative examples of Second Temple Jewish understandings of the nature and role of the fear of God in the salvation of his people.

IV. Summary of the Thesis

This study will demonstrate that, although there is no explicit reference to the fear of God in the catena of Scripture in 6:16c–18, the key to understanding the fear of God in 2 Cor 7:1 can be found in the wider contexts of the OT passages cited in 6:16c–18. The contexts of these OT passages show that the fear of God derives from an awareness of the judgment of God to come and consequently functions as a motivation for righteous behavior. Since the OT passages cited in 6:16c–18 are taken from both the Law (Lev 26:11) and the Prophets (Ezek 20:34; 37:27; Isa 52:11), these features of the fear of God, for Paul, are shown to appear throughout the Scriptures.[88] Furthermore, the contexts from which they are taken are consistently eschatological, pointing forward to the coming redemption of God's people under a new covenant. Thus, Paul's understanding of his present age as the beginning new age of the new covenant leads to his understanding of the fear of God as a motivation for his own ministry (2 Cor 5:11) and also to his exhortation to the Corinthians to pursue a holy life with the same motivation (7:1). Moreover, because Paul understands the fear of God as deriving from the eschatological judgment of God, the judgment context constitutes the background for Paul's fear of God (5:10–11) and also becomes the background to the urgency facing the Corinthians (6:1) as the new covenant temple of God (6:16).

---

87. See Francis Watson (*Paul and the Hermeneutics of Faith* [London; New York: T&T Clark, 2004], 2–5) on this "three-way conversation" between "Pauline letters," "the scriptural texts to which they appeal," and "the non-Christian Jewish literature of the Second Temple period which appeals to the same scriptural texts." Watson, 4, argues that, "To interpret is always to interact with a text, and it is also to be *constrained* by the text. If so, it is essential to retrace the way from the scriptural text to its Pauline and non-Pauline realizations, in a manner that allows the scriptural text a voice of its own within a three-way conversation" (original emphasis).

88. Cf. Rom 3:21.

V. Outline of the Thesis

In Chapter Two, this work examines the fear of God in 2 Cor 7:1 within the immediate context of 6:14–7:1 and shows how 7:1 functions as a summary of Paul's previous argument in 6:14–18. Moreover, through an analysis of the literary structure of 6:14–7:1, this work reveals the semantic relationship between 7:1 and the catena of Scripture in 6:16c–18. It then explores the larger context of 2 Cor 7:1 by examining "the fear of the Lord" in 5:11, which is the only other place in 2 Corinthians where Paul uses fear with a specific reference to God/the Lord. The investigation of the context of "the fear of the Lord" in 5:11 shows that it derives from "the judgment seat of Christ" in 5:10, and that it is inextricably linked to the fear of God. This connection is further supported by the examination of 6:1 as the content of Paul's fear and by the examination of the Isaianic context of 2 Cor 4–6 as a whole, which is significantly by the references to Isaiah in 2 Cor 4–6.[89]

This examination of the Isaianic context of 2 Cor 4–6 provides the ground for Chapter Three, in which we examine the fear of God against the contexts of the OT texts Paul quotes in the catena of Scripture (2 Cor 6:16c–18). The context of Isa 50:4–52:11 shows how the commands in 52:11, cited in 2 Cor 6:17ac, are linked to the fear of God in Isa 50:10 that derives from God's judgment in 50:11. The context of Lev 26:11–12 shows how the fear of God in 26:2, expressed in the corresponding fear of his sanctuary, functions as a motivation for the people to keep the covenant stipulation and receive the covenant blessings that include the two promises Paul quotes in 2 Cor 6:16de. Moreover, the covenant formula expressed in the second promise (6:16e) highlights the connection between Lev 26:11–12 and Ezek 37:27, where the promises reappear in a new covenant context. Moreover, the new covenant context of Ezek 36–37 shows that, despite the promised certainty of inheriting the promises of the everlasting covenant of peace, the people of God are still required to respond properly to God's saving activity, which is expressed in terms of God's sanctuary having been placed among them. Thus, the command to fear God/God's sanctuary in Lev 26:2 is still effective in Ezek 37:26 when God places his sanctuary in the midst of his people.

After showing the OT background of the fear of God in 2 Cor 7:1, Chapter Four examines this motif against the Second Temple Jewish backdrop. The exploring of diverse literature from different genres helps us to map out the spectrum of contemporary Jewish perspectives on the fear of God. The Psalms of Solomon show that the fear of God is closely linked to the judgment theme, and that both function as a motivation for the righteous. The fear of God also characterizes the righteous and describes the reign of the future king in the eschaton, when God's vindication of Israel will be fulfilled. The Book of Jubilees shares many similarities with 2 Cor 6:14–7:1, but the fear of God occurs only a few times with a limited function. Instead of the fear of God, the judgment of God is explicitly mentioned as the motivation for a righteous life, but nevertheless, the

---

89. See note 111 in Chapter Two.

assumed link between the fear of God and his judgment indicates that where judgment is given as the motivation, fearing God is also implied. Likewise, 4 Ezra shows the fear of God in a judgment context and further supports our argument as it also shows that those who fear God in the present, as manifest in their keeping of the law, will not fear God on the day of judgment. In contrast, the stance of the unrighteous ones, who did not fear God in the present and despised his law will fear God on the day of judgment. This motivational function of the fear of God is more deliberately expressed in 6 Ezra, which is a later Christian redaction of 4 Ezra, but shares with it the same conviction regarding God's sovereignty in the eschaton and the same practical intention toward the community. The comparison of the Jewish and Christian backgrounds of the fear of God is further explored in the Testaments of the Twelve Patriarchs, in which the Jewish and Christian elements are closely interwoven. Here, the fear of God summarizes the ethics that are required of the people of God, and expresses itself as an example of what constitutes a righteous life. In the Testaments, the fear of God derives from the last judgment that will come upon both the wicked and the Israelites, and thus motivates the latter to pursue a righteous life.

In Chapter Five, we return to 2 Cor 6:14–7:1 to show how the OT understanding of the fear of God and its receptions in Second Temple Judaism can elucidate the passage in three different respects. First, we evaluate the two predominant approaches to 2 Cor 6:14–7:1, i.e., interpolation theories and the salvation-historical hermeneutic, and demonstrate how our understanding of the fear of God helps to answer the questions raised by these approaches concerning the content and context of the passage. Second, we examine the argument of 2 Cor 7:1 itself. Last, this work then explores the role of the fear of God in Paul's eschatology, and how this understanding further sheds light on two different issues regarding 2 Cor 6:14–7:1: temple purity and the command to separate.

Our sixth and final chapter summarizes Paul's use of the fear of God as evidence of his eschatology. In closing, we thus suggest the implications of the current study by briefly examining the subsequent passages where fear appears in 2 Corinthians.

Chapter 2

THE FEAR OF GOD WITHIN THE CONTEXT OF 2 CORINTHIANS

The previous chapter introduced the theme of "the fear of God" in the OT, the NT at large, and in Paul's writings, explained the need for an analysis of its role within Paul's theology, and presented the rationale for doing so by centering the thesis on 2 Cor 7:1. This chapter serves to summarize the basic interpretative decisions which form the foundation for the present work (which will be expanded in Chapter Five) and also further examines "the fear of God" in 7:1 in light of 5:10–11, arguing that "the fear of God" in 7:1 forms an inclusion to "the fear of the Lord" in 5:11. Before examining 5:10–11 it is therefore important to examine the literary structure of 6:14–7:1 and the semantic relationship between 7:1 and the catena of Scripture in 6:16c–18 in order to understand the significance of the fear of God within the argument of 2 Cor 6:14–7:1 as a whole.

I. The Fear of God within the Immediate Context of 2 Cor 7:1

1. The Literary Structure of 2 Cor 6:14–7:1

The argument of 2 Cor 6:14–7:1 can be divided as follows:

6:14a Do not be bound together with unbelievers.

    14b   For what partnership have righteousness and lawlessness?
    14c   Or what fellowship has light with[1] darkness?
    15a   Or what harmony has Christ with Belial?
    15b   Or what has a believer in common with an unbeliever?
    16a   Or what agreement has the temple of God with idols?

    16b   For we are the temple of the living God.

    16c   Just as God said,

---

1. BDAG 873–5. Πρός with the accusative can mean "friendly *to, toward, with, before* κοινωνία." BDAG lists 2 Cor 6:14 as an example in this category.

16d   I will dwell in them and walk among them.
16e   And I will be their God, and they shall be my people.
17a   Therefore, come out from their midst and be separate,
17b   says the Lord.
17c   And do not touch what is unclean;
17d   Then I will welcome you,
18a   And I will be a father to you, and you shall be sons and daughters to me,
18b   says the Lord Almighty.
7:1a Therefore, beloved ones, having these promises,
1b   let us cleanse ourselves from every defilement of flesh and spirit,
1c   completing holiness
1d   in the fear of God.

Within the paragraph of 6:14–7:1, the argument from Scripture in 6:16c–18 contains two doublets of promise-command: God's promises to dwell among his people in a covenant relationship (v. 16de) are followed by his commands to come out and be separate (v. 17a), and his command not to touch what is unclean (v. 17c), which is followed by his promises of acceptance (vv. 17d–18a).[2] These doublets function as a support (καθώς in v. 16c) for Paul's statement of his identity shared with the Corinthians (v. 16b), which serves as a support (γάρ in v. 16b) for the list of contrasts in vv. 14b–16a that supports Paul's initial exhortation not to be bound together with unbelievers (v. 14a).

Thus, it becomes apparent that Paul's statement of his (and the Corinthians') identity in v. 16b supports not only the last contrast in v. 16a, but also the whole list of contrasts in vv.14b–16a since they, having a similar structure, should be considered as a unit:[3]

6:14b		γὰρ				
14b		τίς	μετοχὴ	δικαιοσύνη	καὶ	ἀνομίᾳ,
14c	ἢ	τίς	κοινωνία	φωτὶ	πρὸς	σκότος;
15a	δὲ	τίς	συμφώνησις	Χριστοῦ	πρὸς	Βελιάρ,
15b	ἢ	τίς	μερὶς	πιστῷ	μετὰ	ἀπίστου;
16a	δὲ	τίς	συγκατάθεσις	ναῷ θεοῦ	μετὰ	εἰδώλων;

This list of contrasts functions, not only as a ground for the preceding exhortation (γάρ in v. 14b), but also as a hinge by which *a shift of argument* is made

---

2. This doublet of promise-command reappears in 7:1 as "having these promises" and "let us cleanse ourselves."

3. Thus, Paul Barnett, *The Second Epistle to the Corinthians*, NICNT (Grand Rapids: Eerdmans, 1997), 345; Ralph P. Martin, *2 Corinthians*, 2nd rev., WBC 40 (Grand Rapids: Zondervan, 2014), 362. Contra Hans Dieter Betz ("2 Cor 6:14–7:1: An Anti-Pauline Fragment?" *JBL* 92 [1973]: 91), who argues that the fifth question stands by itself.

from Paul's initial exhortation to the Corinthians (v. 14a) to his statement of his identity shared with the Corinthians (v. 16b). First of all, there is a shift of motif as the focus narrows from the "antithetical rhetorical questions"[4] in vv. 14b–16a to the theme of the temple of God in v. 16b, so that the final antithesis in v. 16a, with its reference to the temple of God, "is also the genesis of the 'temple of God' motif that is central to the remainder of this paragraph."[5] Second, there is also a shift in the person addressed in Paul's argument: Paul's exhortation is addressed to the Corinthians in the second person plural (v. 14a, μὴ γίνεσθε); but, after the list of contrasts Paul speaks in the first person plural (v. 16b, ἡμεῖς). Paul refers to the Corinthians, whom he identifies with righteousness, light, Christ, the believer, and the temple of God (contrasted against lawlessness, darkness, Belial, the unbeliever, and idols), and then shifts the focus to himself and the Corinthians.[6] This shift of person is especially significant because a similar shift from the second person plural to the first person plural occurs again in 6:17–18 and 7:1. Here, Paul uses three imperatives, ἐξέλθατε (v. 17a), ἀφορίσθητε (v. 17a), μὴ ἅπτεσθε (v. 17c), and three matching indicatives, εἰσδέξομαι (v. 17d), ἔσομαι (v. 18a), ἔσεσθε (v. 18a), all of which address the second person plural ὑμᾶς.[7] He then uses the first person plural subjunctive, καθαρίσωμεν, for his concluding exhortation in 7:1b. This transition from the second person plural to the first person plural highlights the common *identity* of Paul and the Corinthians and also their common *responsibility* regarding the command in 7:1b.

Accordingly, the dialogue in the paragraph of 2 Cor 6:14–7:1 can be diagrammed as follows:

	Speaker	**to**	**Audience**	**(in) Type of Speech**
6:14a	Paul	to	Corinthians	second person plural
14b–16a	List of contrasts			
16b	Paul	to	Paul + Corinthians	first person plural
16c–18	God	to	Paul + Corinthians	(second person plural)[8]
7:1	Paul	to	Paul + Corinthians	first person plural

---

4. Barnett, *Second Corinthians*, 343.

5. Murray J. Harris, *The Second Epistle to the Corinthians: A Commentary on the Greek Text*, NIGTC (Grand Rapids; Milton Keynes: Eerdmans; Paternoster, 2005), 504. Likewise, R. J. McKelvey, *The New Temple: The Church in the New Testament*, Oxford Theological Monographs (London: Oxford University Press, 1969), 94.

6. Thus, McKelvey, *New Temple*, 94.

7. The relative pronoun appears three times in vv. 17d–18a.

8. While the imperatives in 6:17a and 17c are clearly second person plurals, the other OT quotations in 6:16c–18 do not show specific reference to the pronoun ὑμᾶς. However, because Paul applies the OT quotations to himself and the Corinthians (cf. 7:1), and also because the OT quotations follow Paul's statement of the common identity of Paul and the Corinthians in v. 16b, the whole catena of Scripture seems to apply to Paul and the Corinthians. Many commentators argue that the OT quotations indicate the fulfillment of

The sequence of the dialogue in 6:14–7:1 thus clarifies that the focus of Paul's argument in the text does not lie on unbelievers, nor on the contrasting parties, but on the identity (6:16b) and the responsibility (7:1) that Paul and the Corinthians share as believers. What is central to Paul's argument in 6:14–7:1 is, therefore, the believers' *identity* as the temple of the living God (6:16b) that Paul shares with the Corinthians and the *exhortation* to cleanse themselves (thus completing holiness in the fear of God) that is appropriate to their identity (7:1).[9] In this context, Paul's statement about the identity in v. 16b already prepares for his concluding exhortation in 7:1. Thus, in 7:1 Paul does not exhort the Corinthians to cleanse themselves because they must confront their opponents, but rather because this command derives naturally from their identity, which is once more emphasized in their "having (the) promises" delineated in the catena of Scripture.[10]

2. The Semantic Relationship between 2 Cor 7:1 and the Catena of Scripture

In this regard, the catena of Scripture in 6:16c–18 supports Paul's statement of his and the Corinthians' identity in 6:16b and also provides the ground on which Paul exhorts the Corinthians in 7:1. Nevertheless, the OT texts in the catena are difficult to recognize because their wording and structure have been altered.[11] Furthermore, the literary structure of the catena is complicated since the transitions between the quotations are hardly noticeable.[12] Three quotation formulae appear in the catena,

---

the OT promises in the Corinthian church; e.g., Margaret E. Thrall, *A Critical and Exegetical Commentary on the Second Epistle to the Corinthians: Introduction and Commentary on II Corinthians I-VII*, vol. 1, ICC (Edinburgh: T&T Clark, 1994), 477; Barnett, *Second Corinthians*, 351–3; Scott J. Hafemann, *2 Corinthians*, NIVAC (Grand Rapids: Zondervan, 2000), 283–6; Harris, *Second Corinthians*, 505–6; Martin, *2 Corinthians*, 367–8.

9. In this regard, C. K. Barrett (*A Commentary on the Second Epistle to the Corinthians*, BNTC [London: Black, 1973], 351) rightly argues that the life demanded of believers lies in their identity: "Corporately the people whose hearts have been changed by the Spirit are the 'temple of the living God'. Their life comes from the 'living' God through his life-giving Spirit who dwells in them. Corporately they are a living temple of God, indwelt by his Spirit because individually they are temples of God, indwelt by his Spirit (cf. 1 Cor 3:16–17; 6:19). Fundamental to this interpretation is the fulfillment motif, which dominates the apostle's thought within 2 Corinthians."

10. Harris, *Second Corinthians*, 513: "[Paul] includes himself in the exhortation and expands it to incorporate the rejection."

11. Martin (*2 Corinthians*, 354) claims that these OT texts are sometimes a quotation, but many times a paraphrase or a redaction of OT verses. Paul does not "slavishly follow nor cite verbatim the OT text in Greek," but while not corrupting "the true meaning of the texts, he appears to alter the wording so as to continue his theme of the separation of God's people from defiling associations" (p. 368).

12. William J. Webb, *Returning Home: New Covenant and Second Exodus as the Context for 2 Corinthians 6.14–7.1*, JSNTSup 85 (Sheffield: JSOT Press, 1993), 32.

however, that help to clarify the relationship between the OT quotations: καθὼς εἶπεν ὁ θεὸς ὅτι in v. 16c, λέγει κύριος in v. 17b, and λέγει κύριος παντοκράτωρ in v. 18b. These quotation formulae do not indicate the beginning or end of the OT quotations, but rather follow the flow of Paul's argument, as seen in the fact that the quotation formula in v. 17b appears in the middle of the quotation from Isa 52:11.[13] The first quotation formula, καθὼς εἶπεν ὁ θεὸς ὅτι, is an unusual way for Paul to introduce an OT quotation.[14] Because of its unique form, especially in comparison with the other two parallel quotation formulae within vv. 16c–17b, it seems that καθώς in v. 16c introduces the entire catena of Scripture.[15] While the quotation formula in v. 16c works as an *introductory* phrase at the beginning of the catena of Scripture, the other two quotation formulae in vv. 17b and 18b function *retrospectively* at the end of each quotation.[16] These two retrospective quotation formulae function as division markers in the catena and reveal a doublet of promises and imperatives. In other words, because of the quotation formula inserted in v. 17b, the imperatives in v. 17ac, quoted from Isa 52:11, are divided into two, each linked respectively to promises. Moreover, Paul's change of the order of the imperatives in v. 17ac, which otherwise would form a verbatim quotation from

---

13. Cf. Frank J. Matera, *II Corinthians: A Commentary*, NTL (Louisville; London: Westminster John Knox, 2003), 164: "In addition to this strong introductory formula [in v. 16c], Paul employs two other formulas, one in the middle of the quotation ('says the Lord') and another at the end ('says the Lord Almighty'), thereby underscoring the authority of this citation at its beginning, middle, and end."

14. Barrett, *Second Corinthians*, 200; Harris, *Second Corinthians*, 505; Martin, *2 Corinthians*, 368. An introductory phrase using the conjunction καθώς with God as the subject appears only here in the Pauline corpus. The conjunction καθώς is used in Rom 1:17, 2:24; 3:4, 10; 4:17; 8:36; 9:13, 29, 33; 10:15; 11:8, 26; 15:3, 9, 21; 1 Cor 1:31; 2:9; 2 Cor 8:15; 9:9, and most of the time it is used to refer to the Scripture, καθὼς γέγραπται. Only in Rom 9:29 is it used with another personal subject, καθὼς προείρηκεν Ἡσαΐας. This unique quotation formula in 2 Cor 6:16c has led some scholars to posit that this catena is a fragment from Qumran texts; see Joseph A. Fitzmyer, "Use of Explicit Old Testament Quotations in Qumran Literature and in the New Testament," *NTS* 7 (1961): 302; idem, "Qumrân and the Interpolated Paragraph in 2 Cor 6,14–7,1," *CBQ* 23 (1961): 279; Joachim Gnilka, "2 Cor 6:14–7:1 in the Light of the Qumran Texts and the Testaments of the Twelve Patriarchs," in *Paul and Qumran: Studies in New Testament Exegesis*, ed. Jerome Murphy-O'Connor (London: G. Chapman, 1968), 58; Betz, "2 Cor 6:14–7:1," 92. However, Matera (*II Corinthians*, 164) argues that this formula is important for Paul because it discloses that he views the whole of Scripture as God's word, and thus Paul also reinforces what he wants to say by appealing to the authority of God; likewise, Barrett, *Second Corinthians*, 200.

15. As Harris, *Second Corinthians*, 494.

16. Paul's retrospective use of the quotation formula, λέγει κύριος, appears in other places, e.g., Rom 12:19; 1 Cor 14:21. Romans 14:11 can be seen either as a part of the quotation in Isa 49:18 or as a retrospective quotation mark because it is placed in between two quotations (of Isa 49:18 and 45:23).

Isa 52:11, also suggests that the interruption in 2 Cor 6:17a–c is intentional. Thus, instead of a "promises-imperatives-promises" structure,[17] we have a "promises-imperative (break indicated by quotation formula) imperative-promises" structure:[18]

v. 16c Introductory QF (Quotation Formula)	καθὼς εἶπεν ὁ θεὸς ὅτι
v. 16d A1 Promise (God's Presence)	ἐνοικήσω ἐν αὐτοῖς
v. 16e A2 Promise (Covenant Formula)	καὶ ἐμπεριπατήσω καὶ ἔσομαι αὐτῶν θεὸς καὶ αὐτοὶ ἔσονταί μου λαός
v. 17a B Imperative	διὸ ἐξέλθατε ἐκ μέσου αὐτῶν καὶ ἀφορίσθητε
v. 17b Retrospective QF	λέγει κύριος
v. 17c B′ Imperative	καὶ ἀκαθάρτου μὴ ἅπτεσθε
v. 17d A′ 1 Promise (God's Acceptance)	κἀγὼ εἰσδέξομαι ὑμᾶς
v. 18a A′ 2 Promise (Adoption Formula)	καὶ ἔσομαι ὑμῖν εἰς πατέρα καὶ ὑμεῖς ἔσεσθέ μοι εἰς υἱοὺς καὶ θυγατέρας
v. 18b Retrospective QF	λέγει κύριος παντοκράτωρ

In addition, the insertion of the quotation formula in 6:17b shifts the orientation of the second half of the imperatives in v. 17c more closely toward the promise of God's presence in v. 17d, so that this promise becomes contingent upon the fulfillment of the preceding imperative.[19] Therefore, the conjunction, καί (in κἀγώ), in v. 17d can be translated as "then" or "in that case," introducing a result clause.[20] In other words, the promises in v. 16de have been fulfilled in the past (cf. v. 16b),

---

17. Some scholars propose other structural analyses that recognize a chiasm in the catena of Scripture that does not separate the paraenetic portion in v. 17abc. For example, James M. Scott argues that the catena is introduced as a single quotation, thereby forming a chiasm, so that 2 Cor 6:16c–18b "has corresponding beginning and ending premises (ABC/A′B′C′) with concretizing parenesis in the middle." James M. Scott, *Adoption as Sons of God: An Exegetical Investigation into the Background of ΥΙΟΘΕΣΙΑ in the Pauline Corpus*, WUNT 2/48 (Tübingen: J. C. B. Mohr, 1992), 192. Also, see idem, "Use of Scripture," 77; David E. Garland, *2 Corinthians*, NAC 29 (Nashville: Broadman & Holman, 1999), 336.

18. Webb (*Returning Home*, 32–3) argues that the interruption with the introductory formula in 6:17b is intended to impart "a bi-fold structure" to the whole.

19. Thus, Webb, *Returning Home*, 33; George H. Guthrie, *2 Corinthians*, BECNT (Grand Rapids: Baker Academic, 2015), 357.

20. BDAG 494–6. According to BDAG, 495, καί can be used to introduce a result that comes from what precedes: *and then, and so*. Likewise, McKelvey, *New Temple*, 96; Matera, *II Corinthians*, 165; Harris, *Second Corinthians*, 495, 507.

while the promises in vv. 17d–18a still await a future fulfillment, which is contingent on the obedience of believers to the commands (v. 17ac). At the same time, διό in v. 17a, which introduces the paraenesis quotation, indicates that the imperative in v. 17a builds upon the (fulfilled) promises of God in v. 16de. Thus, God's promises in v. 16de become the grounds for his imperatives in v. 17a, and the following imperative in v. 17c leads to (καί) God's promises in vv. 17d–18a.

Nevertheless, the interruption in v. 17b does not signify that the imperatives in vv. 17a and 17c are different from each other, nor does it signify that the promises in v. 16de and vv. 17d–18a are very different. Though this point will be developed in detail later, it should already be noted here that it is difficult to distinguish the promises of God's presence in v. 16d from the promise of God's future acceptance in v. 17d, or the promise of the covenant formula of v. 16e from that of the adoption formula of v. 18a. When comparing the content of the promises and imperatives in vv. 16d–18a, their similarity argues against the idea that the promises of God in vv. 17d–18a are different from the promises of God in v. 16de.[21] In fact, the content of these promises in vv. 16d–16e and vv. 17d–18a overlaps, so that the promises of God's acceptance and his relationship with his people in vv. 17d–18a are already said to be fulfilled in v. 16de. In order to understand the force of Paul's argument, this dual temporal aspect of the promises must be explored in which *they are already fulfilled, but at the same time await their full completion in the future*, being contingent on fulfilling God's commands.

Moreover, as mentioned above, this inextricable relationship between the promises of God and the imperatives, which is expressed in a doublet of promise-command within the catena of Scripture, reappears in Paul's last exhortation in 7:1:

| A | **Promise** | having these promises |
| B | **Imperative** | let us cleanse ourselves |

The exact nature of the relationship between the adverbial participle clause and the exhortation is not immediately clear.[22] However, 6:16c–18b provides a lens through which one can interpret 7:1 due to the close connections between them. First, the conjunction οὖν in v. 7:1a indicates an inferential syntactical connection. Second, the similarity of the promises (the demonstrative ταύτας refers back to the promises that have been mentioned in vv. 16d–18b) and commands (both 6:17ac and 7:1b deal with cleansing and purification) reflects a close semantic and theological relationship between 7:1 and the preceding catena of Scripture. Lastly, within 7:1 the relationship between the promises and commands is further unpacked by the second

---

21. Barnett, *Second Corinthians*, 355–6; Harris, *Second Corinthians*, 511; Martin, *2 Corinthians*, 372.

22. The adverbial participle is often taken as a ground, "since" (e.g., "Since we have these promises" [ESV], "Therefore, since we have these promises" [NIV], and "Because we have these promises" [NLT]). Nevertheless, the question remains whether "having these promises" is intended to indicate that the promises were already fulfilled in the past or will be in the future.

adverbial participle clause, ἐπιτελοῦντες ἁγιωσύνην ἐν φόβῳ θεοῦ (completing holiness in the fear of God), the themes of which will be seen to be Paul's own commentary on the preceding admonition from Scripture. This second adverbial participle clause, as that which clarifies Paul's admonition in view of his own understanding of the OT commands, thus becomes the key to understanding the command in 7:1b, which in turn will help clarify the argument of 6:14–7:1 as a whole.

Though this point will be clarified later in Chapter Five, it should already be noted that "completing holiness" functions as a *result* of "cleansing," which is an ongoing process for believers, and "the fear of God" indicates the *means* by which the process of completing holiness is to be executed by believers. Although Paul uses the fear of God several times in his letters in various forms,[23] he seems to introduce the notion of the fear of God into this concluding statement of his exhortation in 7:1 rather abruptly. Whereas the other themes of 7:1 look back directly to the OT quotations in 6:16c–18 conceptually, the motif of the fear of God does not have an immediately observable connection with the preceding section. Indeed, the only prior reference to "fear" before 7:1 is 5:11. Thus, before we turn our attention to the OT quotations in 2 Cor 6:16c–18, in order to determine their relationship to the fear of God in 7:1, it will be helpful to examine 2 Cor 5:11 within its context for any light it might shed on 7:1.

II. The Fear of God within the Larger Context of 2 Corinthians

1. The Fear of the Lord in 2 Cor 5:11

"The fear of the Lord" (ὁ φόβος τοῦ κυρίου) in 2 Cor 5:11 is the only other place in 2 Corinthians besides 2 Cor 7:1 where Paul uses fear with an explicit reference to its object.[24] Here, Paul refers to "the fear of the Lord" when describing his apostolic ministry:

> Therefore, knowing the fear of the Lord, we are persuading men, and we have been manifested to God, but I am hoping to have been manifested also to your conscience.

Scholars have often observed the connection between 5:11 and 7:1, but the comparison has mostly been limited to vocabulary.[25] Nevertheless, a closer examination of the fear of the Lord in 5:11 will reveal the conceptual parallels

---

23. Cf. note 2 in Chapter One.

24. Cf. 2 Cor 7:5 refers to Paul's fear (and that of his companions); 7:11 and 15 refer to the Corinthians' fear. On the other hand, the verb, φοβέω/φοβέομαι, appears twice in 2 Cor 11:3; 12:20, but they too appear without a referent.

25. E.g., Gordon D. Fee, "II Corinthians vi. 14–vii. 1 and Food Offered to Idols," *NTS* 23 (1977): 147; Victor Paul Furnish, *II Corinthians*, AB 32A (Garden City, NY: Doubleday, 1984), 306; Barnett, *Second Corinthians*, 357n77; Harris, *Second Corinthians*, 514n111.

between these two contexts, and thus further enlighten our understanding of Paul's use of the fear of God in 7:1. In both cases fear functions similarly as a motivating factor to accomplish the task: knowing the fear of the Lord is a motivation for Paul to pursue his ministry for the sake of the Corinthians in 5:11, and the fear of God serves as the basis for the Corinthians to carry out Paul's exhortation to complete holiness through cleansing in 7:1. In addition, in each case fear appears against an OT background: the fear of God in 7:1 follows the catena of Scripture in 6:16c–18, and even though it might not be explicit in the text, many scholars have observed that the context of the fear of the Lord in 5:11 contains an OT background.[26] Lastly, because the fear of God plays a significant role in the new covenant (Jer 32:39–41), the contexts of the fear of the Lord/God in 2 Cor 5:11 and 7:1 are congruent with Paul's argument in 2 Cor 3 regarding the inauguration of the new covenant.[27]

Paul mentions the fear of the Lord in 5:11 as part of the defense of his apostolic ministry, which has been the focus of his discussion throughout 2:14–6:10.[28] According to Paul, this fear of the Lord derives from the judgment seat of Christ (5:10)[29] and functions as a motivation for his ministry.[30] Paul's description of his

---

26. E.g., see Scott (*2 Corinthians*, 117–18, 130–1) for a detailed argument of the various OT backgrounds of 2 Cor 5:11. Also, Garland (*2 Corinthians*, 268), Matera (*II Corinthians*, 130), and Schmeller (*Zweite Korinther*, 309) argue for the background from the OT wisdom literature, while Keener (*1–2 Corinthians*, 183) mentions that the fear of God/the Lord is a prominent OT basis for ethics.

27. For a more detailed argument regarding the new covenant context in 2 Cor 3 with regard to the OT prophecy, see Scott J. Hafemann, *Paul, Moses, and the History of Israel: The Letter/Spirit Contrast and the Argument from Scripture in 2 Corinthians 3*, WUNT 2/81 (Tübingen: J. C. B. Mohr, 1995), 92–186. Also Albert L. A. Hogeterp, "The Eschatological Setting of the New Covenant in 2 Cor 3:4–18," in *Theologizing in the Corinthian Conflict: Studies in the Exegesis and Theology of 2 Corinthians*, ed. Reimund Bieringer et al., BTAS 16 (Leuven: Peeters, 2013), 131–44.

28. Harris, *Second Corinthians*, 411; Barnett, *Second Corinthians*, 280.

29. Even though scholars do not agree to whom the fear of the Lord in 5:11 refers, they agree that the fear of the Lord derives from the judgment seat of Christ in 5:10, e.g., Furnish, *II Corinthians*, 322; Barnett, *Second Corinthians*, 279; Harris, *Second Corinthians*, 412; Martin, *2 Corinthians*, 276; Guthrie, *2 Corinthians*, 296.

30. In 5:11 the adverbial participle, εἰδότες, functions as a motivation for Paul to accomplish his work: "*Because* we know the fear of the Lord, we are persuading men." Cf. "Since, then, we know the fear of the Lord ..." (NIV). For the fact that perfect participles that are used as presents, such as οἶδα, mostly indicate the cause or reason or ground of the action, see Daniel B. Wallace, *Greek Grammar beyond the Basics: An Exegetical Syntax of the New Testament* (Grand Rapids: Zondervan, 1996), 631n47, who also lists the passages in the NT where εἰδότες is used causally. Also, Harris, *Second Corinthians*, 411. On the other hand, Furnish (*II Corinthians*, 304–5) argues that the fear is not just "knowing about" the final judgment before Christ, although it includes that. Furnish argues that the phrase "the fear of the Lord" must be understood primarily in relation to its background in the Hebrew Bible, not only with reference to the judicial bench of Christ (v. 10).

ministry here as "persuading men" is the corollary to his earlier definition of his ministry as that characterized by the new covenant (2 Cor 3:6) established by the Spirit (3:3, 6, 8 cf. 5:5), and as that subsequently described as the ministry of reconciliation (5:18). Hence, by implication, Paul's ministry of the new covenant that has been established by the Spirit and reconciles people to God is inextricably linked motivationally to the fear of the Lord that derives from the judgment seat of Christ.[31]

Paul's declaration of "fear" as a motivation for his ministry in 5:11 is striking in view of the fact that in the wider context Paul repeatedly states his "confidence" as a motivation for fulfilling his calling for ministry (3:4; 4:1, 16; 5:6, 8).[32] At first glance, it seems that Paul switches from the *positive* term "confidence" to the *negative* term "fear" that derives from the judgment seat (5:10). However, as with his "confidence" in God, also his "fear" of the Lord functions in the same motivational way for Paul (5:11), which draws attention to the significance of the function and meaning of "the fear of the Lord."

---

31. Matthew V. Novenson (*Christ among the Messiahs: Christ Language in Paul and Messiah Language in Ancient Judaism* [New York; Oxford: Oxford University Press, 2012], 164) argues that the goal of Paul's ministry of reconciliation in 2 Cor 5:18 is to persuade people in 5:11. Scholars are divided about the nature or subject matter of πείθω ("to persuade") in 5:11. There are three possible options for understanding the verb: "to evangelize," Barnett, *Second Corinthians*, 280n8; "to defend his apostolicity," Rudolf Karl Bultmann, *The Second Letter to the Corinthians*, trans. Erich Dinkler (Minneapolis: Augsburg, 1985), 147; R. Kent Hughes, *2 Corinthians: Power in Weakness* (Wheaton, IL: Crossway, 2006), 186; Furnish, *II Corinthians*, 306; or both, Harris, *Second Corinthians*, 413; Martin, *2 Corinthians*, 278. Based on Paul's claim in 6:12 that he is giving the Corinthians an opportunity "to boast about us" (καυχήματος ὑπὲρ ἡμῶν), so that they will be able to confront Paul's opponents, Paul's action of persuading men is best taken to mean that he intends to defend his apostleship. However, because Paul's action is based on his fear of the Lord (and not on his fear of men, including his opponents), Paul's emphasis is not on preserving himself per se, but on the eschatological judgment (5:10) that befalls all people (including the Corinthians). For Paul sees one's eschatological destiny disclosed in how people respond to his mission (cf. 2 Cor 2:15–17a). Thus, Paul, as the minister of Gentiles, persuades the Corinthians not to receive God's grace in vain (6:1) and reconcile with God (and him) (5:20; 6:13; 7:2).

32. E.g., in 4:1 Paul affirms that his confidence in ministry derives from the mercy (of God) that was shown to him, and in 4:16 Paul does not lose heart because of the hope of resurrection (διό in 4:16). Paul's confidence also stems from the belief that God prepares "our heavenly dwelling" (5:1–2) and guarantees it by the Holy Spirit (5:5). Eventually, these certainties allow Paul the confidence to be of good courage (5:6, 8). Bultmann (*Second Corinthians*, 145) rightly argues that Paul's "confidence" (πεποίθησις) in 3:4 is based on his own calling as the "servant of the new covenant" in 3:6. Likewise, Furnish, *II Corinthians*, 301, comments that the expression of confidence with which Paul starts 5:6–10 reformulates the declaration of his apostolic boldness in 4:16.

Moreover, in 5:9 Paul's confidence leads to his ambition "to be pleasing to the Lord" (εὐάρεστοι αὐτῷ εἶναι). Even though the semantic relationship between Paul's ambition "to be pleasing to the Lord" in v. 9 and his desire "to persuade men and to be manifest before God" in v. 11 is not specifically expressed in the text, both the structural context of vv. 9–11 and Paul's use of "pleasing" (εὐάρεστος) elsewhere support the close connection, if not identity, between the two. First, structurally, the fear of the Lord in v. 11 derives from the judgment seat of Christ in the previous verse and a motivation for Paul to prosecute his ministry (οὖν in v. 11). At the same time, the judgment in v. 10 becomes the grounds for Paul's ambition to be pleasing to God in v. 9 (γάρ in v. 10). Thus, the judgment seat of Christ functions as a motivation both *retrospectively* (for Paul's ambition in v. 9) and *prospectively* (for Paul's ministry in v. 11). Therefore, it is only proper to understand that Paul's ambition is inextricably linked with his ministry. Second, Paul uses "pleasing" (εὐάρεστος) several times in his writings in a way to express (the goal of) his ministry.[33]

Thus, the motivation for Paul's ambition to please the Lord in 5:9 and his ministry to persuade men in v. 11 is based on the reality expressed in v. 10 that everyone will be manifested at "the judgment seat of Christ" (τὸ βῆμα τοῦ Χριστοῦ) and all will be judged according to what they did through the body "either good or evil" (εἴτε ἀγαθὸν εἴτε φαῦλον). In this regard, an examination of the judgment seat of Christ is necessary to clarify Paul's understanding of fear that motivates him to persuade others.

2. The Judgment Seat of Christ in 2 Cor 5:10

As mentioned above, in 2 Cor 5:10 Paul states the support for his ambition to be pleasing to the Lord:

> For all of us must appear before the judgment seat of Christ, so that each may receive recompense for what has been done in the body, whether good or evil.

There are two questions raised regarding the judgment seat of Christ in 5:10 that are significant for our understanding of the fear of the Lord in the next verse. First, "*who is the judge* at the judgment scene?"[34] and second, "*who will be judged* at

---

33. For example, in Rom 12:1–2 Paul "exhorts" (παρακαλῶ) the Romans to present their bodies as "a living sacrifice, holy and pleasing to God" (θυσίαν ζῶσαν ἁγίαν εὐάρεστον τῷ θεῷ), and also to discern the will of God that is "good and pleasing and perfect" (τὸ ἀγαθὸν καὶ εὐάρεστον καὶ τέλειον; cf. Rom 14:18; Eph 5:10; Phil 4:18; Col 3:20).

34. For the scholarly discussion of the option, see, Friedrich Guntermann, *Die Eschatologie des Hl. Paulus*, NTAbh 13 (Münster: Aschendorff, 1932), 204–8; Wilhelm Thüsing, *Per Christum in Deum: Studien zum Verhältnis von Christozentrik und Theozentrik in den Paulinischen Hauptbriefen*, 2nd ed., NTAbh 1 (Münster: Aschendorff, 1969), 30–9; and David Edward Aune, "The Judgment Seat of Christ (2 Cor. 5.10)," in *Pauline Conversations in Context : Essays in Honor of Calvin J. Roetzel*, JSNTSup 221 (London; New York: Sheffield Academic Press, 2002), 68–86.

the judgment scene?" Paul uses "the judgment seat" (τὸ βῆμα) only two times in his writings, but each time, he attributes to it with a different presider:[35] while in 5:10 it is before "the judgment seat of Christ" (τὸ βῆμα τοῦ Χριστοῦ) where all will stand, in Rom 14:10 it is before the "judgment seat of God" (τὸ βῆμα τοῦ θεοῦ).[36] David Edward Aune lists three possible ways to understand the different expressions of "the judgment seat of Christ" and "the judgment seat of God": (1) one can combine the two texts into a single narrative in which Paul had in mind an eschatological judgment scene where Christ presides, after which God will preside in a climactic act of judgment; (2) the two texts represent variants of a single eschatological event, and Christ and God function interchangeably as the presider; and (3) one may focus on how these fragments of latent apocalyptic discourses function in each context where they occur, rather than combining the texts into a single concept.[37]

Aune further argues that the reason why Paul describes diverse judgment scenes is not to provide precise information about a particular episode in the complex unfolding of events in the eschaton, but rather to use these scenes in their respective contexts as "means of argument" (*Argumentationsmittel*) to reinforce the other points he was trying to make.[38] While Aune's argument that Paul was able to use different eschatological judgment scenes to develop his argument is *possible*,

---

35. "Τὸ βῆμα" in the NT consistently refers to a place of judicial decision-making or judgment. E.g., Matt 27:19; John 19:13; Acts 7:5; 12:21; 18:12, 16, 17; 25:6, 10, 17. BDAG 175; Guthrie, *2 Corinthians*, 288. Also Mark A. Seifrid, *The Second Letter to the Corinthians*, PNTC (Grand Rapids; Nottingham, England: Eerdmans; Apollos, 2014), 236: "[it] is most likely the seat on the raised platform that was used for public judgments and declarations." It is also translated as "tribunal," e.g., Barnett, *Second Corinthians*, 274; Thrall, *Second Corinthians*, 1:394; Harris, *Second Corinthians*, 405.

36. There is a textual variant in Rom 14:10 regarding βήματι τοῦ θεοῦ. Some manuscripts read βήματι τοῦ Χριστοῦ, e.g., the later Alexandrian MSS C, 33, and 81, Ψ, the second [Byzantine] corrector of ℵ, two other uncials L, P, and the majority text. Nevertheless, βήματι τοῦ θεοῦ is to be preferred here because of the evidence of the earlier texts, e.g., ℵ, A, B, C, and the wider geographical distribution represented by D, F, G, etc. Scholars have argued that the variant derived from the influence of 2 Cor 5:10, since, in contrast to Rom 14:10, there is no such textual variant in 2 Cor 5. Bruce Manning Metzger, *A Textual Commentary on the Greek New Testament: A Comparison Volume to the United Bible Societies' Greek New Testament*, 3rd ed. (London: United Bible Societies, 1975), 513; Douglas J. Moo, *The Epistle to the Romans*, NICNT (Grand Rapids: Eerdmans, 1996), 834, 846-7.

37. Aune, "Judgment Seat," 81-3.

38. Ibid., 76. Aune, 69, argues that 2 Cor 5:10 is one of more than twenty passages in the Pauline letters "in which fragments of a latent apocalyptic scheme of events find brief and cryptic expression"(cf. Rom 2:6–16; 14:10–12; 1 Cor 3:8, 12–15; 4:5; 6:2–3, 9–10, 14; 13:12; 2 Cor 4:14; 5:1–8; 11:15; Eph 6:8; Phil 1:6, 10–11; 2:16; 3:10–11, 18–21; Col 1:22; 1 Thess 1:10; 5:2–5, 9; 2 Tim 4:14).

it is *not probable* because Aune cannot explain the connection within the one related context of 2 Cor 5:11 and 7:1 between the fear of the "Lord" that derives from the judgment seat of "Christ" and the fear of "God."[39] Furthermore, Aune's argument that Paul simply borrowed the Jewish apocalyptic view of the eschaton overlooks the OT background of the fear of the Lord.[40]

1) Who Will Judge? Although Paul does not provide a detailed description of the eschatological judgment in 2 Cor 5:10, he gives specific explanations of the judgment in other texts. In Rom 2:16 Paul describes the judgment scene as taking place in a "co-operative" manner:[41] "On the day when, according to my gospel, God will judge (κρίνει ὁ θεός) the secret thoughts of all through Jesus Christ (διὰ Χριστοῦ Ἰησοῦ)." Here, Paul explains that *God* is the judge in the final judgment and that he will judge through the agency of *Jesus Christ*. The latter is not excluded from the office of judge, but there is a clear distinction of roles.[42] James D. G. Dunn thus argues that God has a higher authority because it is God who delegates Jesus' role in the final judgment and there is "no scope for the thought that Jesus as judge

---

39. Cf. Brendan Byrne, *Romans*, SP 6 (Collegeville, MN: Liturgical Press, 2007), 414: "Paul can readily interchange the Christological and theological perspective because of his sense of the complete ordination of the work of Christ to that of God." Also, Moo, *Romans*, 847n105: "The shift of terminology [from the judgment seat of Christ to God] does not imply that Paul conceives of two separate 'judgment seats' but that he views God and Christ as so closely related that he can shift almost unconsciously from one to the other."

40. Aune, "Judgment Seat," 86.

41. L. Joseph Kreitzer, *Jesus and God in Paul's Eschatology*, JSNT 19 (Sheffield: JSOT Press, 1987), 110–11. Kreitzer argues that Paul uses the κρίνω word group frequently when speaking of God's judgment (κρίνω appears in Rom 2:1, 3, 12, 16, 27; 3:4, 6, 7; 14:3, 4, 5, 10, 13, 22; 1 Cor 2:2; 4:5; 5:3, 12, 13; 6:1, 2, 3, 6; 7:37; 10:15, 29; 11:13, 31, 32; 2 Cor 2:1; 5:14; Col 2:16; 2 Thess 2:12, συγκρίνω in 1 Cor 2:13; 10:12, ἀνακρίνω in 1 Cor 2:14, 15; 4:3, 4; 9:3; 10:25, 27; 14:24, κατακρίνω in Rom 2:1; 8:3, 34; 14:23; 1 Cor 11:32, κρίσις in 2 Thess 1:5, κατάκρισις in 2 Cor 3:9; 7:3, δικαιοκρίσις in Rom 2:5, κρίμα in Rom 2:2, 3; 3:8; 5:16; 11:33; 13:2; 1 Cor 6:7; 11:29, 34; Gal 5:10, and κατάκριμα in Rom 5:16, 18; 8:1). According to Kreitzer, Paul's use of the judgment is similar to Jewish pseudepigraphal literature (for example, 1 En., T. Ab., T. Mos.), so that "there is a fluctuation between executors of final judgment within several of the Jewish pseudepigraphal documents. This fluctuation involves the ambiguous reference to the executor (whether God or agent) as seated on the Throne of Judgment" (p. 106).

42. God's role as subject in the last judgment is further explained in 1 Thess 3:13, where the context of judgment appears with the same preposition (ἔμπροσθεν) as in 2 Cor 5:10: "And may he so strengthen your hearts in holiness that you may be blameless *before our God and Father* at the coming of our Lord Jesus with all his saints" (emphasis added).

has replaced God, far less usurped God's role."[43] Hence, the relationship between God and Christ at the judgment expressed in Rom 2:16 indicates that there need not be a tension between Rom 14:10 and 2 Cor 5:10. In this regard, Wilhelm Thüsing argues:

> Für diesen Sachverhalt, daß Paulus von Gott als dem Richter spricht, obschon man entsprechend dem Vorhergehenden eine Aussage über Christus als den Richter erwarten würde, gibt es nur eine Erklärung: Der Apostel sieht das Richteramt Gottes und Christi so sehr *in eins*, daß für ihn das eine mit dem

---

43. James D. G. Dunn, "Jesus the Judge: Further Thoughts of Paul's Christology and Soteriology," in *The Convergence of Theology: A Festschrift Honoring Gerald O'Collins, S. J.*, ed. Daniel Kendall and Stephen T. Davis (New York: Paulist, 2001), 43, 45. Dunn argues that it was a commonly accepted Jewish concept that others could play a role in the final judgment, which is combined with Paul's exalted lordship of the risen Christ. Moreover, Paul's understanding of salvation as a two-stage-process (justification and judgment) naturally led him to alternate the role of judgment between God and Christ: "[T]he two-stage soteriology (beginning and end, justified already but not yet finally acquitted) is mirrored in the double role of Jesus in the process of justification: justified through faith in Christ, and Jesus the judge. Affirming Jesus as eschatological judge recognizes that justification is a process, that it is not complete in the moment faith is placed in Christ, and that Christ will also signal its completion, while at the same time giving reassurance that the judge is also the justifier" (p. 42). Even though Dunn provides an understanding of how both God and Christ are in the judgment scene, his argument is lacking in some aspects. First, his argument that it was a commonly accepted Jewish concept that others could play a role in the final judgment needs a more accurate delineation of the roles of the partakers because the functions of the various participants in the final judgment vary. Dunn lists Jub. 4:17-24; 1 En. 12-16; T. Ab. [A] 13:3-10; T. Ab. [B] 11:1-4, 7 as examples. In these passages several characters have roles in the judgment beside God: Abel (T. Ab. [A] 13; T. Ab. [B] 11), Enoch (Jub. 4; 1 En. 13-15; T. Ab. [B] 11), the twelve tribes of Israel (T. Ab. [A] 13), and angels (T. Ab. [A] 13). However, their various roles in the judgment are limited to secondary roles, e.g., writing condemnations, bringing charges, interceding, writing memorial prayers and petitions on behalf of the fallen angels, or recording sins and righteous deeds. Regarding the role as a judge, only Abel and the twelve tribes of Israel are described as judges, but their role is likewise limited. Their role as judge will only last until the great and glorious Parousia, when every person will be judged by the Master-God of all. Only then will there be perfect judgment and recompense, eternal and unalterable, which no one can question (T. Ab. [A] 13:4-7). Second, Dunn's argument that Christ's participation in the final judgment exemplifies Paul's two-stage soteriology is less persuasive in that Paul mostly refers to *God* as the one who judges in the eschaton (e.g., Rom 3:26; 4:5; 8:33). Moreover, instead of describing Christ as the judge in the eschaton, Paul several times refers to Christ as the one who rescues or saves from God's wrath (Rom 5:9-10; 8:33-34; 1 Thess 1:10).

anderen gegeben ist. Er ist ganz davon durchdrungen, daß auf dem Richterstuhl Gottes sein Synthronos Christus sitzt.[44]

In fact, the concept of God's judgment in and/or through Christ is not foreign to 2 Corinthians because Paul twice mentions that he speaks "before God and in Christ" (κατέναντι θεοῦ ἐν Χριστῷ) (see 2:17 and 12:19). Scholars rightly acknowledge that the phrase "before God" implies God's judgment as that which functions, like "the fear of the Lord" in 5:11, as the motivation for Paul's ministry.[45] In 2:17, Paul claims that, different from his opponents, who are "peddling God's word,"[46] he speaks "out of sincerity," since he is "speaking before God and in Christ." Because being "in the presence of God" means to be seen and judged by God, Paul emphasizes that being under the scrutiny of God testifies to his sincerity.[47] Therefore, Paul's consciousness of the coming judgment functions as a source for Paul's concern over the integrity of his apostolic ministry.[48]

In a similar context, Paul insists on the legitimacy of the self-defense of his ministry in 2 Cor 12:11–18, where he advocates his sincerity toward the Corinthians in spite of appearances to the contrary.[49] There Paul states that his self-defense is not for his own sake, but that he aims to build up the Corinthian church (v. 19), and once again emphasizes in support of this contention that he "speaks before God and in Christ" (κατέναντι θεοῦ ἐν Χριστῷ λαλοῦμεν). Once again, Paul thus supports his sincerity by recognizing that not just the Corinthians, but he himself stands under God's judgment.[50] This judgment theme in 12:19 is further highlighted

---

44. Thüsing, *Per Christum*, 36, emphasis added. Likewise, Scott, *2 Corinthians*, 117; Guthrie, *2 Corinthians*, 288.

45. Barnett, *Second Corinthians*, 158; Hafemann, *2 Corinthians*, 114–15; Harris, *Second Corinthians*, 255; Schmeller, *Zweite Korinther*, 309; Martin, *2 Corinthians*, 656; Seifrid, *Second Corinthians*, 95.

46. Scott J. Hafemann (*Suffering and the Spirit: An Exegetical Study of II Cor. 2:14–3:3 within the Context of the Corinthian Correspondence*, WUNT 2/19 [Tübingen: J. C. B. Mohr, 1986], 124) argues that καπηλεύω means "selling the Word of God as a retail dealer sells his wares in the market." For a more detailed discussion about the meaning of καπηλεύω, see ibid., 105–25.

47. Barrett, *Second Corinthians*, 104. The judgment theme in 2:17 is further emphasized in that the previous verse shows the two diverse results produced by Paul's message: to those who respond positively to Paul and his message, Paul is a fragrance that leads to life, but to those who reject Paul, he becomes a means of destruction and loss. Rightly, Martin, *2 Corinthians*, 188. Barrett (*Second Corinthians*, 100) also argues that both the terms and the distinction between the two groups in vv. 15–16 are eschatological since salvation and destruction are consummated at the last day.

48. Hafemann, *Suffering*, 171.

49. Martin, *2 Corinthians*, 624.

50. Thus, Barrett, *Second Corinthians*, 328; Martin, *2 Corinthians*, 656; Seifrid, *Second Corinthians*, 467–8.

by Paul's fear expressed in the next verses that the Corinthians might not have repented from their previous sins (12:20-21).[51] Just as the judgment of God and the fear deriving from it motivate Paul for his ministry, so too he wants the Corinthians to have the same motivation for their own lives, and thus exhorts them to "test themselves whether they are in the faith" (13:5). In this regard, Mark A. Seifrid rightly comments:

> In the conclusion of the letter, Paul once again returns to the formulation that he uses here [in 2:17]: 'before God, in Christ we speak' (12:19). There, too, he makes a claim to sincerity, even if it is implicit. There, too, he recalls his good conscience and the anticipation of the judgment in which he will be manifest to God (cf. 5:11), as well as the presence of Christ in him, who grants him faith to and the power to speak (cf. 13:3, 5).[52]

Therefore, a close connection exists between the references to "before God and in Christ" in 2:17 and 12:19, and "the fear of the Lord" that derives from "the judgment seat of Christ" in 5:10 (cf. Rom 2:16; 14:10). Moyer Hubbard thus argues that 5:11-13 picks up the theme of 2:17, and that the parallels between these two texts "are unmistakable."[53] The same is true of the parallels between 12:19 and 5:10-11, in which Paul states his concern for the Corinthian church that they might not be under God's judgment. In 2:17, 5:10, and 12:19 Paul continually refers to the judgment that functions as a motivation (through his fear of the Lord/God) for his ministry; and, moreover, implicitly and explicitly exhorts the Corinthians to have the same motivation (cf. 13:5). Hence, just as Paul speaks "in Christ and before God" in 2:17 and 12:19, so too all must stand before Christ as they are judged by God in 5:10-11 (cf. again Rom 2:16; 14:10).[54] Clearly, then, the judgment seat of Christ in 5:10 functions as a reference to the eschatological judgment of God.

2) Who Will Be Judged? Scholarly opinion is divided over the identity of those who in 2 Cor 5:10 will stand at the final judgment seat of Christ: some argue that the judgment is a universal judgment that applies to everyone, including believers;[55] others argue that the judgment applies only to believers.[56] While the former

---

51. Martin, *2 Corinthians*, 649.

52. Seifrid, *Second Corinthians*, 95.

53. Moyer V. Hubbard, *New Creation in Paul's Letters and Thoughts*, SNTSMS 119 (Cambridge; New York: Cambridge University Press, 2002), 165.

54. Note the move from being "manifest before the judgment seat of Christ" (φανερωθῆναι ἔμπροσθεν τοῦ βήματος τοῦ Χριστοῦ) in 5:10 to "having been manifest to God (θεῷ δὲ πεφανερώμεθα)" in 5:11, using the same verb.

55. Scott, *2 Corinthians*, 116; Garland, *2 Corinthians*, 269.

56. Thrall, *Second Corinthians*, 1:394; Harris, *Second Corinthians*, 406; Martin, *2 Corinthians*, 270-1; Guthrie, *2 Corinthians*, 289-90.

position emphasizes the reality of condemnation at the judgment, which is thus seen to flow smoothly to the fear of the Lord in the next verse, the latter position raises questions regarding the purpose of the judgment, i.e., what does it mean that believers are "to receive recompense" (κομίζω) according to their good or evil work? Moreover, how can this latter position explain "the fear of the Lord" which derives from the judgment and motivates the holy life of believers? For example, Ralph P. Martin, who argues that the judgment in view applies only to believers, emphasizes the solemnity of the judgment (that leads to the fear of the Lord), but does not explain further *how* the judgment can motivate believers, who are already being saved.[57] In this regard, in arguing that the judgment applies only to believers, George H. Guthrie suggests that the verb in 5:10, κομίζω, should be understood in terms of "evaluation" rather than "condemnation" (cf. Rom 5:16, 18; 8:1; 1 Cor 3:10–15; 4:5). Thus, according to Guthrie:

> These rewards play a part in motivating those who have been saved to live well for Christ in the world, reminding believers that God has saved us to participate in the advancement of his cause in the world. On the other hand, "suffering loss" may be a form of recompense for believers who do not live well for the Lord (1 Cor. 3:15), who though forgiven, will experience a forfeiture of reward or privilege ... Both reward and withholding of reward, therefore, seem to play a role in motivating believers concerning their choices in life.[58]

The most fundamental objection to Guthrie is whether κομίζω can be understood to mean "to evaluate." Guthrie refers to BDAG, which lists 2 Cor 5:10 under "to come into possession of something or experience something, carry off, get (for oneself), receive as a recompense."[59] As Guthrie admits, he imports this idea of "evaluation" only because he cannot accept the idea that both believers and unbelievers will be judged and "receive recompense" according to deeds.[60] Moreover, despite his effort to hold both the solemnity of the judgment (and the fear of the Lord that derives from it) and the surety of salvation of believers, Guthrie's argument does not sufficiently explain how then in the transition from 5:10 to 5:11 the fear of the Lord that derives from judgment (in his view, a negative reality) applies to believers to motivate their lives (in his view, a positive reality). In other words, Guthrie's proposal raises the question of how the fear of the Lord, deriving from the possibility of "suffering loss" at the judgment, is distinct from the

---

57. Martin, *2 Corinthians*, 271: "The tribunal of Christ, for the Christians, is needed to complete God's justice, both in terms of holiness and impartiality ... The life of faith does not free the Christian from the life of obedience."

58. Guthrie, *2 Corinthians*, 289–90.

59. BDAG 557.

60. Guthrie, *2 Corinthians*, 289: "One view understands believers to have been brought into relationship with Christ by grace but kept in, or judged, by works ... Yet this view must be ruled out in light of Paul's treatment of justification."

fear that derives from the "condemnation" at the judgment of unbelievers. Guthrie's proposal thus results in adding yet another category of "fear," i.e., the negative fear experienced only by believers, to the traditional dual approach to the meaning of the fear of God in biblical texts (see Chapter One).

As I have suggested earlier, it is more proper to understand "the fear of God" as referring only to the *one kind of fear* that derives from God's judgment that functions differently according to the person (believer and unbeliever) and time (present or eschatological future).[61] A closer examination of the content of the fear of the Lord/God in 5:10–11 is thus necessary at this point in the light of this thesis to see if it will elucidate more clearly what is at stake for Paul at the judgment seat of Christ and in doing so shed light upon our understanding of the fear of the Lord/God in Paul's thought. To examine the content of the fear of the Lord/God in 5:10–11 more closely, we therefore turn to 2 Cor 6:1 as a key for understanding the judgment scene in 5:10. For as Margaret E. Thrall argues:

> [O]ne cannot rule out the possibility that Paul envisaged an adverse, punitive recompense for sinful Christians which might conceivably threaten their salvation. Salvation is a matter of grace, not to be secured by good works, but grace may be received in vain (6.1).[62]

3. The Content of Paul's Fear in 2 Cor 6:1

In 2 Cor 6:1 Paul exhorts the Corinthians not to receive God's grace in vain because (γάρ in 6:2) now is the "eschatological now" prophesied in Isa 49:8:

> As we work together (with God), we urge you also not to receive the grace of God in vain.

While no "fear" language explicitly occurs in 2 Cor 6:1, its context indicates that here Paul describes the content or subject of his fear concerning the Corinthians,

---

61. In this regard, Schmeller (*Zweite Korinther*, 309) rightly argues that the focus in 2 Cor 5:10–11 is not on the judgment scene, but rather on the fear of the Lord that derives from it.

62. Thrall, *Second Corinthians*, 1:395. Likewise, Seifrid (*Second Corinthians*, 238) argues that Paul's warning in 2 Cor 6:1 is connected to his ministry in 5:11 in that the salvation of the Corinthians, which is directly connected to the mission of the apostle, is at stake. Also, Barnett, *Second Corinthians*, 375. In this regard, John M. G. Barclay's observation about Paul's use of grace (gift) in his recent monograph, *Paul and the Gift* (Grand Rapids: Eerdmans, 2015) is meaningful: "a gift can be *unconditioned* (free of prior conditions regarding the recipient) without also being *unconditional* (free of expectations that the recipient will offer some 'return'). Paul has provided a parade example of this phenomemon, since he simultaneously emphasizes the incongruity of grace and the expectation that those who are 'under grace' (and wholly refashioned by it) will be reoriented in the 'obedience of faith'" (pp. 562–3, original emphasis).

since Paul's other uses of "in vain" (κενός) elucidate the fearful nature of such an outcome, whether it be regarding his own ministry or the faith of those in his churches.[63] For as Judith M. Gundry Volf observes:

> Paul does not always express certainty about the long-term effectiveness of his apostolic labor. He voices his concern not to "labor in vain" (Phil 2:16; 1 Thess 3:5; Gal 2:2; 4:11) and be forced to stand empty-handed at the final test of Christian service. Does Paul's *fear* imply the possibility of his converts' falling away? Does Paul manifest such a *fear* in the expressions "believe in vain" (1 Cor 15:2) and "receive the grace of God in vain" (2 Cor 6:1)?[64]

However, even though Gundry Volf acknowledges that Paul warns of the eschatological significance of his converts' becoming apostates, she rejects the idea that such a fear actually plays an operative role in Paul's theology. She does so mainly because, as we saw above for Guthrie, the view that Paul actually fears apostasy "is hard to reconcile with Paul's expressions of confidence regarding the successfulness of divine salvific activity."[65] Thus, for Gundry Volf, Paul's "fear" that the Corinthians might receive the grace of God in vain (2 Cor 6:1) is put forth for the sake of argument only, since Paul is counting on his converts not to deny the gospel of their salvation by denying its minister.[66] However, if the possibility of receiving God's grace in vain, and hence Paul's fear relating to that reality, is only hypothetical, it is hard to understand how such a hypothetical fear in 5:11 could in fact be derived from the final judgment in 5:10, or how it could be motivational for Paul's ministry.[67]

On the other hand, B. J. Oropeza emphasizes the rhetorical weight that Paul's fear carries in the "in vain" (κενός) language by examining the parallel between the

---

63. Paul uses κενός in 1 Cor 15:10, 14 (2x), 58; 2 Cor 6:1; Gal 2:2; Eph 5:6; Phil 2:16 (2x); Col 2:8; 1 Thess 2:1; 3:5. Of significance for our purposes are the uses in 1 Cor 15; 2 Cor 6; Gal 2; Phil 2; 1 Thess 2; 3, where it refers to the content of Paul's fear.

64. Judith M. Gundry Volf, *Paul and Perseverance: Staying In and Falling Away* (Louisville: Westminster John Knox, 1990), 261, emphasis added.

65. Ibid., 271.

66. Ibid., 280. Gundry Volf nevertheless acknowledges the real danger of falling away from God's grace: "While Paul recognizes the real danger of exclusion from salvation through absence or abandonment of faith in Christ, his fundamental belief in God's faithfulness accounts for the apostle's hope and even conviction of the final perseverance in faith of the elect, which in his discussions emerges as his dominant perspective" (p. 229). However, because the real danger of exclusion from salvation is hard to reconcile with the view about perseverance that she prioritizes, she does not understand Paul's fear of apostasy as real.

67. Gundry Volf (ibid., 100) acknowledges that the judgment in 2 Cor 5:10 is a "future eschatological judgment according to works, which Christian also await," but does not explain it with regard to "the fear of the Lord" in 5:11.

Israelites in the wilderness and the Corinthian congregation in 1 Cor 10:1–13. Oropeza argues that Paul warns the Corinthian congregation about the real possibility of apostasy in 10:12: "So if you think you are standing, watch out (βλεπέτω) that you do not fall (μὴ πέσῃ)." Oropeza states that, here, πίπτω means "a falling from salvific grace, the result of which leads to eschatological consequence of divine rejection."[68] As the Israelites were tested in the desert before entering Canaan, in which most were overthrown in the wilderness due to the displeasure of the Lord and 23,000 "fell" in a single day for their idolatry (1 Cor 10:5–8), the same challenge is awaiting the Corinthians, including the same danger of apostasy that leads to divine judgment.[69] Oropeza further argues that in 2 Corinthians the danger of apostasy was still apparent, as shown by the apostle's continuing warning and fear for the congregation (cf. 5:20–6:2; 11:3ff; 12:20–21).[70] Thus, at the final

---

68. B. J. Oropeza, *Paul and Apostasy: Eschatology, Perseverance, and Falling Away in the Corinthian Congregation*, WUNT 2/115 (Tübingen: Mohr Siebeck, 2000), 196. Similarly, Calvin Roetzel argues that the fall "means more than falling into sin or unbelief; it refers to the danger of falling out of grace (Gal 5:4) or into eschatological ruin (Rom 11:22). The Corinthians are forewarned that the end of the age(s) is imminent when the judgment will be manifest (10:11)." Calvin J. Roetzel, *Judgement in the Community: A Study of the Relationship between Eschatology and Ecclesiology in Paul* (Leiden: Brill, 1972), 172–73. Contra Gundry Volf (*Perseverance*, 127), who argues that "falling" refers not to losing salvation but to losing the appearance of salvation. Oropeza (*Apostasy*, 28–33) criticizes Gundry Volf for her topical-exegetical approach which fails to take the entire Pauline epistles (including many passages about apostasy) into account. Oropeza argues that this failure derives from her attempt to examine the texts according to her Reformed understanding of election and predestination.

69. Thus, Oropeza, *Apostasy*, 128: "There is an implicit *warning* here in [1 Cor] 10:5 to the Corinthian congregation" (original emphasis). Oropeza is rather vague in differentiating the corporate notion of the Corinthians as a whole from the notion of the Corinthians as individuals with regard to the judgment. On the one hand, Oropeza, 190, argues that Paul is warning the Corinthian congregation that their coveting food and committing idolatry might result in their apostasy and divine judgment *en masse*. However, on the other hand, Oropeza, 183, also argues that Paul has in view the individual scope of judgment: "Even though Paul is using corporate language, he does not appear to have a fully corporate, representational view in mind. Namely, the entire Corinthian community will not be judged because of some members who commit various vices." Oropeza later concludes, "In 1 Corinthians 10:1–12 Paul may be supporting the irrevocable perseverance of the elect people of God *as a whole* ('all'), but he still believes that some members who were once part of that elect community can fall away so as to lose the salvific benefits of the elect community. One's identity as an elect individual may only find meaning if that individual belongs to the elect community" (p. 205, original emphasis). Thus, Paul might address the Corinthian congregation as whole, but he makes clear that the judgment will be according to the individual's deeds (2 Cor 5:10).

70. Ibid., 211.

judgment (2 Cor 5:10) not only will Paul's opponents and accusers face severe consequences, but also there will be reciprocation for believers:

> The reciprocation for those who claim to be Christ's followers but have done reprehensible things includes the possibility of punishment on that day, and that punishment is strong enough to justify the fear Paul promotes in 5:11. For the Corinthians, it will turn out that no less than their final salvation will be at stake on judgment day; Paul will warn against members receiving saving grace in vain (see 6:1–2).[71]

Hence, with the "in vain" (κενός) language, Paul consistently warns about the danger into which he or his followers might fall. In 1 Cor 15:10 Paul warns of the danger that God's grace in his own life might be "in vain."[72] This danger is further expressed in Paul's fear that his proclamation (1 Cor 15:14), his running (Gal 2:2; Phil 2:16), his labor (Phil 2:16; 1 Thess 3:5), or his coming to believers (1 Thess 2:1) might have been in vain. Furthermore, Paul's fear is not only for himself, but it is also for believers because their work can fall into jeopardy as well. Paul fears that God's grace towards believers (2 Cor 6:1), their faith (1 Cor 15:14), and their labor (1 Cor 15:58) might be in vain, or that they would be deceived by vain words and suffer the wrath of God (Eph 5:6; Col 2:8). Paul also uses the adverb εἰκῇ ("vainly") in a similar way. Paul fears that his work (Gal 4:11),[73] the faith (1 Cor 15:2), and the suffering (Gal 3:4) of believers might be undergone "vainly."

However, contra the perspective of Gundry Volf, Paul's use of fear does not justify drawing a difference between Paul's fear and that of the believers.[74] As 1 Cor 15:2, 10, 14, 58 clearly show, Paul's fear that his work might be in vain is closely linked with his fear that the believers' work might be in vain. The failure of the Corinthians means at the same time failure for Paul's ministry. Likewise, because

---

71. B. J. Oropeza, *Exploring Second Corinthians: Death and Life, Hardship and Rivalry*, RRA 3 (Atlanta: SBL Press, 2016), 324.

72. The conjunction ἀλλά informs how Paul's hard working functions as the grounds of God's grace not being in vain. Thus, David E. Garland, *1 Corinthians*, BECNT (Grand Rapids: Baker Academic, 2003), 692.

73. In Gal 4:11 Paul specifically mentions his fear in regard to his work being in vain: "I am *afraid* that my work for you may have been *in vain* (φοβοῦμαι ὑμᾶς μή πως εἰκῇ κεκοπίακα εἰς ὑμᾶς)" (emphasis added).

74. Gundry Volf (*Perseverance*, 267) argues that Paul's fear of laboring in vain merely signifies his loss of an eschatological boast at the day of Christ and that this statement is therefore primarily an expression of his self-concern. For her, Paul's fear is thus distinguished from the fear of believers—whether they might be excluded from final salvation: "It is hard to say, however, whether [Paul's] converts' final exclusion from salvation as the implication of Paul's possible labor in vain would imply their apostasy or the falling away of those who falsely professed faith. The statements about laboring in vain themselves do not make this distinction" (p. 267).

Paul knows that everyone, including the Corinthians, will stand before the final judgment seat, he persuades them and exhorts them with the fear of the Lord (2 Cor 5:10-11). In this context, as the fear functions as motivation for Paul's ministry (2 Cor 5:11), he wants the fear to work in the same way for believers' life (2 Cor 7:1). This affirms that Paul's fear about himself is not different from his fear about the believers. Moreover, the connection between Paul and the Corinthians is further emphasized in the significance of the resurrection of Christ in 1 Cor 15:14, where Paul states that without the resurrection, *both* his proclamation and the faith of the Corinthians might be in vain.

It is also noteworthy that Paul's argument concerning the danger in view in 1 Cor 15 has the final judgment of God as its context, when God will put all things in subjection under his feet (15:24–28). In this context of God's eschatological judgment, Paul uses the "in vain" language in 15:2 to warn the Corinthians, which is similar to his warning in 2 Cor 6:1.[75] As Gordon D. Fee rightly comments, "[1 Cor 15:10] points back to v. 2 and forward to v. 14, where there is considerable danger that if they persist in their present folly, God's grace to them will have turned out to be 'in vain.'"[76]

Thus, the above survey shows that Paul and the Corinthians share not only the motivation that leads them to live according to the gospel, but also the danger that God's grace and all their work will be jeopardized if they do not continue to live properly. The salvation announced in the gospel, which Paul received and preached to the Corinthians, and which they received, is conditional on their persevering faith. The danger of rendering God's grace and labor in vain is not a hypothetical one, but contains a real possibility. For this reason, the fear of the Lord/God regarding this danger does not derive from a mere "suffering of loss" at the judgment.[77]

4. Who Is the Lord in 2 Cor 5:11?

The examination so far has focused on the subject and object in view in relationship to Paul's understanding of the eschatological "judgment seat" and also on the related content of Paul's fear of the Lord/God. To complete the connection between the fear of the Lord in 2 Cor 5:11 and the fear of God in 7:1, it is necessary to examine the referent of the "Lord" whom Paul fears. The exact referent of κύριος in 5:11, however, is much debated and scholars have not reached a consensus. Some

---

75. Similarly, Paul exhorts the Corinthians in 15:58 to be steadfast and immovable, which for them too will be shown by abounding in the work of the Lord always. In other words, knowing that their labor is not in vain in the Lord becomes the motivation for the Corinthians to be always abounding in their work for the Lord. Wallace (*Beyond the Basics*, 631) takes εἰδότες in 15:58 as causal.

76. Gordon D. Fee, *The First Epistle to the Corinthians*, NICNT (Grand Rapids: Eerdmans, 1987), 735.

77. Contra Barnett, *Second Corinthians*, 276; Hughes, *2 Corinthians*, 182.

scholars argue that "Lord" refers to Christ in the previous verse,[78] while others argue that it refers to God.[79] There are also scholars who argue that the Lord in 5:11 can refer to either God or Christ, since both are seated together on the *merkabah* (throne-chariot) and perform activities interchangeably.[80] Rudolf Karl Bultmann suggests an alternative explanation that "Lord" in v. 11 refers to Christ in v. 10, but the fear to which Paul is referring is the fear before the judge, which is linked to the יראת יהוה ("fear of God") from the OT, now transferred to the κύριος.[81] Fee agrees with Bultmann that the fear of the Lord in 5:11 indicates a distinctive OT phrase regarding Yahweh that is now applied directly to Christ, but also rightly stresses the context of eschatological judgment, since the "Lord" is the exalted Lord before whom both Paul and the Corinthians must appear at the end of the age.[82]

Yet, in support of the position argued by Victor Paul Furnish, who argues that the Lord in 2 Cor 5:11 "must be understood *primarily* in relation to its background in the Jewish Bible and tradition,"[83] we have seen that the judgment seat of Christ in 5:10 refers to the final judgment in which elsewhere for Paul God will be the judge. Thus, the most natural theological reading of Paul's point here would be that "the fear of the Lord" in 5:11 refers to the fear of God. Moreover, the following evidence further supports the reading of κύριος with reference to God: the context

---

78. E.g., Barnett, *Second Corinthians*, 279n3; Matera, *II Corinthians*, 125–26; Harris, *Second Corinthians*, 412. Harris takes the fear as "reverential awe" which is directed to the risen Christ.

79. E.g., Garland, *2 Corinthians*, 265; Furnish, *II Corinthians*, 306.

80. E.g., Scott, *2 Corinthians*, 117.

81. Bultmann, *Second Corinthians*, 146. Bultmann (ibid.) concludes that the fear of the Lord means "simply consciousness of responsibility." While I agree with Bultmann about the OT context of the fear of God motif and its motivating function in Paul's argument, his argument that fear refers to a consciousness of responsibility underestimates the eschatological function that fear takes for Paul. For Paul, the fear of God is a *realistic* factor that derives from the eschatological judgment (5:10), i.e., from a real danger facing those who profess faith (cf. 6:1).

82. Gordon D. Fee, *Pauline Christology: An Exegetical-Theological Study* (Peabody, MA: Hendrickson, 2007), 572. Fee, following the traditional "dual understanding" of the fear of God in the Scriptures, argues however that this fear "is not cringing or fearful 'fear'; rather, it has to do with living with proper reverence and awe of the Lord (Christ), before whom all will appear finally for judgment" (p. 572). Fee, 192, argues that the fear of the Lord is a key idea derived from the canonical wisdom literature and "moves along a spectrum of meaning from being 'fearful' to having proper 'awe' before God, while the latter tends to dominate."

83. Furnish, *II Corinthians*, 306, emphasis added. Furnish, 306, lists 1 Chr 19:7 LXX, 9; Ps 18 [19]:9; Isa 2:10, 19, 21; as well as Proverbs, Sirach, and the Testaments of the Twelve Patriarchs as evidence. Contra Barnett (*Second Corinthians*, 279), who argues that Furnish's comment is only valid if the fear in view can be connected to the fear of the Lord in OT wisdom literature, a connection which Barnett rejects. Our study of the non-wisdom literature context for "the fear of God" in 2 Cor 7:1, however, counters Barnett's objection.

of 2 Cor 5:11, the solitary use of κύριος in 2 Corinthians, and the OT background of 5:10–11.

1) The Context   In 2 Cor 5:1–15 Paul states that God is the one who validates Paul's mission by preparing for him and his churches an eternal house (5:1), which is guaranteed through sending the Spirit (5:5). Paul then uses κύριος as a clear reference back to God in 5:6 and mentions that God is the reference point for his ministry in vv. 9, 13. In these ways, Paul clearly states that the source of his ministry is God. In contrast, Christ appears only two times in 5:1–15, and in both cases the references are limited to Christ's role as an agent of God's work: first in a reference to the final judgment ("the judgment seat of Christ" in v. 11), and then as another motivation for his ministry ("for the love of Christ urges us on" in v. 14).[84]

Moreover, the appearance of Christ in v. 14 as another motivation for Paul's ministry works as a hinge that leads to his argument concerning his ministry of reconciliation (2 Cor 5:16–21). In this section Christ appears more often, but here too he remains in the role of agent, while God takes the leading initiative. It is God who reconciles the people and the world to himself through Christ (διὰ Χριστοῦ in v. 18, ἐν Χριστῷ in v. 19), it is God who makes his appeal through Paul (δι' ἡμῶν in v. 20), and it is God's righteousness that comes about as a result of Paul's ministry (ἵνα ἡμεῖς γενώμεθα δικαιοσύνη θεοῦ ἐν αὐτῷ in v. 21). Therefore, as Martin rightly comments that the flow of Paul's argument is to show how God himself is personally involved, both in his acting through the agency of Christ (v. 18: διὰ Χριστοῦ) and by coming himself in Christ (v. 19: ἐν Χριστῷ) to our world.[85] In addition, Paul warns the Corinthians not to accept the grace of *God* in vain in 6:1, emphasizing once again the role of God as subject in the previous section. Contextually, therefore, the judgment seat of Christ in 5:10 is best taken not to refer to Christ's leading role in the final judgment, but functions as a reference to the final judgment when God will judge everyone through Christ (cf. again Rom 2:16; 14:10). Therefore, against this backdrop, on top of Paul's statements elsewhere in 2 Cor 2:17 and 12:19 (cf. Rom 14:10), the "Lord" in 5:11 is more likely to refer to God.

2) The Solitary Use of Κύριος   Second, Paul's use of κύριος in 2 Corinthians, when used without a corresponding reference to "Jesus" and/or "Christ," supports reading "Lord" in 5:11 as referring to God. Paul uses κύριος 29 times in 27 verses in 2 Corinthians, though he uses it together with Ἰησοῦς or Ἰησοῦς Χριστός only on a handful of occasions (eight times), so that κύριος occurs by itself twenty-one times.

---

84. The genitive (τοῦ Χριστοῦ) can be either subjective (Christ's love) or objective (love for Christ); but, as Martin (*2 Corinthians*, 285) argues, the consensus among the scholars is the former.

85. Martin, *2 Corinthians*, 301. Also see Harris (*Second Corinthians*, 436–9), who argues that God the Father is both the initiator and goal of reconciliation and that Christ is God's agent in achieving reconciliation.

T Usage	Frequency	2 Corinthians Texts
ὁ κύριος + Ἰησοῦς Χριστός	5	1:2, 3; 4:5; 8:9; 13:14
ὁ κύριος + Ἰησοῦς	3	1:14; 4:14; 11:31
ὁ κύριος alone	21	2:12; 3:16, 17 (2x), 18 (2x); 5:6, 8, 11; 6:17, 18; 8:5, 19, 21; 10:8, 17, 18; 11:17; 12:1, 8; 13:10

It is by far the most common for Paul to use κύριος with reference to Jesus. Larry W. Hurtado argues that in the 200 occurrences of κύριος in the undisputed Pauline epistles, Paul applies it to Jesus about 180 times.[86] However, Hurtado argues that Paul also uses the same term to designate God, especially when dealing with OT quotations.[87] In fact, among the twenty-one solitary usages of κύριος in 2 Corinthians, Paul uses the term to refer to God with specific OT allusions in 2 Cor 3:16–18 (Exod 34:34), 6:17–18 (Isa 52:11; Ezek 20:34; 2 Sam 7:14), 8:21 (Prov 3:4), and 10:17–18 (Jer 9:22).[88]

---

86. Larry W. Hurtado, *Lord Jesus Christ: Devotion to Jesus in Earliest Christianity* (Grand Rapids: Eerdmans, 2003), 115–17. According to Hurtado, there are three main kinds of contexts and statements in which Jesus is characteristically referred to as κύριος: (1) In hortatory statements and passages Jesus is the Lord/Master whose teaching and example are authoritative for believers (Rom 14:4–12; 16:2–20; 1 Cor 4:19; 5:58; 6:12–7:40; 16:7; 1 Thess 4:1–2); (2) in reference to eschatological expectations, Jesus is designated as the Lord who will come again as the agent of God (1 Cor 4:1–5; Phil 4:5); and (3) in formulae and passages reflecting actions of the worship setting, κύριος designates the unequaled status given to Jesus by God and is the characteristic title given to Jesus in the worship practices of early Christians (1 Cor 5:1–5; 11:17–33). In this regard, it is not easy to determine in which category the context of 2 Cor 5:10–11 would fit. The fear of the Lord functions as the motivation for Paul's apostleship (which is closer to the first category), but it should also be noticed that the fear of the Lord derives from the eschatological judgment seat in v. 10 (which brings it close to the second case). Unfortunately, Hurtado does not deal with 2 Cor 5:11 in detail in his argument, and admits that these distinctions are artificial and unrealistic, so that the development of convictions about Jesus can be rather complex (pp. 117–18). By comparison, Wright argues that 2 Cor 5:10 furthers the messianic identity of Jesus as the coming judge. He compares Rom 14:11 with Phil 2:11 where Isa 45:23 is quoted and referred to Jesus and concludes: "[Paul] clearly intends in these passages that the *kyrios*, which in the original stands for YHWH, should now be understood to refer to Jesus himself." N. T. Wright, *Paul and the Faithfulness of God*, COQG 4 (London: SPCK, 2013), 702.

87. Hurtado, *Lord*, 112. For example, Rom 4:8 (Ps 32:1–2); 9:28–29 (Isa 28:22; 1:9), 10:16 (Isa 53:1); 11:3 (1 Kgs 19:10), 34 (Isa 40:13), 12:19 (Deut 32:35), 15:11 (Ps 117:1); 1 Cor 3:20 (Ps 94:11) 14:21 (Isa 28:11); 2 Cor 6:17–18 (Isa 52:11; 2 Sam 7:14).

88. Furnish (*II Corinthians*, 211) argues that in Paul κύριος "generally means Christ, except when the apostle is quoting Scripture or working closely with a scriptural text." Likewise, Hafemann (*Paul, Moses, and the History of Israel: The Letter/Spirit Contrast and the Argument from Scripture in 2 Corinthians 3*, WUNT 2/81 [Tübingen: J. C. B. Mohr, 1995], 397–401) argues that κύριος in 2 Cor 3:16–18 refers to God.

Moreover, even without a specific OT quotation, κύριος, when it is used by itself in 2 Corinthians, can refer to God.[89] For example, in 2 Cor 2:12 the Lord is the one who opens the door for Paul to proclaim the good news: "And when I came to Troas for the good news of Christ (τοῦ Χριστοῦ), and a door was opened by the Lord (ἐν κυρίῳ)."[90] Here Χριστός is used as the object of the gospel and κύριος is the subject who opens a door. The referent of κύριος is ambiguous here, but in Col 4:3 Paul uses the same expression with "God" as the subject:

> At the same time praying for us as well that *God will open a door* (θεὸς ἀνοίξη ἡμῖν θύραν) of the word to us, in order that we may declare the mystery *of Christ* (τοῦ Χριστοῦ), for which I am in prison (emphasis added).

Here God is specifically mentioned as the subject who opens a door for Paul for his ministry, while Christ is the content of the mystery that is declared. Therefore, κύριος in 2 Cor 2:12 probably also refers to God.[91]

Similarly, in 8:5 Paul explains how the Macedonians gave themselves "first to the Lord (πρῶτον τῷ κυρίῳ) and to us, by the will of God (διὰ θελήματος θεοῦ)." Not only is "God" the closest referent of κύριος in vv. 1 and 5,[92] but also the context shows that κύριος in 8:5 refers to God in view of the fact that the prepositional phrase "by the will of God" modifies both "to the Lord" and "to us."[93] For Paul uses this phrase in other places when he introduces his apostleship,[94] so that the Macedonians' giving themselves to the κύριος likely denotes that they acknowledged not only that their collection was an act of God's grace, but also that Paul had an ambassadorial role in administrating it. In other words, the Macedonians' generous action shows their submission to Paul's apostleship as *God*-given by means of/

---

89. In this regard, notable is Novenson's argument (*Christ*, 118–19), where he compares the titles, "Jesus," "Christ," and "Lord" and concludes: "The words Ἰησοῦς, χριστός, and κύριος, because they are different words, have their own respective ranges of meaning. It is true that their joint association with the person Jesus sometimes will have led to conflation of different degrees and kinds in certain Christian authors, but it is not the case that Christian authors simply redefined all of the terms to mean 'Jesus.'"

90. Contra Barnett (*Second Corinthians*, 135), who takes the ἐν as indicating sphere of opportunity rather than agency. Though Barnett does not understand ἐν as agency, he argues that "[t]he phrase 'a door was opened for me' expresses Paul's conviction that God was actively responsible for the opportunity to minister that he found on coming to Troas."

91. Contra Harris (*Second Corinthians*, 238) and Martin (*2 Corinthians*, 179), who argue that Christ is portrayed in 2 Cor 2:12 as both the content of the gospel and the one who provided the opportunities to present it.

92. Note the reference to "grace" in vv. 6 and 7, which picks up "the grace *of God*" from v. 1, thus providing an inclusio around 8:1–7 by virtue of this reference to God's grace.

93. Barnett, *Second Corinthians*, 398; Harris, *Second Corinthians*, 568–9.

94. E.g., 1 Cor 1:1; 2 Cor 1:1; Eph 1:1; Col 1:1; 2 Tim 1:1.

through God's will,[95] which supports the argument that the referent of κύριος in v. 5 is God.

In 8:19 and 21 Paul mentions the commendation of Titus:

> And not only that, but he has also been appointed by the churches to travel with us while we are administrating this generous undertaking for the glory of the Lord (τοῦ κυρίου δόξαν) himself and to show our goodwill.

> For we intend to do what is right not only in the Lord's sight (ἐνώπιον κυρίου), but also in the sight of others.

Not only is "God" in v. 16 the closest preceding referent of κύριος in v. 21, but also v. 21 alludes to Prov 3:4, which strengthens the argument that κύριος in both v. 19 and v. 21 refers to God.[96]

In the same way, Paul uses κύριος in 10:8 and 13:10 to refer to the origin of Paul's given authority. Paul states in 10:7 that he belongs to Christ (cf. Χριστοῦ εἶναι), which limits the reference of κύριος to Jesus in the next, conceptually related, sentence. However, Paul then describes the "field" of his ministry to be given by God in 10:13 and in 13:10 Paul describes his authority as that which the κύριος gave him for "building up and not tearing down," which is an allusion to God's activity on behalf of Jeremiah in Jer 1:10; 24:6.[97] In other words, while Paul can refer to Christ as the source of his authority, Paul also uses the OT prophet's commission by God to refer to the authority that the κύριος gave him, and therefore the κύριος who gave Paul his ministry in 13:10 most probably refers to God.[98]

In 11:17 Paul states that when he speaks, "he does not speak as the Lord would (κατὰ κύριον),[99] but as a fool." Although other scholars interpret κύριος in this text

---

95. James M. Scott, *2 Corinthians*, NIBCNT 8 (Peabody, MA: Carlisle: Hendrickson; Paternoster, 1998), 177–8; Barnett, *Second Corinthians*, 399–400.

96. Harris, *Second Corinthians*, 607; Martin, *2 Corinthians*, 455; Barnett, *Second Corinthians*, 424. Barnett further supports the link between the Lord in v. 21 and God because Paul repeatedly states "in the sight of God" (4:2; cf. 2:17; 5:11).

97. Harris, *Second Corinthians*, 695; Jeffrey W. Aernie, *Is Paul also among the Prophets? An Examination of the Relationship between Paul and the Old Testament Prophetic Tradition in 2 Corinthians*, LNTS 467 (London: T&T Clark, 2012), 166–75.

98. Contra Barnett (*Second Corinthians*, 472) who argues that the Lord is the ascended, glorious Christ, and Harris, *Second Corinthians*, 568, 693, who argues that although God was also actively involved in Paul's call into apostleship and service, it is more probable that κύριος here is the Lord Jesus. However, Harris neglects the other passages where κύριος refers to God and is not necessarily limited to Jesus, especially when it is used in relation to the OT context. Harris denies the Jeremiah context in 10:8.

99. Literally, the phrase κατὰ κύριον is "according to the Lord," but is taken variously as "after the Lord" (KJV), "as the Lord would" (ESV, NAS, NIV), "with the Lord's authority" (NRSV), "at the Lord's direction" (Harris). For a more detailed argument on this, see Harris, *Second Corinthians*, 780–1.

as Christ,[100] Martin suggests that κύριος in 11:17-18 refers back to the κύριος in 10:17 who appointed and authorized Paul to his service.[101] Moreover, Paul's statement in 10:17, "Let the one who boasts, boast in the Lord," is followed and supported (γάρ) by his biblical appeal to Jer 9:22-23 (LXX), which furthers the connection between κύριος and God.[102]

In the remaining passages where κύριος is used by itself (12:1, 8) its referent is not specifically mentioned and it is the context that decides whether it refers to God or to Jesus.[103] Based on Paul's common usage of the solitary κύριος in 2 Corinthians, the word itself cannot determine its referent, but if it is related contextually to an OT background, it adds weight to interpreting κύριος as referring to God.

3) The OT Background The fact that the theme of the final judgment, and the consequent fear of God as judge, is a common theme in the OT therefore supports taking the κύριος in 2 Cor 5:11 to refer to God in his role as judge in the final judgment mentioned in v. 10.[104] Paul alludes to such OT passages when he discusses

---

100. Ibid., 781; Hughes, *2 Corinthians*, 398.
101. Martin, *2 Corinthians*, 547.
102. Aernie, *Paul*, 175-83.
103. Although Paul refers to a revelation of both God and Jesus in other epistles (cf. revelation with Jesus as referent in 1 Cor 1:7; Gal 1:12; 2 Thess 1:7; revelation with God as referent in Eph 1:17; 3:3), the revelation of κύριος in 12:1 probably refers to Christ since it appears as the closest referent in v. 2. Regarding 12:8, most scholars argue that κύριος as the personal object of prayer in v. 8 refers to Christ because of the mention of "the power of Christ" (ἡ δύναμις τοῦ Χριστοῦ) in the next verse. E.g., Hurtado, *Lord*, 140; Harris, *Second Corinthians*, 859-61; Fee, *Pauline Christology*, 194-95; Martin, *2 Corinthians*, 612. Paul normally refers to God as the object of prayer (2 Cor 13:7; Phil 1:3; 4:6). Note also that in Eph 2:18 Paul states that all believers have access to God the Father through Christ: "for through (δι' αὐτοῦ) him both of us have access (ἔχομεν τὴν προσαγωγὴν) in one Spirit to the Father (πρὸς τὸν πατέρα)." Harris (*Second Corinthians*, 860), lists 1 Cor 1:2; 16:22 as other examples in the Pauline corpus where Christ is the object of prayer besides 2 Cor 12:8 and concludes, "Such a practice occasions no surprise, given the early Christian belief in the deity of Christ." However, 1 Cor 16:22 contains Paul's curse formula, and not a prayer formula. Roy E. Ciampa and Brian S. Rosner, *The First Letter to the Corinthians*, PNTC (Grand Rapids; Nottingham, England: Eerdmans; Apollos, 2010), 864-5. Therefore, the support for Christ as the object in Paul's prayer is rather limited.
104. Fee (*Pauline Christology*, 192) argues that "[2 Cor 5:10-11 is a] key OT phrase where the κυρίος = Yahweh of the Septuagint has been appropriated and applied to Christ." Fee rightly sees the OT background of 2 Cor 5:10-11, but fails to distinguish the Christ in v. 10 from the Lord in v. 11. Kreitzer (Eschatology, 107) argues that there is an allusion to the judgment scene of Eccl 12:14 in 2 Cor 5:10. Also, Barnett, *Second Corinthians*, 279. For a more detailed reference of this theme in the OT, see Kent L. Yinger, *Paul, Judaism, and Judgement according to Deeds*, SNTSMS 105 (Cambridge: Cambridge University Press, 1999), 19-63.

these themes elsewhere.[105] Besides Paul's description of the judgment scene in Rom 14:10–11, with its quotation of Isa 45:23 LXX, Phil 2:9–11 is also noteworthy, where Paul refers to the same passage from Isaiah, but this time equates YHWH with Christ, thus showing that Paul can use κύριος to refer to either God or Christ depending on the context:

> Therefore, God (θεός) also exalted him and gave him the name that is above all names, so that in the name of Jesus every knee shall bow in heaven and on earth and under the earth, and every tongue shall confess that Jesus Christ is Lord (κύριος Ἰησοῦς Χριστός), for the glory of God (θεός) the Father.

In Phil 2:9–11, unlike Rom 14:10–11, the Isaiah text applies to Jesus and implicitly identifies Christ with the OT reference to God. Thus, "Jesus Christ the righteous Savior bears the name of the one Lord, Yahweh."[106] Of significance for 2 Cor 5:10–11, however, is that God's judgment appears implicitly in the OT text, and Paul confirms the judgment scene of Phil 2:10–11 by his concluding exhortation to the Philippians to work out their salvation with *fear* and trembling:[107]

---

105. For example, Paul speaks of "the judgment seat of God" in Rom 14:10, which is further supported (γάρ) by the quotation from Isa 45:23 LXX in the following verse. According to Kreitzer (*Eschatology*, 108), Paul makes a referential shift from the Christological argument in v. 9 to God in vv. 10–11: "We must not overlook the fact that 'Lord' most probably refers to *God himself* (via the force of τοῦ θεοῦ in v. 10), and that this, while quite natural, does represent a referential shift from the preceding Christological use of the verb κυριεύσῃ in v. 9" (emphasis added). Also Yinger, *Deeds*, 269. Both Kreitzer and Yinger mention the connection to Eccl 12:13–14, where both themes of the judgment seat and the fear of God appear. Although Paul probably also had the Ecclesiastes context in the background when mentioning the judgment and the fear of God, this thesis will focus on the Isaianic context since Paul directly alludes to passages from Isaiah in 2 Cor 5:17; 6:1, 17; Rom 14:10–11; Phil 2:9–12.

106. Moisés Silva, "Philippians," *Commentary on the New Testament Use of the Old Testament*, eds. G. K. Beale and D. A. Carson (Grand Rapids: Baker Academic, 2007), 838. Because Isa 45:23 in Phil 2 applies to Christ, scholars such as Wright argue that the same quotation in Rom 14:10–11 also applies to Christ. According to Wright, in Rom 14:11 Jesus is referred to as the Lord within a scriptural quotation where "Lord" stands for the divine name. Wright thus comments on Rom 14:11, "We have here, then, a probable further coupling of Jesus' messianic identity (as the coming judge) with his embodiment of the returning YHWH himself." Wright, *Faithfulness*, 702. However, Rom 14:10–11 clearly has God in view because this is the only referent that appears in vv. 10–12 ("the judgment seat of God" in v. 10; God as the object of praise in v. 11; God as the subject of reckoning in v. 12).

107. John Oswalt (*The Book of Isaiah*, NICOT [Grand Rapids: Eerdmans, 1998], 224) argues that this verse implies God's role as the only judge and savior of the world, which has implication both for Israel and also Israel's enemies (v. 24). According to Oswalt, 224, "*bowing down* may be the act of a condemned criminal, but it may also be that of pardoned

Therefore, my beloved ones, just as you have obeyed me always, not only in my presence, but now much more in my absence, with fear and trembling (μετὰ φόβου καὶ τρόμου), work out your salvation.

As in 2 Cor 5:10–11, here too the believers' "fear" refers to the fear of God that derives from the eschatological judgment in which Christ plays a central role. Therefore, the same OT context in other Pauline passages most likely also indicates a close connection between the judgment scene and the fear of God that derives from it.[108]

---

worshiper, and here one may exclude neither possibility" (original emphasis). Likewise, Matthew S. Harmon (*She Must and Shall Go Free: Paul's Isaianic Gospel in Galatians*, BZNW 168 [Berlin; New York: de Gruyter, 2010], 95–6) argues that this verse describes God's acting as the norm in carrying out judgment. Also, Kreitzer (*Eschatology*, 114–17) argues that the context (vv. 22 and 24) of Isa 45:23 clearly indicates the judgment theme.

108. Kreitzer (*Eschatology*, 107) sees the allusion to Eccl 12:13 in Rom 14:10 and 2 Cor 5:10 signaled by the reference to the judgment seat (βῆμα) and concludes that "[t]he important point to note here is the fact that the thrust of the concluding verse of this Old Testament book is a clear reference to the Final Judgment by God." The OT background behind the judgment theme in Paul is also apparent in his usage of "the day of the Lord:" "It appears clear that for Paul, the fact that Christology and eschatology are so closely linked is what determines his use of 'Day of the Lord' texts from the Old Testament as a means of expressing his understanding of the Christian faith" (p. 129). As Kreitzer, 99, argues, the day of the Lord is a concept that is closely related to the Parousia and the final judgment in Paul, both deriving from the OT: "we note the way in which Paul continues the Old Testament concept of the Day of the Lord, especially with reference to God's wrath and judgment as being made manifest in that Day." The day of the Lord appears in Paul in various terms: the day of the Lord (1 Cor 5:5 [textual variant]; 1 Thess 5:2; 2 Thess 2:2); the day of the Lord Jesus (1 Cor 1:8 [textual variant]; 2 Cor 1:14); the day of the Lord Jesus Christ (1 Cor 1:8 [textual variant]); the day of Christ Jesus (Phil 1:6); the day of Christ (Phil 1:10; 2:16); other uses of "the day," such as *the day* of God's wrath and revelation of righteous judgment (Rom 2:5); *the day* God judges . . . through Christ Jesus (Rom 2:16); each work will be manifest, for *the day* will declare (1 Cor 3:13); behold, now is *the day* of salvation (2 Cor 6:2); *the day* of redemption (Eph 4:30); *the day* should overtake you like a thief (1 Thess 5:4); on *that day* he comes to be glorified (2 Thess 1:10); he is able to guard what I have entrusted to him until *that day* (2 Tim 1:12); may the Lord grant to him to find from the Lord on *that day* (2 Tim 1:18); The Lord, the righteous judge, shall give to me on *that day* (2 Tim 4:8). Two observations can be made from these passages. First, "the day" connotes the final judgment in the eschaton. Second, there is a clear referential overlap, or even a transition between the Lord (YHWH in the OT) and Jesus Christ in Paul's use of "the day." As Kreitzer, 113, argues, "a referential confusion and conceptual overlap between God and his messianic representative is frequently present in those Pauline passages which speak of the Day of the Lord and are reliant upon theocentric Old Testament texts which have been Christologically reinterpreted." Kreitzer argues further that the transference of description from God to

Therefore, these conceptually parallel Pauline passages, read against their OT backdrops, further confirm the reading of 2 Cor 5:11 in which Paul's fear derives from the final judgment where God is the judge, which is identified in v. 10 with the judgment seat of Christ. If then the fear of the Lord in 5:11 is read as referring to the fear of God, the close parallel between 5:11 and 7:1 becomes more apparent.

III. The Isaianic Context of 2 Cor 4–6 and the Fear of God

As seen above, in 6:1–2 Paul understands his present age as the beginning of the eschaton which the prophet Isaiah had proclaimed in that Paul's exhortation in 6:1 is based on (γάρ in 6:2) Isa 49:8. By citing the announcement of Isa 49:8, Paul affirms that the eschatological salvation, i.e., "the day of salvation" promised by Isaiah, is now coming to pass in the lives of the Corinthians as a result of his ministry.[109] Paul's recognition of the dawning reality of Isa 49:8 means that the reality of the eschatological judgment at the judgment seat of Christ affirmed in 2 Cor 5:10 is now impending. Paul's fear of the possibility that one might receive God's grace in vain in 6:1 is thus the same fear inspired by the judgment seat of Christ in 5:10–11. It is this fear that motivates Paul for his ministry, and it is this fear that Paul exhorts the Corinthians to share with him in 7:1. Also, as seen in Rom 14:10–11 and Phil 2:6–12, Paul cites the Isaiah text to support his argument concerning God's final judgment, which leads to the fear of God among believers. Thus, a closer examination of the Isaianic context of 2 Cor 4–6 will shed further light on Paul's understanding of the fear of God. For though Paul often uses Scripture to support his argument in 2 Cor 2:14–7:1,[110] he turns to Isaiah for

---

Christ in these texts is based on the OT background (for example, Joel 2:32/Rom 10:13; Isa 45:23/Phil 2:10–11; Zech 14:5/1 Thess 3:13; Zech 14:5/1 Thess 4:14; Zech 14:5/2 Thess 1:7–10; Isa 66:4–6, 15/2 Thess 1:6–12; Isa 2:10/2 Thess 1:9; Isa 28:16/Rom 9:33; Isa 59:20/Rom 11:26; Isa 59:17/1 Thess 5:8). Kreitzer therefore concludes that there is a "co-operation" between God and Messiah with respect to the day of judgment in the eschaton, also witnessed to by the Jewish Pseudepigrapha (p. 106), and that, as a result, "there exists a conceptual ambiguity within sections of the eschatological teaching of the Pauline epistles" (p. 129). Nevertheless, it should be noticed that in the context of these passages God remains the subject who carries out the judgment (Rom 2:2–3, 5; 13:2; 14:3–4; 1 Cor 4:5).

109. Beale, "Reconciliation," 230. Also, T. Ryan Jackson, *New Creation in Paul's Letters: A Study of the Historical and Social Setting of a Pauline Concept*, WUNT 2/272 (Tübingen: Mohr Siebeck, 2010), 179; Mark Gignilliat, "2 Corinthians 6:2: Paul's Eschatological 'Now' and Hermeneutical Invitation," *WTJ* 67 (2005): 155.

110. Thus, Mark Gignilliat, *Paul and Isaiah's Servants: Paul's Theological Reading of Isaiah 40–66 in 2 Corinthians 5:14–6:10*, LNTS 330 (London: T&T Clark, 2007), 37: "[F]or Paul, Scripture plays a major, if not leading, role in his self-apologetic in 2 Cor 2:14–7:1."

support in 2 Cor 4–6.[111] Moreover, because most of the Isaiah texts Paul quotes or alludes to in 2 Cor 4–6 are from Isa 40–66, the larger context of Isa 40–66 provides the theological and eschatological framework for Paul's argument.[112]

In this regard, both G. K. Beale and William J. Webb persuasively demonstrate the influence of the Isaianic context on Paul's argument in 2 Corinthians, especially, chs 5–6. According to Beale, Paul understands reconciliation in Christ (2 Cor 5:17–21) to be the fulfillment of Isaiah's promise of a new creation, in which Israel would be restored into a peaceful relationship with God, a theme which extends through the beginning of 2 Cor 7.[113] In a similar way, Webb argues that the new covenant and new Exodus traditions found in Isa 40–66 are the background for Paul's argument in 2 Cor 5–6.[114] The role of the Isaianic background for Paul's argument further appears when Paul identifies his ministry in 6:1–2 with the ministry of the servant of God from Isa 49:8. For both Beale and Webb, Paul's adoption of the title "God's servant" (corresponding to *ebed Yahweh*) for himself is essential evidence that Paul understands Isaiah's prophecy to be fulfilled in and through his own ministry.[115]

Mark Gignilliat agrees with Webb and Beale that Paul's adoption of the title "God's servant" in several places of his writings (2 Cor 4:5; 6:2; Gal 1:10; Phil 1:1) appears against the Isaianic background.[116] However, Gignilliat criticizes Beale and Webb for not making a more precise distinction in these passages between the singular Servant (represented by Christ) and the plural servants (represented by

---

111. For example, NA[28] lists as a citation or allusion Isa 43:18 in 2 Cor 5:17, Isa 49:8 in 2 Cor 6:2; Isa 52:11 in 2 Cor 6:17; and Isa 43:6 in 2 Cor 6:18, but scholars have presented the Isaianic influence on 2 Corinthians in much greater detail, e.g., Isa 9:1–2 in 2 Cor 4:6; Isa 8:16–22 in 2 Cor 3:14–4:8; Isa 53:12 in 2 Cor 4:11; Isa 43:18–19; 42:9; 48:3, 6–7 in 2 Cor 5:17; Isa 49:8 in 2 Cor 6:2; Isa 52:11 in 2 Cor 6:17; Isa 43:6 in 2 Cor 6:18; Isa 49:13 in 2 Cor 7:6; Isa 55:10 in 2 Cor 9:10. Craig A. Evans, "From Gospel to Gospel: The Function of Isaiah in the New Testament," in *Writing and Reading the Scroll of Isaiah: Studies of an Interpretive Tradition*, ed. Craig C. Broyles and Craig A. Evans, vol. 2, VTSup 70 (Leiden; New York: Brill, 1997), 682–91; Florian Wilk, "Paulus als Nutzer, Interpret und Leser des Jesajabuches," in *Die Bibel im Dialog* (Tübingen; Basel: Francke, 2005), 93–116; and Gignilliat, *Servants*, 37. In addition, Florian Wilk ("Isaiah in 1 and 2 Corinthians," in *Isaiah in the New Testament* [London: T&T Clark, 2005], 149) recognizes the following allusions to Isaiah in the beginning of 2 Cor 4: e.g., 2 Cor 4:3 (Isa 53:1), 2 Cor 4:4 (Isa 52:14), 2 Cor 4:5 (Isa 52:11, 15), 2 Cor 4:6 (Isa 52:13), 2 Cor 4:9 (Isa 54:6). Wilk (149–50) also argues that Paul alludes to Isa 43:18–19; 42:9; 48:3, 6–7 in 2 Cor 5:16–17. However, Wilk does not include 2 Cor 6:17 in his argument because he doubts the Pauline authorship of the passage. Also, see Aernie, *Paul*, 195–214, for Paul's use of prophetic rhetoric (mostly from Isaiah) in 2 Cor 4:1–6.

112. Gignilliat, *Servants*, 70.

113. Beale, "Reconciliation," 228–31.

114. Webb, Returning Home, 158 (cf. see note 16 in Chapter One).

115. Ibid., 112–13, 128–58; Beale, "Reconciliation," 230–1.

116. Gignilliat, *Servants*, 108.

the followers, including Paul). Examining Paul's quotation of Isa 49:8 in 2 Cor 6:2, Gignilliat agrees with Beale and Webb that Paul's emphasis is on the eschatological "now," but claims that reading 2 Cor 6:2 as Paul's identification with the Servant goes beyond Paul's own intention.[117] For Gignilliat, Paul does not equate himself with the Servant addressed in Isa 49:8 because in 2 Cor 5:14–21 Paul identifies the typological significance of the Servant with the person and work of Christ.[118] Gignilliat thus argues that it is more appropriate in 6:2 to view Paul identifying himself not with the "Servant" in Isaiah's servant songs, but rather with the "servants" in the last part of Isaiah.[119]

However, whether Gignilliat is correct or not regarding whether Paul views himself as the Servant of Isa 49:8, which is beyond the scope of this present study,[120] his work points to the significance of the relationship in Isaiah between the Servant and his servants, in which the fear of God, which is to characterize the Servant (Isa 11:2–3), is also to be the attitude of his obedient followers (i.e., the servants) (Isa 50:10).[121] In the same way, Paul speaks of fearing God both in relationship to himself as an apostle (as a motivation of his ministry in 2 Cor 5:11) and in relationship to the Corinthians (as a motivation for the perfection of their holiness in 2 Cor 7:1). Moreover, the Isaianic background to 2 Cor 6:1 is further emphasized in that Isa 49:4 LXX describes the Servant's statement regarding his own ministry with language similar to that in 2 Cor 6:1:

> But I said, "I have labored *vainly* (κενῶς), and I have given my strength *in vain and for nothing* (εἰς μάταιον καὶ εἰς οὐδὲν); therefore my judgment is with the Lord, and my toil before my God"
>
> NETS, emphasis added.[122]

Although the Servant's work of restoring Israel has appeared largely to be "in vain," there is nevertheless a significant effect of this work on "the preserved ones"

---

117. Gignilliat, "2 Corinthians 6:2," 148–9, 155–6.

118. Gignilliat, *Servants*, 108–9.

119. Ibid., 137–38. Gignilliat, 112–31, emphasizes the shift from servant (singular) in Isa 40–55 to the servants (plural) in Isa 54–66. Gignilliat argues that Paul's identity as one of the servants of the Servant is especially apparent in his identity as the herald (2 Cor 5:14–21; 6:1–10), sufferer (6:3–10), and one of the righteous (5:21; 6:6–7), in addition to Paul's emphasis in 6:3–10 on the eschatological tension of the present age, during which Paul argues that he is possessed by Christ (pp. 132–42).

120. For a detailed argument concerning this issue, see Aernie, *Paul*, 133–58.

121. Brevard S. Childs, *Isaiah*, OTL (Louisville: Westminster John Knox, 2001), 102. Also Albert L. A. Hogeterp (*Paul and God's Temple: A Historical Interpretation of Cultic Imagery in the Corinthian Correspondence*, BTAS 2 [Leuven; Dudley, MA: Peeters, 2006], 371) argues that the fear of God in 7:1 links to Isa 11:2.

122. The Isaiah LXX text is from Joseph Ziegler, ed., *Isaias*, 3rd ed., SVTG 14 (Göttingen: Vandenhoeck & Ruprecht, 1983).

in Israel and also on the Gentiles (Isa 49:6, 8).[123] Moreover, this hopeful expectation is further emphasized in Isa 65:22–23 LXX, which has a strong linguistic connection with Isa 49:4 LXX. Here, God promises that:

> And they shall not build, and others inhabit; they shall not plant, and others eat, for according to the days of the tree of life shall the days of my people be; they shall make old the works of their labors. And my chosen ones shall not labor *in vain* (εἰς κενόν), nor bear children for a curse, because they are an offspring blessed by God
>
> NETS, emphasis added).

God assures his Servant in 49:5–6 that his labor will not be in vain,[124] and he assures the same promise to his people in 65:23. Thus, the promise in Isa 65:23 echoes the servant's mention from 49:4 that he has labored in vain, but nevertheless he does not lose hope and confidence in God and reflects the confident trust that God will not fail to reward his faithful ministry in the eschatological future.[125] It is this reward that Paul sees now coming about in his own ministry among the Corinthians.

---

123. Beale, "Reconciliation," 228.

124. Jan Leunis Koole, *Isaiah III*, vol. 2, HCOT (Leuven: Peeters, 1998), 2, 21–25: "the Servant receives recompense and satisfaction (v. 4) for his futile work on Israel in the more honourable tasks (v. 5b) of being 'a light to the nations'" (p. 21).

125. This insight derives from a conversation with Isaac Blois.

Chapter 3

THE FEAR OF GOD WITHIN THE CONTEXT OF THE CATENA OF SCRIPTURE

Chapter Two examined the larger context of 2 Corinthians, in which Paul mentions the fear of God with regard to the last judgment, and revealed the Isaianic framework that forms the background of Paul's argument in chs 4–6. Chapter Three now examines the role of the fear of God in the specific OT contexts of Isa 52:11 and Lev 26:11–12, both cited in the catena of Scripture in 2 Cor 16c–18, and its relationship to the related themes of Ezek 20:34; 37:27; and Jer 31:31–34; 32:36–40. In doing so, we will see that in these OT passages the fear of God both derives from the expectation of God's coming judgment and motivates the righteous in anticipation of that day. At the same time, the fear of God is evoked by the presence of God, represented by his sanctuary, which is promised in the new covenant. This observation will then shed light on the meaning and significance of Paul's use of the fear of God in 2 Cor 7:1 as he summarizes and concludes his argument in 6:14–18.

I. *The Fear of God within its Isaianic Context*

In the middle of the catena of Scripture in 2 Cor 6:17ac, Paul quotes two commands from Isa 52:11: "come out from their midst and be separate" and "do not touch what is unclean." Paul's summary of this previous argument in 2 Cor 7:1 picks up these commands in its admonition for the Corinthians "to cleanse themselves" and its related reference "to completing holiness." What has not been noticed, however, is that Paul's reference to "the fear of God" in 7:1 is also related to these commands once Isa 52:11 is read in its larger context of Isa 50:4–52:11, where the fear of God in 50:10 appears in both MT and LXX.[1] Specifically, the verb "to fear" (ירא) with

---

1. In contrast to the other Isaiah-text used in 2 Cor 6:16c–18 (e.g., allusion to Isa 43:6 in 2 Cor 6:18a), which is used as supplementary to 2 Sam 7:8 and 14, Isa 52:11 is quoted independently and without modification (except for the order), see William J. Webb, *Returning Home: New Covenant and Second Exodus as the Context for 2 Corinthians 6.14–7.1*, JSNTSup 85 (Sheffield: JSOT Press, 1993), 40–3.

God as referent appears in Isa 50:10; 57:11; 59:19.[2] The reference to the fear of God, which Paul uses to support his argument both in 2 Cor 5:11 and 7:1, thus appears right in the center of the argument of Isa 50:4–52:11, the context that Paul has in view in 2 Cor 5:10–7:1.[3]

As we will observe, the context of Isa 50:4–52:12 reveals the close relationship between the fear of God and the judgment of God, providing further insights into the context of 2 Cor 7:1. Inasmuch as Isa 50:10 mentions the fear of God within the context of his judgment in relation to God's commands as developed in 51:9–52:12, this most likely explains why Paul, who quotes the commands from Isa 52:11 in 2 Cor 6:17ac, goes on to conclude his argument with the fear of God in 7:1d, especially if the role of the fear of God in Paul's argument matches that of Isaiah. Hence, the fact that Paul frames his direct appeal to the Isaiah passages in 2 Cor 5:10–7:1, by reference to the fear of God in 5:11 and 7:1, appears at first surprising and unrelated, but is best explained as deriving from the connection between the fear of God (Isa 50:10), God's commands (Isa 51:9, 17; 52:11), and the judgment of God (Isa 50:9, 11; 51:6, 8) that exists within the wider Isaianic context of Isa 50:4–

---

2. Cf. the noun יראה with God as referent appears in Isa 11:2, 3; 33:6; 63:17. In Isaiah the verb ירא appears 27 times in 26 verses (Isa 7:4; 8:12; 10:24; 18:2, 7; 21:1; 25:3; 29:13; 35:4; 37:6; 40:9; 41:5, 10, 13, 14; 43:1, 5; 44:2; 50:10; 51:7, 12; 54:4, 14; 57:11 [2x]; 59:19; 64:2), and the noun יראה appears five times (Isa 7:25; 11:2, 3; 33:6; 63:17). In addition, the noun מורא ("fear"), which is similar to ירא, appears in 8:12 and 8:13, where in the latter case it is used with God as its referent. In these texts, LXX renders ירא as φοβέω ("to fear," Isa 7:4; 8:12; 10:24; 35:4; 37:6; 40:9; 41:5, 10, 13; 43:1, 5; 44:2; 50:10; 51:7, 12; 54:4, 14; 57:11 [2x]; 59:19) or φοβερός ("fearful," Isa 21:1), and יראה as φόβος ("fear," Isa 7:25; 11:3), φοβέω ("to fear," Isa 63:17), or εὐσέβεια ("piety, godliness," Isa 11:2; 33:6). In addition, in rendering other related Hebrew words for "fear," LXX has θεός as the object of fear in Isa 29:23 (φοβέομαι/ערץ in MT) and κύριος as its object in Isa 2:10 (φόβος/פחד in MT), 19 (φόβος/פחד in MT), 21 (φόβος/פחד in MT); 8:13 (φόβος/ערץ in MT). The Isaiah LXX text is from Joseph Ziegler, ed., *Isaias*, 3rd ed., SVTG 14 (Göttingen: Vandenhoeck & Ruprecht, 1983) unless otherwise indicated. All LXX translations are mine unless otherwise indicated.

3. As observed in Chapter Two, Paul uses the broader Isaianic context of Isa 40–66 within his argument in 2 Cor 4–6. Thus, Florian Wilk, "Gottes Wort und Gottes Verheißungen. Zur Eigenart der Schriftverwendung in 2 Kor 6,14–7,1," in *Die Septuaginta – Texte, Kontexte, Lebenswelten: Internationale Fachtagung Veranstaltet von Septuaginta Deutsch (LXX.D), Wuppertal 20.–23. Juli 2006*, ed. Martin Karrer and Wolfgang Kraus, WUNT 213 (Tübingen: Mohr Siebeck, 2008), 693n94: "Dabei werden, auch im zweiten Korintherbrief, gerade Jes 40–45; 49–56 intensiv genutzt." In this context, Beale argues that the theme of reconciliation in Christ, which continues throughout 2 Cor 6–7, is Paul's way of explaining Isaiah's promises of "restoration." G. K. Beale, "The Old Testament Background of Reconciliation in 2 Corinthians 5–7 and Its Bearing on the Literary Problem of 2 Corinthians 6:14–7:1," in *The Right Doctrine from the Wrong Texts? Essays on the Use of the Old Testament in the New* (Grand Rapids: Baker Books, 1994), 217–44; idem, *A New Testament Biblical Theology: The Unfolding of the Old Testament in the New* (Grand Rapids: Baker Academic, 2011), 711–19.

52:12.[4] Within this context, the fear of God derives from the judgment of God that befalls those who do not respond faithfully to God's deliverance, and thus motivates the people of God to keep his commandments; as such, the fear of God consequently characterizes the faithful.

Before examining the fear of God in Isa 50:10 and its context, two things should be addressed regarding Paul's use of the Isaianic text: the question regarding Paul's *Vorlage(n)* for his use of the Isaianic text and the fact that Paul's quotations in 2 Cor 6:2 and 6:17ac all derive from Isa 40–66. The former question clarifies the exegetical basis of our examination, while the latter fact provides the conceptual background of it.

1. The Isaiah Text

Regarding the issue of Paul's OT quotations, much ink has been expended on the question of whether Paul employed a single *Vorlage* or multiple *Vorlagen* in his use of the OT.[5] Paul, a Greek-speaking Jew who could read Aramaic and Hebrew, probably had various options when approaching the OT.[6] Hence, although Paul's OT quotations usually overlap strongly with a known LXX form,[7] scholars also

---

4. Cf. Florian Wilk, "Gottes Wort," 695: "Das gemeinsame *Thema* der Gottesworte in 2Kor 6, 16ff. wird durch die Gedankenlinie von 5, 16a über 6, 17a–c zu 7, 1c angezeigt" (original emphasis). Wilk does not acknowledge the theme of the fear of God in 2 Cor 6:14–7:1 in his article.

5. Dietrich-Alex Koch, *Die Schrift als Zeuge des Evangeliums: Untersuchungen zur Verwendung und zum Verständnis der Schrift bei Paulus*, BHT 69 (Tübingen: Mohr Siebeck, 1986), 57–71, 81–101; Christopher D. Stanley, *Paul and the Language of Scripture*, SNTSMS 74 (Cambridge: Cambridge University Press, 1992), 67–72; idem, *Arguing with Scripture: The Rhetoric of Quotations in the Letters of Paul* (New York: T&T Clark, 2004), 38–71; E. Earle Ellis, *The Old Testament in Early Christianity: Canon and Interpretation in the Light of Modern Research*, WUNT 54 (Tübingen: J. C. B. Mohr, 1991), 77–121; Timothy H. Lim, *Holy Scripture in the Qumran Commentaries and Pauline Letters* (Oxford; New York: Clarendon; Oxford University Press, 1977), 123–76; Florian Wilk, *Die Bedeutung des Jesajabuches für Paulus*, FRLANT 179 (Göttingen: Vandenhoeck & Ruprecht, 1998), 340–80; idem, "Isaiah in 1 and 2 Corinthians," in *Isaiah in the New Testament* (London: T&T Clark, 2005), 133–58; Mark Gignilliat, *Paul and Isaiah's Servants: Paul's Theological Reading of Isaiah 40–66 in 2 Corinthians 5:14–6:10*, LNTS 330 (London: T&T Clark, 2007), 13–30; Richard B. Hays, *Echoes of Scripture in the Letters of Paul* (New Haven: Yale University Press, 1989), 154–92; J. Ross Wagner, *Heralds of the Good News: Isaiah and Paul "in Concert" in the Letter to the Romans*, NovTSup 101 (Leiden: Brill, 2002), 341–60; Steve Moyise, *Paul and Scripture: Studying the New Testament Use of the Old Testament* (Grand Rapids: Baker Academic, 2010), 111–25.

6. Lim, *Holy Scripture*, 26–7.

7. Henry Barclay Swete, *An Introduction to the Old Testament in Greek*, ed. Richard Rusden Ottley, 2nd ed. (Cambridge: Cambridge University Press, 1991), 400; Wilk, "Gottes Wort," 694; D. Moody Smith, "The Pauline Literature," in *It Is Written: Scripture Citing Scripture: Essays in Honour of Barnabas Lindars*, ed. D. A. Carson and H. G. M. Williamson (Cambridge: Cambridge University Press, 1988), 272–3.

have suggested that on occasion Paul's quotation might have been influenced by MT as well, or derive from an unknown Hebrew or LXX-tradition.[8] For example, Christopher D. Stanley argues that five passages (Rom 10:5; 11:4; 12:19; 1 Cor 3:19; and 15:54) of Paul's 83 explicitly marked quotations show a measure of agreement with MT over against the LXX tradition, and even these five are accompanied by deviations from the Masoretic tradition that make direct resort to the Hebrew unlikely.[9] Paul thus seems to rely on a Hebraizing or Graecizing revision of the common OG, or even a different translation altogether.[10] Moreover, not only the variety of sources, but also Paul's understanding of the new eschatological situation no doubt influenced his reading of the OT.[11] Consequently, rather than focusing on reconstructing Paul's *Vorlage*, this work will focus on Paul's reading of the OT on a conceptual and theological level and not a text-critical one.[12] This work will

---

8. Cf. Wagner, *Heralds*, 16n60: "where Paul's citations or allusions differ from the 'LXX' (as critically reconstructed) and appear to reflect a text closer to that now preserved in MT, *this does not prove that Paul was drawing directly on a Hebrew text*. Rather, he may well have been using a text of the LXX that had previously been revised toward a Hebrew exemplar" (original emphasis).

9. Stanley, *Arguing*, 67. Cf., Moisés Silva, ("Old Testament in Paul," *DPL* 631) argues that seven out of 107 explicit quotations in the Pauline corpus agree with MT over against the LXX tradition (Rom 1:17; 11:4, 35; 12:19; 1 Cor 3:19; Gal 3:11; 2 Tim 2:19a).

10. Koch, *Schrift*, 57–81; Stanley, *Arguing*, 67. Likewise, Silva ("Old Testament in Paul," 632) argues that Paul's "dependence on the current Greek translation of his day is clearly established, but there is good reason to think that he was familiar with the original Hebrew and that the latter, in at least some cases, determined how he used the OT." Regarding whether Paul used biblical texts that belong to any particular strand in the extant Septuagint manuscript tradition, Stanley (*Arguing*, 68–69) argues that "the results are decidedly mixed" because there is no consistent preference for a certain text-family in Paul. With Koch, Stanley too thinks that over half of the irregularities in Paul's quotations over against the known texts, are due to Paul's own adaptations in light of how they are to function in his context (37–51). Nevertheless, despite the practical conflicting data, the evidence in Paul's citations shows that the great majority of Paul's uses were taken directly from written texts of some sort (71, 79).

11. Gignilliat, *Servants*, 16.

12. Thus following Frances M. Young and David Ford, *Meaning and Truth in 2 Corinthians*, BFT (London: SPCK Publishing, 1987), 63; Smith, "Pauline Literature," 279; Gignilliat, *Servants*, 16. As Wagner (*Heralds*, 15) claims, the text-critical examination of Paul's *Vorlage* serves as a tool for exposing Paul's interpretative strategies and aims. In this study I use the term LXX to refer to the Greek translation of a biblical book, most of the time following the critically-reconstructed text in the Göttingen LXX. By using this text, I do not assume that Paul's *Vorlage* exactly matches the reconstructed *Urtext* of the Göttingen edition, but it serves as a critical text for our study (cf. Wagner, *Heralds*, 7n23). Also in this study I use the term MT to refer to Israel's Bible in Hebrew and Aramaic, most of the time following the critical edition of the *BHS*. Emmanuel Tov ("*The Status of the Masoretic Text*

follow MT in the narrative description of Isaiah unless there are significant differences between LXX and MT.[13]

2. The Fear of God as a Response to God's Deliverance

As mentioned above, Paul's quotations in 2 Cor 6:2 and 6:17ac all come from Isa 40–66, which "is clearly dominated by the proclamations that the exile has come to an end, implying that YHWH has returned to his people."[14] Isaiah as a whole highlights both the already-established and the yet-to-be-established relationship between God and his people, but this eschatological emphasis in Isa 40–66 places a distinctive focus on the salvific act of God still to come, with its corresponding exhortation that Israel is to live in a way that is appropriate for God's chosen people. God's eschatological salvation will consist of the restoration of his people and the judgment of his enemies, including his own people who have not lived according to his commandments.[15] The fear of God in 50:10 appears against this backdrop, and plays a significant role for the redeemed people of God.

---

in Modern Text Editions of the Hebrew Bible: The Relevance of Canon," in *The Canon Debate: On the Origins and Formation of the Bible*, eds. Lee Martin McDonald and James A. Sanders [Peabody, MA: Hendrickson, 2002], 245) argues that the *BHS* presents codex Leningrad, a representative of the medieval MT, as the main text, while a critical apparatus presents the variants. According to Tov, a critical edition should either present the best available manuscript as the central text, while recording variants and emendations in its apparatus, or create an eclectic text. But because the MT does not necessarily reflect the original text and contains many early errors, the choice of the MT as the best manuscript might involve problems and perpetuate its assumed centrality.

13. For a more detailed comparative study of Isa 50:4–11 MT and LXX, significant is Eugene Robert Ekblad Jr., *Isaiah's Servant Poems According to the Septuagint: An Exegetical and Theological Study*, CBET 23 (Leuven: Peeters, 1999), 125–65. Cf. Wilk ("Gottes Wort," 694–6), who argues that LXX appears to be the text basis for the references in 2 Cor 6:16c–18. Nevertheless, in his article, "Isaiah," 155–8, Wilk examines Paul's quotations and allusions to Isaiah in 1, 2 Corinthians, and concludes that although Paul relies constantly on the Greek version, in some cases the texts deviate from LXX, testifying that it was revised towards Hebrew. According to Wilk, Paul's modifications of the text have been done intentionally in order to adapt the texts from Isaiah to Paul's argumentations and to underline his understanding of those texts. Wilk excludes 2 Cor 6:18 in his article, "Isaiah," because he doubts its authenticity, but he treats the Isaianic quotation in 2 Cor 6:17ac and 6:17d–18a in "Gottes Wort," 688–91.

14. Blaženka Scheuer, *The Return of YHWH: The Tension between Deliverance and Repentance in Isaiah 40–55*, BZAW 377 (Berlin; New York: de Gruyter, 2008), 80.

15. In Isa 41:1–20, God is described as the judge or prosecutor against the nations. Jerome T. Walsh, "Summons to Judgement: A Close Reading of Isaiah XLI 1–20," *VT* 43 (1993): 351–71. However, in Isa 50:4–51:8 the identity of the opponents of God's people is rather vague and is not limited to the other nations. This will be discussed later.

This emphasis on the fear of God is part of a larger theme within Isa 40–66 which repeatedly emphasizes the relationship between God and his people in various terms: God is described as the maker/creator of his people (40:21–31; 43:1, 7, 15–16, 21; 44:2, 21, 24–8; 45:11; 49:5, 8), and also as the one who chose them as his people (41:8–9; 42:1; 43:10, 20; 44:1–2; 45:4; 49:7).[16] This relationship established by God in the past leads to the expectation of a new relationship to be accomplished by God's restoration of his people in the future.[17] Moreover, Isa 40–66 emphasizes that the new relationship to be established through God's act of restoration demands a response from his people. Blaženka Scheuer argues that this reciprocal relationship between God and his people is the focus of the deliverance in Isaiah, so that when God exhorts his people to repent in Isa 44:21–2 and 55:6–7, "repentance" is not a condition for their deliverance, but a sign of their acceptance of their renewed relationship.[18] In other words, God's salvation of his people establishes the foundation for the people to regain their confidence in God, and their repentance is the confirmation from their side of this confidence as a result of their having been delivered by God.[19]

Hence, although having already been delivered in the past unconditionally, a subsequent condition still remains for maintaining the covenant relationship in the present. Scheuer rightly acknowledges the bilateral demand existing in the reestablished relationship between God and his people, but Scheuer's argument falls short in that it does not deal with the consequence (or the possibility) of failing the command.[20] Just as repentance is the people's positive response to God's deliverance, its refusal is a negative response that brings God's condemnation.[21] In

---

16. John Oswalt (*The Book of Isaiah*, NICOT [Grand Rapids: Eerdmans, 1998], 231) thus comments: "the argument here [Isa 40–66] is quite consistent: he who made you and the whole world, who has providentially sustained you, is able to deliver you from anything." For a more detailed description of the passages dealing with the relationship between God and his people, see Shalom M. Paul, *Isaiah 40–66: Translation and Commentary*, ECC (Grand Rapids; Cambridge: Eerdmans, 2012), 23–4.

17. E.g., Isa 46:3–4.

18. Scheuer, *Return*, 125, 141. According to Scheuer, 133, God's deliverance demands the response of the people in a form of "repentance" that can be defined as "the people's 'positive move' towards YHWH, with a view to the reestablishment of the relationship." Scheuer, 132, lists a number of exhortations in Isaiah that demonstrate the calling for repentance: Isa 40:3, 9, 11; 41:10, 13, 14; 42:10–12, 18, 23; 43:1, 5; 44:1, 2, 8; 46:3, 12; 48:1; 51:1, 7; 52:11; 54:1; 55:1, 3, 6.

19. Ibid., 81: "In spite of the people's rebellion, YHWH delivers, and because YHWH delivers, the people need to return. Their repentance does not condition their deliverance, but it conditions their relationship with YHWH."

20. Ibid., 137.

21. In Isaiah God's judgment falls on those who do not meet the condition (e.g., 50:9, 11; 51:6, 8). Thus, Henk Leene ("History and Eschatology in Deutero-Isaiah," in *Studies in the Book of Isaiah: Festschrift Willem A.M. Beuken*, ed. Jacque Van Ruiten and Marc Vervenne,

other words, Scheuer's argument reveals only one of the motivations for obedience to God's commands as the people's proper response to God's deliverance that it is initiated by and made possible as a result of God's redemption in the past. However, it misses the other motivation for obedience, i.e., the new awareness of the future consequences of failing to keep God's commands. There are therefore two "sides" to the covenant stipulations: God's deliverance in the *past* and his promised deliverance and condemnation in the *future*. The role of the fear of God is thus significant because it helps us to see the future side that Scheuer misses—the fear of God that leads to obedience functions as the people's proper response to God's initial salvific action in view of the final judgment still to come.[22] Thus, examining the context of Isa 50:4–52:11, where the connection between the fear of God (50:10), God's judgment (50:9, 11; 51:6, 8), and his commands (51:9, 17; 52:1, 11) is established, will further our understanding of the fear of God as the proper responsive attitude of God's people. In turn, the examination will also elucidate the significance of Paul's quotation of the commands from 52:11 in 2 Cor 6:17ac and his mention of the fear of God in 2 Cor 7:1.

BETL 132 [Leuven: Leuven University Press; Peeters, 1997], 236–37) argues: "I do not believe that according to Deutero-Isaiah whole peoples would turn to Yhwh en masse ... whoever may count him- or her-self as part of Israel's historical remnant, Jews by birth (46,3), is far from righteousness and only belongs to the seed of the Servant by listening (48,17ff.; cf. 50,10)." Contra Klaus Koch, *The Prophets. Vol. 2: The Babylonian and Persian Periods* (London: SCM, 1983), 150: "For nothing is said [in Deutero-Isaiah] about what happens to the people who refuse to be converted, and who resist belief in the prophetic word. There is not the slightest indication that there are men and women in the nation [including the Israelites] who are not going to experience the impending turn to salvation, but who will have to die first, because of their wickedness or lack of faith." Scheuer (*Return*, 79) agrees with Koch that neither in the accusations nor in the calls to repentance in Isa 44:21–2 and 55:6–7 is there any threat against those who answer the call negatively. However, Scheuer acknowledges the possibility of the people's negative response in Isa 40–66: "On several occasions, the prophet proclaims condemnation and misfortune for those that do not turn to YHWH but put their trust in idols (Isa 42:17; 44:20; 45:24). The people's actions, demonstrated by the choices they make in the present, ought to be decisive for their future: freedom of choice always comes with responsibility for the consequences of that choice" (p. 133). Again, "the proclamation of deliverance can either be ignored completely or responded to wholeheartedly" (p. 142).

22. Cf. Scheuer, *Return*, 132: "There are calls to demonstrate one's faith by speaking of and rejoicing in YHWH's salvation, by not being afraid, or by putting one's trust in YHWH. There are calls to willingness to listen and to understand and also a call geographically to leave the place of the exile." Scheuer does not deal with the fear of God, and mentions only briefly that, "The true service of YHWH, which is to have faith in YHWH (Isa 50:10), to believe in the proclaimed salvation, and to do what YHWH demands, is presented as a contrast [to the concepts of sin in Deutero-Isa]" (p. 129).

II. The Fear of God in the Context of Isa 50:4–52:11

The catena of double commands in Isa 50:4–52:11 (51:9, 17; 52:1, 11), of which 52:11 is the last, starts immediately after the section spanning 50:4–51:8, where the fear of God (50:10) functions as the focal point in describing the positive response from the people to God's salvation, i.e., pursuing righteousness (51:1), knowing righteousness (51:7), and having God's Torah in their hearts (51:7). The fear of God, as the positive response of the people, forms a sharp contrast to the response of those who fear the reproach of others (51:7) and whose end is condemnation at God's judgment (50:9, 11; 51:6, 8). In this regard, the fear of God derives from an awareness of the consequences of the last judgment and functions as a decisive motivating factor in determining who will respond properly to God's deliverance and who will undergo God's condemnation.

1. The Literary Structure of Isa 50:4–51:8

The first major section of our passage, Isa 50:4–51:8, is a complex text and scholars have argued over how to divide it.[23] However, most scholars agree that the section starts at 50:4 because of the clear change of speaker from God in 49:8–50:3 to his servant in 50:4.[24] Since 50:4 starts with אדני יהוה/κύριος, which does not appear previously in the chapter but reoccurs in vv. 5, 7, and 9, the section of 50:4–11 can be divided as follows:[25]

---

23. Most scholars agree that a new section of text starts in 50:4, but there is less agreement on the end of the section. For example, Klaus Baltzer (*Deutero-Isaiah: A Commentary on Isaiah 40–55*, Hermeneia [Minneapolis: Fortress, 2001], 338–49) divides the section as 50:4–8; 9–11; 51:1–3; 4–8. Oswalt (*Isaiah*, 320–27) divides it as 50:4–9; 50:10–51:8. John Goldingay (*The Message of Isaiah 40–55: A Literary-Theological Commentary* [London: T&T Clark, 2005], 418) sees 50:9–11 as a unit, and divides Isa 51 into 51:1–3; 4–5; 7–8. Roy F. Melugin (*The Formation of Isaiah 40–55*, BZAW 141 [Berlin; New York: de Gruyter, 1976], 71–73, 152–59) divides it as 50:4–9; 10–11; 51:1–3; 4–5; 6;7–8. Brevard S. Childs (*Isaiah*, OTL [Louisville: Westminster John Knox, 2001], 401) divides it as 50:4–9; 10–11; 51:1–3; 4–6; 7–8. Pierre Bonnard (*Le Second Isaïe, Son Disciple et Leurs Éditeurs: Isaïe 40–66*, Ebib [Paris: Gabalda, 1972], 237, 244) sees that 50:4–11 reflects on the prophet's assurance and that the prophet further communicates with the faithful people in 51:1–8, which he divides into 51:1–3, 4–6, 7–8. MT marks 51:8 as the end of a *seder*, while 1QIsa[a] has a space after v. 9, implying a break. For a more detailed discussion, see Jan Leunis Koole, *Isaiah III*, vol. 2, HCOT (Leuven: Peeters, 1998), 102–4.

24. Melugin, *Formation*, 152–56; Baltzer, *Deutero-Isaiah*, 338–39; Goldingay, *Message*, 401–2; Paul, *Isaiah*, 349–50.

25. Following Oswalt (*Isaiah*, 323), who calls this use of the phrase "highly intentional."

50:4	God made me listen
50:5–6	Obedience as a result or as a mode of listening[26]
50:7–8	God's vindication is near
50:9	God's vindication in contrast to his judgment
50:10	Listen to God's servant (= Fear God)
50:11	God's judgment

These verses function as the introduction to the section that follows in 51:1–8, which is closely linked in that the themes in 50:4–11 reoccur in 51:1–8:[27] First, "to hear" in 50:4 reappears in 50:10, 51:1, 4 (2x), 7.[28] The difference between these passages is that in 50:4 God grants his servant (or the speaker) an ear to hear, while in 51:1, 4, 7 God directly exhorts his people (or the audience) to listen to him. Yet in all cases the object of hearing/listening is either God himself (51:1, 4, 7) or his servant (50:10).

Second, the obedience which appears as a result of God's opening his servant's ears to listen in 50:5–6 reappears in 51:2 in relation to the example of Abraham and Sarah. The text does not describe specific obedient behaviors of Abraham and Sarah, but nevertheless their faithful trust in God's promise stands in parallel with the obedient behavior described in 50:5–6.[29] Moreover, the rock and the quarry in 51:1 and Abraham and Sarah in 51:2 are closely connected because the same imperative "look to" (הביטו/ἐμβλέπω) appears in both verses. Both imperatives

---

26. It is not easy to decide whether Isa 50:5–6 describes the *result* of God's awaking the servant's ear to listen or the *mode* of the servant's listening (that is, how it appears). In v. 7, God helps the servant and "therefore" (על־כן/διὰ τοῦτο) he is not ashamed. The state of the servant here is clearly the result of God's action. On the other hand, in other passages where שמע appears, the mode of hearing is then described. For example, Isa 50:10, "Who among you fears the Lord, (that is) listens to the voice of the servant," 51:1, "Listen to me, you who pursue righteousness and seek the Lord," or 51:7, "Listen to me, you who know righteousness, you people who have my teaching in their hearts." Thus, Goldingay, *Message*, 418.

27. Likewise, Melugin, *Formation*, 159: "Isaiah 51, 1–8 is related to the forgoing context by verbal repetition."

28. In MT, שמע ("to hear") appears in 50:4, 10; 51:1, 7. In 51:4, שמע does not appear, but is replaced by קשב ("to pay attention") and אזן ("to listen"), both are used in parallel to שמע elsewhere in Isaiah; cf., e.g., Isa 28:23: "Give ear (אזן), and hear (שמע) my voice; give attention (קשב), and hear (שמע) my speech." Here, both verbs, אזן and קשב, are used as synonyms for שמע. See also Isa 42:23: "Who among you will give ear to (אזן) this, will attend (קשב) and listen (שמע) for the time to come?" Here, both verbs have the same meaning as שמע. It is also noteworthy that in all occurrences of אזן in Isaiah, it always appears with שמע (1:2, 10; 28:23) 32:9; 42:23; 64:6). In this sense, Roger Norman Whybray (*Isaiah 40–66*, CB [London: Oliphants, 1975], 154) rightly comments that there is a threefold exhortation in Isa 51, namely, hearken to me (v. 1); listen to me (v. 4); hearken to me (v. 7). Likewise, Childs, *Isaiah*, 401.

29. Oswalt, *Isaiah*, 335.

address those who pursue righteousness and seek for God (51:1), and the context shows that Abraham and Sarah are an example of those who do so. Verse 3 further expands the blessings on Abraham and Sarah in v. 2 to include the restored blessings in Zion, which is a common motif in Isa 40–66.[30]

Third, the theme of vindication appears as the vindication of the servant (50:7–8) and then reoccurs as the restoration of Zion (51:3) and of God's people (51:5). While the blessing on Abraham and Sarah in v. 2 is clearly in the past, the context of God's restoration of Zion in v. 3 and of his people in v. 5 are in the future. In addition, the same word "near" (קרוב/ ἐγγίζω), representing the nearness of God's vindication of his servant in 50:8, also appears in 51:5 describing his vindication of the people.

Lastly, God's vindication and restoration of his people in 50:9 are juxtaposed with the destiny of the mortal opponents, who will be judged so that they wear out like a moth-eaten "garment" (בגד/ἱμάτιον). The theme of the garment reoccurs in 51:6 and 51:8 as a description of the opponents' mortal state and their destiny of judgment.[31]

In conclusion, 51:1–8, as the extension of 50:4–11, can be divided as follows:

51:1	Exhortation to listen
51:2	Obedience and restoration of Abraham and Sarah
51:3	Zion's restoration
51:4	Exhortation to listen
51:5	God's salvation is near
51:6	God's salvation in contrast to his judgment over the people
51:7	Exhortation to listen
51:8	God's salvation in contrast to his judgment over the people

The whole section of Isa 50:4–51:8 can thus be divided thematically as follows:

50:4	Listen	
	50:5–6	Testimony of obedience
	50:7–8	God's vindication
	50:9	God's salvation and his judgment
50:10	Listen to God's servant (= Fear God)	
	50:11	God's judgment
51:1	Exhortation to listen	
	51:2	Testimony of obedience and restoration
	51:3	God's restoration
51:4	Exhortation to listen	

---

30. Ibid; J. Gerald Janzen, "Rivers in the Desert of Abraham and Sarah and Zion (Isaiah 51:1–3)," *HAR* 10 (1986): 141; Goldingay, *Message*, 420–21; Paul, *Isaiah*, 358–60.

31. Thus, Koole, *Isaiah III*, 2: 119–20. Melugin (*Formation*, 157–58) also observes the repetition of words in 51:1–8, but does not make any connection between judgment and the garment.

		51:5	God's restoration
		51:6	God's restoration and his judgment
51:7	Exhortation to listen		
		51:8	God's restoration and his judgment

From the above analysis, we can observe the following. First, the repetitive themes of hearing (obeying), God's vindication, and his judgment show that 50:4–51:8 forms a closely linked unit. Second, in this structure two choices are presented to the people, each choice followed by specific consequences. God's judgment is repetitively presented in a visual and dramatic way (50:9; 51:6, 8) thus functioning as a warning to those who do not obey. Third, the double commands (51:9, 17; 52:1, 11) are given after these two choices are laid before the people, which indicates that these commands are specific ways for the people of God to live according to their restoration. Lastly, in the section spanning 50:4–51:8, 50:10–11 stands out from the other sections in that it uses different vocabulary despite its similar themes (obedience and God's judgment).[32]

2. The Immediate Context of the Fear of God

As mentioned above, there are several factors that distinguish Isa 50:10–11 from the section spanning 50:4–51:8. First, "to hear" appears in 50:10 not with God, but with his servant as referent, which parallels fearing God.[33] Second, 50:11 uses unique terms to describe God's judgment, such as a "burning torch" (זיקות/φλόξ) and "place of torment" (מעצבה/λύπη), which distinguishes it from other appearances of God's judgment in 50:9; 51:6, 8.[34] Thus, even though 50:10–11 continues the themes of hearing and judgment, which are congruent with the immediate context, because of its unique terms scholars have argued that these two verses form an independent section that functions as one of the transitional segments in 50:4–51:8.[35]

---

32. For this reason Joseph Blenkinsopp (*Isaiah 40–55: A New Translation with Introduction and Commentary*, AB 19A [New York: Doubleday, 2000], 79) argues vv. 10–11 is an editorial addition by a later hand.

33. This is the only place in Isaiah where the voice of the servant of God is the object of "to hear." Based on 50:10, which does not distinguish the addressees but describes them as a whole, the servant of God is probably not the recipient of God's redemption for his people, but the agent of it or even God himself. For a more detailed discussion and argument among scholars about this issue, see Roger Norman Whybray, *The Second Isaiah*, OTG 1 (Sheffield: JSOT Press, 1983), 68–78; Oswalt, *Isaiah*, 323.

34. MT has מעצבה, which appears only here in Isaiah, while LXX renders it as λύπη, which appears in a handful of places (Isa 1:5; 35:10; 40:29; 50:11; 51:11). Thus, Michael E. W. Thompson, *Isaiah: chs 40–66*, EC (London: Epworth, 2001), 89: "[The problem of v. 11 is] the very harsh word of judgment we have in v. 11, so harsh that it is on its own in Isa. 40–55."

35. E.g., Oswalt, *Isaiah*, 328, who argues that in this section while "the voice of his servant" clearly points backward (50:4), "fearing God" clearly points forward (51:1, 7). Also Koole, *Isaiah III*, 2:102; Melugin, *Formation*, 73.

Furthermore, the translation of 50:10 is a matter of debate:

50:10a   Who (מִי) among you fears the Lord (יְרֵא יהוה)
50:10b   hearing (שֹׁמֵעַ) the voice of his servant (בְּקוֹל עַבְדּוֹ)?
50:10c   who (אֲשֶׁר) walks in the darkness and has no light.
50:10d   who trusts/let him trust (יִבְטַח)[36] in the name of the Lord and relies/ let him rely (וְיִשָּׁעֵן)[37] upon his God (בֵּאלֹהָיו).

Jan Leunis Koole provides four possible ways of translating 50:10.[38] First, the מִי clause may be confined to v. 10ab, and v. 10c starts a new sentence: "Who among you fears the Lord, let him obey the voice of his servant. He who walks in darkness and there is no light for him . . ." Second, all of v. 10 can be construed as dependent on מִי as an interrogative particle. In this case, v. 10c may refer back to the servant in v. 10b: "Who among you fears the Lord and obeys the voice of his servant, who (the servant) walks in darkness and there is no light for him . . ." or "Who among you fears the Lord and obeys the voice of his servant, who (among you) walks in darkness and there is no light for him . . ." Third, the question may be taken to extend to v. 10c and to lead up to the encouragement of v. 10d. In this case, too, v. 10c may refer back to the servant or מִי, the question is confined to v. 10ab, and the text mentions not only the suffering but also the resolve of the servant: "Who among you fears the Lord and obeys the voice of his servant, who (the servant) walks in darkness and there is no light for him? Let him . . ." or "Who among you fears the Lord and obeys the voice of his servant, who (among you) walks in darkness and there is no light for him? Let him . . ." Fourth, the question can be confined to v. 10a, basically corresponds to the one who is mentioned. In this case, a point of secondary importance is whether אֲשֶׁר functions as a relative, "Who among you fears the Lord and obeys the voice of his servant, *he who* walks in the darkness . . ."; or as a conditional, "Who among you fears the Lord and obeys the voice of his servant, *if he* walks in the darkness . . ."; or as a concessive particle, "Who among you fears the Lord and obeys the voice of his servant, *although he* walks in the darkness . . ."

Koole's options present two central questions in translating v. 10. The first is how to understand the relationship between v. 10ab and v. 10c, i.e., whether v. 10c is a description of *the servant* in v. 10b[39] or a continuous description of *those* (מִי) in v. 10a.[40]

---

36. This verb is *Qal* imperfect third person masculine singular of חטב, but can be jussive in meaning since there is no unique form for the jussive.

37. This verb is *Niphal* imperfect third person masculine singular of שׁען, but can be jussive in meaning since there is no unique form for the jussive.

38. Koole, *Isaiah III*, 2:124–25.

39. "Who among you fears the Lord and obeys the voice of *his servant who* (i.e., the servant) walks in darkness and there is no light for him . . ."

40. "Who among you fears the Lord and obeys the voice of *his servant, who* (i.e., among you) walks in darkness and there is no light for him . . ."

Against the first option, W. A. M. Beuken argues that the tense change of the Hebrew verbs (הלך and יבטח) from perfect to imperfect makes it less probable since the latter does not usually follow the former asyndetically.[41] Thus, v. 10c is more likely a continuous description of מי in v. 10a.[42] The second question regarding Koole's option concerns how to render יבטח and ישען in v. 10d, which has three possibilities: first, these verbs apply to the servant in v. 10b, "... the voice of his servant ... who trusts in the name of the Lord and relies on his God"; second, the jussive verbs apply to the ones called in v. 10a, "Who among you ... Let him trust in the name of the Lord and rely on his God"; third, they apply to the ones in v. 10c, "Let him who walks in darkness and has no light trust in the name of the Lord and rely on his God." The first choice is less convincing because, as argued above, v. 10cd is not a description of the servant in v. 10b. The difference between the second and third options is reducible to the question of whether v. 10ab and v. 10c describe different groups of people. In other words, are those "who fear God and obey the voice of his servant" different from those "who walk in the darkness"? If so, how are they different? The syntax does not clearly answer this, but the context of vv. 10–11 sheds light on this question.

In contrast to the previous verse, v. 11 describes the faithless ones, who refuse to fear God and listen to the word of his servant, by using similar images of light and darkness.[43] While the faithful ones trust in the Lord even in the darkness, the faithless ones kindle their own fire and walk in the light of that fire. The condemnation against them comes from God himself, and their own flame will devour them; furthermore, their destiny is the "place of torment" (MT, מעצבה) or the "place of sorrow" (LXX, λύπη).[44] The emphasis of 50:10–11 thus lies on the *difference* between the faithful and the faithless responses, which will bring

---

41. W. A. M. Beuken, "Jes 50:10-11, Eine Kultische Paränese zur Dritten Ebed-Prophetie," *ZAW* 85 (1973): 169–70. Contra Melugin, *Formation*, 73; Baltzer, *Deutero-Isaiah*, 342–3.

42. Most of the English translations seem to prefer the latter: ESV, NIV, KJV, NRSV, etc. (KJV and NRSV seem to allow a possibility of the other option by using a relative pronoun: "... the voice of his servant, *who* walks ...," while ESV and NIV do not allow this by putting v. 10b and v. 10c together: "... the voice of his servant? Let him who walks in darkness and has no light trust ..." On the contrary, the Targum and the Vulgate choose the first option. In 1QIsa, the servant is changed to plural, which strengthens the connection between the servants and the following verbs in v. 10b; pluralizing servant "makes this singular relative clause refer back to the reverer." John Goldingay and David Payne, *A Critical and Exegetical Commentary on Isaiah 40–55*, vol. 2, ICC (London: T&T Clark, 2005), 216. The Vulgate also takes v. 10b as referring to the servant: "quis ex vobis timens Dominum audiens vocem *servi sui qui* ambulavit in tenebris et non est lumen," emphasis added.

43. Oswalt, *Isaiah*, 329; Paul, *Isaiah*, 355–6.

44. In MT, the word מעצבה ("place of torment") is a hapax legomenon that probably derives from עצב ("pain," "hurt"). Goldingay (*Isaiah*, NIBCOT 13 [Peabody, MA: Carlisle: Hendrickson; Paternoster, 2001], 291) comments that this "imagery will later develop into the notion of Gehenna, but it has not done so yet." Also Paul (*Isaiah*, 356) comments that the verb שכב is a euphemism for "to die."

corresponding consequences.⁴⁵ Therefore, v. 11 does not refer to two different groups of people, but describes one group, i.e., the unfaithful. In this regard, v. 10, which lies in contrast to v. 11, seems to read best as describing different features of one group, i.e., the faithful one who fears the Lord (v. 10a), obeys the voice of his servant (v. 10b), and trusts in the name of the Lord and relies on his God (v. 10d), even while walking in darkness (v. 10c).⁴⁶ In view of the above considerations, the MT text should be rendered as follows:

50:10a   Who among you fears the Lord
50:10b   and hears the voice of his servant?
50:10c   Who (among you) walks in the darkness and has no light?
50:10d   Let him trust in the name of the Lord and rely on his God
         [He trusts in the name of the Lord and relies on his God].
50:11   Behold, all of you who light up a fire and gird yourselves with a burning torch. (You) walk in the flame of your fire, and among the burning torch that you have burned. This is what you shall become from my hand. And you shall lie down in the place of torment.

Moreover, LXX further supports this translation because, unlike MT, three commands appear in 50:10 LXX rather than two:

50:10a   Who (τίς) among you is the one who fears the Lord (ὁ φοβούμενος τὸν κύριον)?
50:10b   Let him hear (ἀκουσάτω) the voice of his servant.
50:10c   Those who walk (οἱ πορευόμενοι) in the darkness—they have no light;
50:10d   You all, trust (πεποίθατε) in the name of the Lord, and lean upon (ἀντιστηρίσασθε) God.

LXX renders 50:10b as a command to the one addressed in 50:10a. Therefore, three commands are given to two groups of people: the one who fears the Lord is to hear the voice of his servant; those who walk in the darkness are to trust in the name of the Lord and lean upon God. In v. 10c LXX uses the plural form, οἱ πορευόμενοι ("those who walk"), which excludes any possible connection with the servant, and in v. 10d it uses second person plural imperatives, which shows that these commands directly address the audience.⁴⁷

45. Melugin, *Formation*, 155; Whybray, *Isaiah 40–66*, 152–53; Koole, *Isaiah III*, 2:121.
46. Beuken ("Jes 50," 171) further supports reading 50:10 as a description of the faithful one *in toto*: "Der Sprecher setzt nicht voraus, daß unter seiner Zuhörerschaft Leute sind, die Gott fürchten und dabei auf den Knecht hören, sondern er fragt, ob es solche Menschen gibt."
47. For a more detailed comparative study of Isa 50:4–11 MT and LXX, see Ekblad Jr., *Servant Poems*, 125–65, especially 155–65. Ekblad Jr., 155, argues, "The LXX of Isaiah 50:10-11 reflects the translator's tendency to clarify where MT is less clear and to distinguish the addressees in a way that permits his contemporaries (and future readers) to find themselves among those addressed."

3. The Significance of the Fear of God in Isa 50:10–11

A comparative examination of MT and LXX of Isa 50:10–11 reveals the following points regarding the fear of God. First, the juxtaposition of two groups of people and their consequences in 50:10–11 leads to the exhortation to the people to live as the faithful by fearing God. The two addressees in v. 10ab and v. 10c appear as the same group since they both represent the faithful people of God, while v. 10bcd give details of what "to fear the Lord" in v. 10a means.[48] Likewise, 50:10 LXX takes the description of those who fear the Lord in MT of v. 10b as a command to hear the servant. The faithful people are further characterized in v. 10d: if one fears the Lord, he or she will hear/obey the voice of the servant, which entails trusting in the name of the Lord and leaning upon God.[49] Within Isa 50:10, fearing God thus parallels listening to/obeying the voice of God's servant. Even though the objects of obedience and fear are different, the context does not indicate a distinction between the two actions in that both describe the appropriate response to God's deliverance, so that obeying the voice of God's servant seems to be an expression of the fact that one fears God. In other words, the fear of God characterizes the people who are obedient to God's commands just as the failure to fear God characterizes those who disobey God and consequently fall under his judgment (50:11). Moreover, as the individual servant is portrayed as both faithful and suffering in 50:6–8, 50:10 requires the same attitude of the addressees:[50]

> Die vorangehende Abschweifung bestätigt unsere früher vorgeschlagene Interpretation, daß in Jes 50₁₀ die Angeredeten gefragt werden, ob es unter ihnen einen gibt, der Gott fürchtet und auf die Stimme seines Knechtes hört. Weil die Determination fehlt, enthält die Frage eigentlich *eine Aufforderung, zu fürchten und zu hören*, nicht die Bitte zu melden.[51]

Second, the exhortation in 50:10–11 is further emphasized since the identity of the faithless ones is, in fact, not very far from that of the faithful ones. The opponents of the servant in vv. 7–8 are described only vaguely, and the opponents in v. 11 appear as faithless people who do not fear or obey, but only rely on being led by their own "fire." The fact that the faithless ones in v. 11 are placed in the *same situation* of darkness as the faithful ones in v. 10 is noticeable because it emphasizes

---

48. Thus, Childs, *Isaiah*, 396: "A challenge is extended to anyone who rightly fears the Lord, and thus identifies with the message of the servant, to trust in God even though it still involves walking on a path of darkness, just like the servant."

49. Note the repetitive exhortations "to hear" in 51:1, 4, 7. Thus, Ekblad Jr., (*Servant Poems*, 160) argues: "These commands [in 50:11] may also reflect an understanding of the servant as the one who invites people to make their choice."

50. Thompson, *Isaiah*, 89.

51. Beuken, "Jes 50," 174, emphasis added.

the commonality of the faithful and the faithless.[52] It is not their different situation, but their *different response* that determines their destiny: if you do not show the right response, i.e., fear God, obey the voice of his servant, trust in the Lord, and rely upon God, then your own fire will devour you.[53] Moreover, after exhorting the faithful ones in v. 10 with בכם ("among you all"), the speaker (probably God) addresses the faithless ones in v. 11 with כלכם ("all of you").[54] Therefore, the opponents are not very different from, if not identical to, the Israelites who have experienced the deliverance of God. If so, one can conclude that the judgment of God on the faithless ones (cf. 50:9, 11; 51:6, 8) is the judgment towards his own people, who failed to show the right response and live according to their reestablished relationship with God.[55]

Third, in this context, fearing God functions as the main characteristic of the positive response of God's faithful people.[56] The fear of God stands parallel to listening to God's servant and forms an explicit contrast to those who "fear others" (cf. 51:7) and "walk in the flame of their own fire" (50:11).[57] In fact, fear appears in Isa 40–66 mostly in the context of prohibition, such as אל־תירא ("do not fear"), in which God exhorts his people not to fear others or the circumstances of their lives.[58] God exhorts the people to fear the right one, i.e., only God himself (50:10; 57:11; 59:19; 63:17), and rebukes his people when they fear others (51:7-8) or fail

---

52. Melugin (*Formation*, 159) makes a similar observation: "The term 'pursuers of righteousness' [in 51:1] apart from ch. 50 probably meant simply, 'Israelite'. But when it follows ch. 50, the term comes to mean the faithful as opposed to those who neither 'fear Yahweh nor obey the voice of his servant'. . . . 'Fear not the reproach of men' (51, 7) also takes on a larger significance in the context of ch. 50. In the context of 51, 1–8, it seems to be an exhortation not to fear the reproach of the 'peoples'. In the context of ch. 50 it retains the same meaning, but it also *includes disobedient Israelites as well*" (emphasis added).

53. Ekblad Jr., *Servant Poems*, 161: "In the LXX of Isaiah the combination of καίω with πῦρ and/or φλόξ is almost always associated with God's judgment."

54. LXX also shows that both judgments in vv. 9, 11 will be upon πάντες ὑμεῖς ("all of you"). Ibid., 132.

55. Likewise, Childs, *Isaiah*, 396.

56. J. Alec Motyer (*The Prophecy of Isaiah* [Downers Grove, IL: InterVarsity Press, 1993], 401) thus comments that fear functions as a mark of the remnant.

57. Also in Isa 50:10 LXX, "fearing the Lord is identified with hearing the servant's voice." Ekblad Jr., *Servant Poems*, 134.

58. E.g., Isa 40:9; 41:10, 13, 14: 43:1, 5; 44:2; 51:7, 12; 54:4, 14. In most Isaianic passages where the command "do not fear" appears, it is accompanied with a description of God's deeds toward his people or of his relationship to them as the reason or grounds for not fearing anything other than God. In these texts God introduces himself as "your God" (41:10, 13), "creator" (43:1; 44:2; 54:5), "helper" (41:13, 14), "comforter" (51:12), "redeemer" (43:1; 54:5), or "husband" (54:5), who "is with you" (43:5) and "will redeem you" (43:5; 44:2; 51:8). For example, 63:16 introduces God as father and redeemer, before addressing God as the proper object of fear in v. 17.

to fear God (57:11),⁵⁹ of which state is identical with having a "hardened heart" (63:17).⁶⁰

Lastly, 50:11 shows the close connection between the fear of God and the future judgment that will be upon those who do not heed the call for a proper response in the present. This connection between the fear of God and his judgment is further highlighted in Isa 59:18–21, where the future judgment of God's enemies according to their deeds (59:18) will lead to the fearing of the name of the Lord (59:19) when he comes as the Redeemer of his people (59:20), which is all part of his covenant promises to his own people (59:21). Even though the judgment in Isa 59 is against God's enemies, the identity of the enemies is not necessarily limited to nations outside Israel because the enemies of God include both other nations and certain fallen Israelites.⁶¹ The correspondence of 59:20 with 1:21–31 shows especially that the enemy is not limited to the nations outside Israel:

> Diese wesentliche Rückbindung von Jes 59 an den an innerisraelitischen Feinden Jahwes orienentierten (*sic*) Text Jes 1, 21ff bestätigt das ebenfalls aus dem engsten Kontext (59, 20a) gewonnene Bild, daß in den Kreis der Widersacher und Feinde Jahwes, die statt Heil sein Gericht zu gewärtigen haben, neben der Völkerwelt *auch unbußfertige Israeliten eingeschlossen sind.*⁶²

Moreover, the judgment of God in 59:18 does not necessarily limit his response to his foes, as was already shown in 57:18–19. In this regard, fear has *both* negative and positive connotations: even though they do not do so, those who exalt themselves against the power and holiness of God have good cause to have fear of the judgment, because he is a devouring fire and will consume them in a moment (cf. Isa. 30:27). At the same time, those who know him in all his attributes, the glad ones as well as the fearsome ones, and order their lives in accordance with them, are those who "fear God," and as a result share his secrets with him (cf. Ps. 25:14).⁶³ The place of fear in 59:19 is significant because it is a distinguishing factor between God's judgment against the faithless in v. 18 and God's restoration for the faithful in v. 20.⁶⁴ This leaves us the possibility to interpret the fearing of the name of the

---

59. E.g., the judgment in 51:8 grounds (כי/ὥσπερ) God's exhortation in 51:7, "do not fear."

60. Cf. Exod 6:9; Deut 9:6, 13; 10:16; 31:27; Neh 9:16–17.

61. Odil Hannes Steck, "Jahwes Feinde in Jesaja 59," in *Studien zu Tritojesaja*, BZAW 203 (Berlin; New York: de Gruyter, 1991), 187: "V.18b deutet auf Einschluß der Völker in diese dem Zorngericht Jahwes verfallenen Feinde, und V.20a zeigt, daß auch ein bestimmter Kreis *von Israeliten* mitbetroffen sein wird" (emphasis added). Likewise, Jan Leunis Koole, *Isaiah III*, vol. 3, HCOT (Leuven: Peeters, 2001), 165.

62. Steck, "Feinde," 189, emphasis added. Also Childs, *Isaiah*, 486.

63. Thus, Oswalt, *Isaiah*, 529.

64. Childs, *Isaiah*, 488: "What follows next is [God's] dual reaction to this intolerable human condition. Verses 9–15a present faithful Israel's reply, and vv. 15b–20 offer the divine response, first to vv. 1–8 and then to vv. 9–15a."

Lord and his glory, which are hypostases for God himself (cf. 30:27; 40:5),[65] as applying not only to the enemies of God, but also to the faithful remnants of Israel.[66]

Hence, Isa 40–66 exhorts all the Israelites who experienced God's deliverance to fear God since fear functions as the expression of their appropriate response to their reestablished relationship. Those who do not fear God are therefore stubborn (63:17) and doomed under God's judgment (50:11). Moreover, the fear of God does not remain a static condition of the faithful people, but rather becomes an ongoing motivation for the people to continue to practice their obedience of faith, expressed in the double commands that follow in 51:9–52:12.

4. The Fear of God and God's Commands in Isa 52:11

The faithful ones, those who fear God, are described in Isa 50:10ab as those who listen (MT), or are exhorted to listen (LXX), to the voice of his servant.[67] The features of the faithful ones are further represented by the following section, i.e., they are those who "walk in darkness and have no light" (50:10c), "pursue righteousness" (51:1), "seek the Lord" (51:1), "know righteousness" (51:7), and "have God's Torah in their hearts" (51:7). Together with these descriptions, several commands are given to them, "trust in the name of the Lord and lean upon God" (50:10d), "listen to God" (51:1, 4, 7),[68] "look to the rock and quarry" (51:1), "look to Abraham and Sarah" (51:2), "lift up your eyes" (51:6), "do not fear the reproach of others" (51:7), and "do not be dismayed by their contempt" (51:7). These imperatives instruct the people how to respond faithfully to God's deliverance in view of the judgment against the faithless declared in 51:6, 8.

---

65. Oswalt, *Isaiah*, 529.

66. Steck ("Feinde," 187) thus argues that the identity of the addressees in 59:19 remains open to interpretation. Also Koole (*Isaiah III*, 3:205) questions why 59:18 does not mention Israel's neighboring nations, continually hostile to Israel, but coastlands that were *not* Israel's enemies. This makes it more likely that the fearing in v. 19 is not limited to the enemies of God, but also open to others, including God's own people.

67. The structure of v. 10ab shows that fearing God can be substituted for listening to his servant. Thus, Beuken, "Jes 50," 181: "Der Mensch, der Gott fürchtet, ist gleichzeitig derjenige, der auf den Knecht hört, dadurch in Finsternisse geraten kann bzw. wird und dann auf den Namen des Herrn sich stützen soll." Also, George Angus Fulton Knight, *Servant Theology: A Commentary on the Book of Isaiah 40–55*, ITC (Edinburgh: Handsel, 1984), 146: "In this note, [Isa 40–55] makes an extraordinary equation: the voice (i.e. words) of the Servant *is* the Word of God; he who obeys the voice of the Servant finds himself leaning upon *God*," original emphasis.

68. The referent in Isa 51:1, "listen to me," can refer to God or to his servant. Given the first person indicative in v. 2, and since the same command appears addressing "my people" in v. 4, the referent in vv. 1, 2, 7 seems to be God. Goldingay, *Message*, 463.

It is against this background that the following double commands in 51:9, 17; 52:1, 12 appear. The four double commands function as a literary marker and form Isa 51:9–52:12 as a distinct unit.[69] The first double command (51:9) presents God's deliverance of his people and the last three (51:17; 52:1, 11) call for the corresponding actions of the people. Isaiah 51:9–11, with the first double command "awake, awake" in v. 9, contain the prayer of the faithful for God to be awake and to deliver them, to which God responds in vv. 12–16.[70] MT and LXX of 51:9 differ in that they have God or the people (Jerusalem) respectively as the referent of the command "to awake."[71] Nevertheless, whoever is in view for the command, the context of God's deliverance of his people remains the same.[72] As promised in 50:7–9; 51:3, 5–6, 8, God will turn to deliver his people, and the covenant formula, "I am the Lord your God ... You are my people" in 51:15–16 exemplifies this redeemed relationship. Moreover, as seen in 51:16, God's redemption grants the people not only a new identity ("you are my people"), but also a new task in accord with their identity ("I have put my words in your mouth"). This task closely resembles the task with which God commissioned his servant in 49:6. Thus, the faithful ones, who were following in the footsteps of the servant (50:10), are now given the *task* of the servant.[73]

This newly given task as the faithful people of God is then further explored in the repetition of the double commands, "awake, awake" in 51:17 (התעוררי התעוררי/ ἐξεγείρου ἐξεγείρου) and 52:1 (עורי עורי/ἐξεγείρου ἐξεγείρου). Though the command to "awake" is the same as that given in 51:9 in relation to God, here both commands represent the response of the people, exhorting Jerusalem and Zion to awake from their helpless condition and prepare to receive their salvation. The consummate salvation of the people is not dependent on God's willingness (51:9–16), nor on the severity of their punishment (51:17–23), but on their response of faith.[74] Moreover, even though the commands in 51:17 and 52:1 share the same verb, they are distinct in that the latter deals specifically with the *holiness of the city*, i.e., God's people: "Jerusalem is to become the holy city, a dwelling that reflects the nature of God's holiness."[75] This is significant in that the faithful one, the one who fears God, is now asked to pursue the holiness of God.[76]

---

69. Tryggve N. D. Mettinger, "In Search of the Hidden Structure: YHWH as King in Isaiah 40–55," in *Writing and Reading the Scroll of Isaiah*, vol. 1 (Leiden: Brill, 1997), 147.

70. Koole, *Isaiah III*, 2:163.

71. LXX renders 51:19: "ἐξεγείρου ἐξεγείρου Ιερουσαλημ."

72. The arm of God (MT) represents his judgment and salvation, as in Isa 51:5, 9; 52:10 (cf. 30:30, 32; 33:2; 40:10, 11; 44:12; 48:14; 49:22; 53:1; 59:16; 62:8, etc.).

73. Thus, Childs, *Isaiah*, 404; Koole, *Isaiah III*, 2:165.

74. Oswalt, *Isaiah*, 352, 359; Goldingay, *Message*, 446.

75. Childs, *Isaiah*, 405. Contra Goldingay and Payne (*Isaiah 40–55*, 2:248), who argue that the variation is mainly stylistic.

76. Cf. Lev 19:2.

The commands in 52:11, from which Paul quotes in 2 Cor 6:17ac, appear in this context of holiness:

> Depart, depart, go out from there; touch no unclean thing; go out from the midst of it; purify yourselves, you who carry the vessels of the Lord.

Because these commands represent the correct response of God's faithful people to his deliverance by indicating the holiness that they must pursue,[77] the focus of the commands is on the purification of the people, rather than on the location from which they are to depart, i.e., Babylon.[78] Thus, the commands in 52:11 exhort the people to respond to God's deliverance by pursuing holiness, which entails leaving the place where God's holiness is not respected.

The fact that the addressees of the commands in 52:11 are the ones who "carry the vessels of the Lord" (נֹשְׂאֵי כְּלֵי יְהוָה/οἱ φέροντες τὰ σκεύη κυρίου) further highlights this point. These people are not necessarily Levites (cf. Num 1:50) or priests (cf. Josh 3:6) since the context addresses the people of Israel in general ("Zion" in 52:1, 2, 7, 8 and "Jerusalem" in vv. 1, 2, 9). This indeed indicates the fulfillment of the promise in Exod 19:6 that the carriers of the vessels of God have become "a kingdom of priests and a holy nation."[79] J. Alec Moyter thus rightly summarizes the significance of the commands in 52:11 in view of the double commands in 51:17 and 52:1:

> A great salvation has been effected in which the Lord's wrath is gone (51:17–23) and his people are established in holiness as a royal priesthood (52:1ff.). Now they are called to live according to their God-given dignity, which is what was asked of the Sinai people but could not be accomplished... In context, however, the call [in 52:11] is to leave the whole setting and ambience of the old sinful life behind.[80]

Therefore, the context of the commands of Isa 52:11, established by the way in which the double commands of 51:17 and 52:1 tie them back to the beginning of this conceptual unit in 51:9, unpack the overarching theme of the fear of God as the people's proper response to God's salvation in 50:10. This contextual link between Isa 52:11 and 50:10 thus reveals how Paul, who quotes the commands from Isa 52:11 in 2 Cor 6:17ac, can later conclude his argument with the exhortation to cleanse oneself that leads to completing holiness in the fear of God. As seen in Isaiah, the fear of God is a characteristic of the faithful remnant and motivates the

---

77. Wilk, "Gottes Wort," 695.

78. Thus, Childs, *Isaiah*, 406–7; Oswalt, *Isaiah*, 371; Koole, *Isaiah III*, 2:244; Motyer, *Prophecy*, 421. Contra Goldingay, *Message*, 458: "The departing involves a literal leaving of a literal Babylon, urged from the perspective of Jerusalem."

79. Thus, Koole, *Isaiah III*, 2:246; Oswalt, *Isaiah*, 373.

80. Motyer, *Prophecy*, 421.

people to show a proper response to God's redemption. The fear of God in view of the coming judgment leads God's people in the present to the obedience of faith that will be vindicated on the day of God's wrath, as opposed to that disobedience which results from not fearing God, which will result in condemnation. Hence, against this backdrop, Paul naturally exhorts the Corinthians to live as faithful believers by completing holiness in the fear of God.

III. The Fear of God in the Context of Lev 26:11–12

This work will now examine the fear of God in the context of Lev 26:11–12, which is quoted in 2 Cor 6:16de. Most scholars detect the presence of Lev 26:11–12 LXX in 2 Cor 6:16de because of the almost verbatim match with the OG as represented in the Göttingen edition,[81] but the change of the pronouns from the second person plural in Lev 26:12 LXX to the third person plural in 2 Cor 6:16e causes many scholars to take this as a "mixed quotation" or "composite citation" with the related passage of Ezek 37:27, from which the change in person is said to derive.[82] As I argued in Chapter One, the OT citations in 2 Cor 6:16de meet the criteria for determining a "composite citation," in which "a literary borrowing occurs in a

---

81. For the sake of argument, this work will follow the MT text of Leviticus, including the chapter numbering. In using MT, I make no statement about its priority over LXX. Unless noted otherwise, the Hebrew quotations are translated closely in the OG as presented in LXX, as found in John William Wevers and U. Quast, eds., *Leviticus*, SVTG v. II, 2 (Göttingen: Vandenhoeck & Ruprecht, 1986). For the establishment of the quotation based on the LXX tradition, see Jan Lambrecht, "The Fragment 2 Cor 6:14–7:1: A Plea for Its Authenticity," in *Miscellanea Neotestamentica*, vol. 2 (Leiden: Brill, 1978), 154; Hans Dieter Betz, "2 Cor 6:14–7:1: An Anti-Pauline Fragment?" *JBL* 92 (1973): 93, 103; Joachim Gnilka, "2 Cor 6:14–7:1 in the Light of the Qumran Texts and the Testaments of the Twelve Patriarchs," in *Paul and Qumran: Studies in New Testament Exegesis*, ed. Jerome Murphy-O'Connor (London: G. Chapman, 1968), 88; Ralph P. Martin, *2 Corinthians*, 2nd rev., WBC 40 (Grand Rapids: Zondervan, 2014), 368–69; Scott J. Hafemann, *2 Corinthians*, NIVAC (Grand Rapids: Zondervan, 2000), 283–4.

82. Betz, "2 Cor 6:14–7:1," 93; Gordon D. Fee, "II Corinthians vi. 14–vii. 1 and Food Offered to Idols," *NTS* 23 (1977): 159; Victor Paul Furnish, *II Corinthians*, AB 32A (Garden City, NY: Doubleday, 1984), 363, 373–74; Webb, *Returning Home*, 33–40; James M. Scott, *Adoption as Sons of God: An Exegetical Investigation into the Background of* ΥΙΟΘΕΣΙΑ *in the Pauline Corpus*, WUNT 2/48 (Tübingen: J. C. B. Mohr, 1992), 195–6; R. Kent Hughes, *2 Corinthians: Power in Weakness* (Wheaton, IL: Crossway, 2006), 253; Martin, *2 Corinthians*, 368–69. For a dissenting opinion, see Christopher D. Stanley, *Paul and the Language of Scripture*, SNTSMS 74 (Cambridge: Cambridge University Press, 1992), 217–21. Stanley argues that because of (1) the absence of quotations from Ezekiel in the rest of the Pauline literature, and (2) the difficulty of explaining the reason for Paul's modification of the pronouns, the passage is the product of a careful reshaping of Lev 26:11–12 to suit a

manner that includes two or more passages from the same or different authors fused together and conveyed as though they are only one."[83] Paul was of course quite capable of changing the direct address of the original to the third person in a quotation, but here the simplest hypothesis is that, as elsewhere, Paul combined two very similar, and even literarily dependent passages into a single citation.[84]

1. Fear in Leviticus

Although the noun, "fear" (יראה/φόβος), does not occur, the verb, "to fear" (ירא/φοβέω, φοβέομαι), appears eight times in the book of Leviticus, and all occurrences are found in chs 19, 25, and 26:

Passage	The Object of Fear	MT	LXX
19:3	Parents	ואביו תיראו	ητέρα αὐτοῦ φοβείσθω
19:14	God	ויראת מאלהיך	καὶ φοβηθήσῃ κύριον τὸν θεόν σου
19:30	My [God's] sanctuary	ומקדשי תיראו	ἀπὸ τῶν ἁγίων μου φοβηθήσεσθε
19:32	God	ויראת מאלהיך	καὶ φοβηθήσῃ τὸν θεόν σου
25:17	God	ויראת מאלהיך	καὶ φοβηθήσῃ κύριον τὸν θεόν σου
25:36	God	ויראת מאלהיך	καὶ φοβηθήσῃ τὸν θεόν σου
25:43	God	ויראת מאלהיך	καὶ φοβηθήσῃ κύριον τὸν θεόν σου
26:2	My [God's] sanctuary	ומקדשי תיראו	ἀπὸ τῶν ἁγίων μου φοβηθήσεσθε

In these eight occurrences, fear appears with reference to God (five times), to his sanctuary (twice), and to parents (once). In all five of its occurrences the fear of God accompanies God's commands to the Israelites regarding other people: "do not show contempt for the disabled ones" (19:14), "respect the elder" (19:32), "do not cheat one another" (25:17), "do not take advantage of fellow Israelite who became poor" (25:36), and "do not rule over the fellow Israelite who is working as an indentured servant" (25:43). All these commands—both positive (19:32) and negative (19:14; 25:17, 36, 43)—function as parallels to the command "to fear God" (ויראת מאלהיך/καὶ φοβηθήσῃ [κύριον] τὸν θεόν σου), thus indicating that the fear

---

particular argumentative context (v. 16b) under the influence of a thoroughly Christian view of existence, and not a loose conflation of Lev 26:11-12 with Ezek 37:27 (p. 219). However, Stanley, 225, argues that the following verse (2 Cor 6:17) is a conflated citation of Isa 52:11 and *Ezek* 20:34. Moreover, as it will be discussed below, the Ezekiel context is essential to understand Paul's argument in 2 Cor 6:14-7:1.

83. Definition by Sean A. Adams and Seth M. Ehorn, "What Is a Composite Citation? An Introduction," in *Composite Citations in Antiquity. Vol. 1*, eds. Sean A. Adams and Seth M. Ehorn, LNTS 525 (London: T&T Clark, 2016), 4.

84. Following Scott, *Adoption*, 196-7; idem, "The Use of Scripture in 2 Corinthians 6.16c-18 and Paul's Restoration Theology," *JSNT* 56 (1994): 78-82. Contra Gnilka, "2 Cor 6:14-7:1," 51; Lambrecht, "Fragment," 2:154.

of God entails God's instructions for the manner in which his people may achieve moral holiness.

It is also significant to notice that in both of its occurrences the command "to fear God's sanctuary" functions similarly as the command to fear God (see 19:30; 26:2). The call to fear God's sanctuary first appears in 19:30, where it follows the command not to profane one's daughter by making her a prostitute, which will lead to desecration of the land.[85] In fact, the reference of the fear of God's sanctuary to God's commandments and God's declaration, "I am the Lord," in 19:29–30 is almost identical to that in 19:14 and 32, where the fear of God functions as the equivalent for the fear of God's sanctuary since the presence of God can be identified with the place of his abode. In all three cases in ch. 19 where fear with regard to God/God's sanctuary appears (vv. 14, 30, 32), it functions as the ground for the commands and is marked by the introductory formula, "I am the Lord." Moreover, in Lev 20:3 God's sanctuary parallels his "name" in that God warns his people against idolatry, which is a profaning of both his sanctuary *and* his name.[86] God's "name," as the indication of his person and character, is thus to be associated with the sanctuary in which God's presence and nature are revealed. The juxtaposition of the defilement of God's sanctuary and the desecration of God's name therefore highlights the consequence that idolatry can bring in both cases, and it also declares God's judgment that will be upon it (vv. 2–3).

Therefore, in Leviticus God's sanctuary (מִקְדָּשׁ/τὰ ἅγιοι) indicates the place where God manifests his presence and character among his people, so that the sanctuary itself demands from the people not only ritual purity (cf. 12:4; 16:33; 21:12, 23) and sacrificial offerings (cf. 26:31), but also a proper attitude (fear) that leads to ethical behavior (19:30; 26:2). In this regard, God's sanctuary, as the place of God's presence, functions as an essential factor in maintaining the covenant between God and his people.[87] If the sanctuary is polluted by idolatry, God's judgment will be the consequence (20:3). Hence, the function of the fear of God's sanctuary in Leviticus is very similar, if not identical, to that of the fear of God in that they both are to elicit the proper attitude that expresses itself in keeping God's commandments, a primary focus of which is the prohibition against idolatry.[88] Andreas Ruwe thus rightly argues:

---

85. Erhard S. Gerstenberger, *Leviticus: A Commentary*, OTL (Louisville: Westminster John Knox, 1996), 277: "desecration is the destruction or removal of the holiness demanded by Yahweh."

86. Jacob Milgrom (*Leviticus 17–22: A New Translation with Introduction and Commentary*, AB 3A [New York: Doubleday, 2000], 1734–5) thus argues that Lev 20:3 is the first (and the only one in the Torah) explicit statement that idolatry pollutes God's sanctuary, which is more frequent in the prophetic writings (cf. Jer 7:30; 32:34; Ezek 5:11; 23:38).

87. John E. Hartley, *Leviticus*, WBC 4 (Nashville: Thomas Nelson, 1992), 321.

88. That the command to fear God's sanctuary is closely connected to the command to fear God himself is further emphasized in Deuteronomy (Deut 4:10; 5:26; 6:2, 13; 8:6; 10:20; 13:5; 14:23; 17:19; 25:18; 28:58; 31:12f.).

> Die Forderung, das Heiligtum zu fürchten, hängt angesichts des Fehlens von parallel Formulierungen im Alten Testament sicher eng mit der Forderung, JHWH zu fürchten ... *Möglicherweise stellt die Forderung, das Heiligtum zu fürchten, die unter dem Eindruck des Bilderverbots modifizierte Forderung, JHWH zu fürchten,* dar, die die Grundorientierung zur Gewinnung von Rechtsbestimmungen nicht mehr direkt auf Gott selbst richtet, sondern indirekter auf das Heiligtum als den besonderen Ort der Gottesgegenwart.[89]

In view of this link between the fear of God and the fear of his sanctuary, it is significant, reflecting the cultic concerns of Leviticus as a whole, that the last reference to fear in Leviticus refers to the fear of God's sanctuary in 26:2, which parallels other commands in 26:1 that allude to the Sinai event in the Exodus (see below).[90] As in its earlier use in 19:30, here too fearing God's sanctuary represents the proper response of God's people to God's manifestation of his presence and motivates them to keep his commandments. In other words, the command to fear God's sanctuary reminds the people of the presence of God among them and his covenant between them, and thus leads them to a proper attitude that fits their covenant status. The fear of God's sanctuary (26:2) thus functions not only as the covenant stipulation that determines God's covenant blessings (vv. 4–13) and curses (vv. 14–39), since it is the motivation for the people to follow God's statues and to keep his commandments faithfully (v. 3). Hence, in all of its occurrences in Leviticus the call to fear God/God's sanctuary, usually as the opposite of behavior that is prohibited, supplies the motivation for the people to pursue holiness.[91] This function and the significance of the command to fear God's sanctuary become more evident once we examine the structure of Lev 26 and the covenant formula in 26:12.

2. The Structure of Lev 26

Even though Lev 25–6 function together as one unit,[92] certain markers indicate that the two chapters present distinct, but related arguments. First, while ch. 25 contains God's instruction about the Sabbatical year and the year of Jubilee, 26:1

---

89. Andreas Ruwe, *"Heiligkeitsgesetz" und "Priesterschrift": Literaturgeschichtliche und Rechtssystematische Untersuchungen zu Leviticus 17,1–26,2*, FAT 26 (Tübingen: Mohr Siebeck, 1999), 102, emphasis added.

90. Gordon J. Wenham, *The Book of Leviticus*, NICOT (Grand Rapids: Eerdmans, 1979), 328; Timothy M. Willis, *Leviticus*, AOTC (Nashville: Abingdon, 2009), 221.

91. Cf. Milgrom, *Leviticus 17–22*, 1596: "the purpose of all the enumerated laws [in Leviticus] is to set the people of Israel on the road to holiness."

92. For example, in addition to certain themes that Lev 25 and 26 share, such as the Exodus narrative (25:38, 55; 26:13, 45) and the Sinai event (25:1; 26:1–2, 46), Milgrom (*Leviticus 23–27: A New Translation with Introduction and Commentary*, AB 3B [New York: Doubleday, 2001], 2150–51, 2274–75) lists the following reasons to support taking Lev 25–26 as one unit:

introduces the new theme of idols, which last appeared in Lev 19:4 (cf. 26:30).[93] Second, the covenant stipulations do not appear in ch. 25, but play a significant role in ch. 26.[94] Last, the theme of the sabbatical year that appears in both chs 25 and 26 functions differently in each chapter: while in ch. 25 the sabbatical year is God's instruction to his people in the new land (25:2), in ch. 26 the sabbatical year given by God to the land expresses God's punishment upon his people (26:34–35, 43).[95]

The structure of Lev 26:1-2 is as follows:

1a	You shall not make for yourselves idols
1b	and you shall not erect for yourselves carved images or pillars,
1c	and you shall not place figured stones in your land to worship at them;
1d	for I am the Lord your God
2a	You shall keep my Sabbaths
2b	and fear my sanctuary;
2c	I am the Lord

Verses 1–2 clearly allude to the Sinai event: v. 1 is a variant of the prohibition of idolatry (cf. Exod 20:4–5), and v. 2a refers to the command of Sabbath keeping (cf. Exod 20:8).[96] In contrast, the command to fear God's sanctuary seems strange against this Exodus backdrop because, although Exod 25–31; 35–40 contain commandments about God's sanctuary, a reference to *fearing* the sanctuary does not appear in those sections. However, fear with reference to God appears frequently in Exodus, where its function is similar to the fear of God's sanctuary in Leviticus in that it motivates the people of God to pursue holiness and refrain from sinning (cf. Exod 20:20).[97]

Leviticus 26 lacks the preface "God spoke to Moses" that introduces its surrounding units (cf. 24:1; 25:1; 27:1); the inclusion "Mount Sinai" (25:1; 26:46) envelopes both chapters; the deliverance from Egypt runs as a refrain through both chapters (25:38, 42, 55; 26:13, 45); both chapters refer to the sabbatical year (25:1–7; 26:34–35, 43); both chapters have the same theme of Israel's violation of God's commandments which leads to their exile; lastly, both chapters share the same theme of Israel's redemption, i.e., God grants Israel the power to redeem its land and those brethren enslaved to non-Israelites. Moreover, if the Israelites demonstrate contrition for their sinful past, God will redeem them from exile (26:39–45).

93. Likewise, Ruwe, *Heiligkeitsgesetz*, 98.
94. Roy Gane, *Leviticus, Numbers*, The NIVAC (Grand Rapids: Zondervan, 2004), 457–8.
95. Contra Milgrom, *Leviticus 23–27*, 2274.
96. Milgrom (*Leviticus 23–27*, 2285) compares the five commandments in Lev 26:1-2 with Exod 20 and Lev 19, and puts "fear my sanctuary" with the commandment "keep my Sabbaths" because "both the temporal and spatial spheres of YHWH must be respected." However, this is contrary to his later argument when he argues that God's promise of his presence in 26:11 cannot mean space or location (p. 2292).
97. Fear with regard to God appears in Exod 1:17, 21; 3:6; 9:20, 30; 14:31; 18:21; 20:20.

Moreover, Lev 26:1-2 is distinct not only from what precedes, but also from the rest of its own chapter in that it functions as a general summary of God's commands. The first two verses of ch. 26 are thus isolated within their own narrow context in that they are neither a component of the immediately preceding nor the immediately following sections.[98] Even Jacob Milgrom, who argues that chs 25-26 form a unit, nevertheless notes the unique function and purpose of 26:1-2:

> Thus 26:1-2 forms *a transitional unit* that functions as *both summary and prolepsis*: a capsule containing the essence of God's commandments, which are determinative for the survival or destruction of Israel's national existence, the subject of the following verses, 26:3-46. It also serves as a prolepsis of the notion of covenant, a leitmotif in the entire chapter.[99]

This observation is important in that it supports the fact that the command to fear God's sanctuary in 26:2 functions as the overarching motivation not only for the parallel commands in v. 1, but also for the following implied admonition in the form of a condition in v. 3 that if Israel keeps God's commands that will lead to receiving God's promises (vv. 4-13), including the two promises that Paul cites in 2 Cor 6:16de.[100]

3. The Covenant Formula

The role of the fear of God/God's sanctuary as an overarching covenant stipulation in Leviticus becomes a central aspect of Lev 26 in that references to "covenant" (ברית/διαθήκη) are distributed throughout the chapter in relationship to God's covenant blessings (v. 9), curses (vv. 15, 25), and promises of restoration (vv. 42 [3x], 44, 45).[101] Leviticus 26 thus reflects the reality that the covenant is seen to be the essence of the relationship between God and his people: keeping his promises defines what it means for God to maintain his covenant (v. 9), so that God's covenant commitment becomes the grounds for God's future restoration (vv. 42, 44, 45);[102] conversely, the people's obedience in response to God's salvific provisions (cf. v. 13) and future promises (vv. 4-12) is likewise necessary in order to maintain the covenant relationship with God (v. 9) and receive his blessings (vv. 4-13), including the two promises of God's presence among his people as expressed in

---

98. Ruwe, *Heiligkeitsgesetz*, 99. Also, Wenham, *Leviticus*, 327-29; Gerstenberger, *Leviticus*, 402.
99. Milgrom, *Leviticus 23-27*, 2277, emphasis added.
100. Gane, *Leviticus*, 457-8.
101. Ibid., 455.
102. According to Milgrom (*Leviticus 23-27*, 2343), the verb קום in *hifil* form can mean "maintain/uphold" when it is used with ברית (covenant) as in v. 9 (cf. e.g., Gen 15:18; 21:27, 32; 26:28; 31:44; Exod 23:32; 24:8; 34:10, 12, 15, 27).

the covenant formula (vv. 11-12), so that the disobedience of the people is interpreted as breaking the covenant (v. 15), which brings God's curse on them (v. 25).[103] In this covenant context, the fear of God, here expressed as the fear of his sanctuary, thus functions as a motivation for the faithful obedience of the people whom God has delivered.

It is thus striking that in Lev 26:12 this covenant relationship is expressed in the twofold, bilateral formula, "I will be your God, and you shall be my people." For Rolf Rendtorff has observed how the covenant formulae in the OT occurs in three versions: (A) "I will be your God" (with its variations); (B) "You shall be my people" (with its variations); and (C) a bilateral combination of the two statements in a single formula, i.e., "I will be your God, and you shall be my people" (with its variations).[104] Rendtorff then points out that the bilateral covenant formula (C) in Lev 26:12 is striking because in the first four books of the Pentateuch formula (A) occurs almost exclusively, while formula (C) appears only twice (Exod 6:7; Lev 26:12).[105] On the other hand, formula (C) appears almost exclusively in the prophetic books, with the exception of formula (A) in Ezek 34:24 and formula (B) in Jer 13:11.[106] Rendtorff consequently argues that the *bilateral* form of the covenant formula in Lev 26:12 is significant because it points to the establishment of the new covenant in the prophetic books, where the bilateral covenant formula is more prominent.[107]

These observations of Rendtorff lead to two points concerning Paul's use of the covenant formula from Lev 26:12 in 2 Cor 6:16de. First, implicitly, the bilateral covenant formula strengthens the allusion to the Exodus event in Lev 26, in addition to the allusions to the Decalogue in Lev 26:1-2; 46.[108] The Exodus event highlights the relationship already established between God and his people that it

---

103. Hartley, *Leviticus*, 459. According to Hartley, lxiii, the fear of God is the proper human response to the manifestation of the holy God that people show by practicing the laws of justice and mercy.

104. For a more detailed discussion regarding the form of the covenant formula, see Rolf Rendtorff, *The Covenant Formula: An Exegetical and Theological Investigation* (Edinburgh: T&T Clark, 1998), 11-13.

105. Formula (B) does not appear at all in this section. On the contrary, in Deuteronomy formula (B) appears several times (Deut 4:20; 7:6; 14:2; 27:9; 28:9), while formula (A) does not appear, and formula (C) appears twice (Deut 26:17-19; 29:12-13).

106. The bilateral covenant formula (C) appears in Jer 7:23; 11:4; 32:38 [39:28 LXX]; Ezek 14:11; 34:24; 37:27; Zech 8:8. Rendtorff, *Covenant Formula*, 13-14.

107. Ibid., 72.

108. As mentioned, Exod 6:7 is the only place beside Lev 26:12 where the bilateral covenant formula (C) appears in the first four books of the Pentateuch: "I will take (ולקחתי, λήμψομαι) you as my people, and I will be your God. You shall know (וידעתם, γνώσεσθε) that I am the Lord your God, who has freed you from the burdens of the Egyptians." Milgrom (*Leviticus 23-27*, 2296) rightly comments that there are parallels between Lev 26:9-13 and Exod 6:4-7, in which God promises Moses to establish the covenantal relationship through

brought about (26:13) and in doing so emphasizes the proper response of the people of keeping the covenant stipulations outlined paradigmatically in the Decalogue. For example, in Exod 29:45–46, which scholars have noticed has close links with Lev 26:11–12, the promises of God's dwelling and covenant relationship with his people are conditional in nature in that they presuppose the consecration of the people.[109] The call to fear God's sanctuary in Lev 26:2 and the conditional nature of the promises in Lev 26:11–12 both appear against this "Exodus" backdrop. Second, more explicitly, the bilateral covenant formula (C) further emphasizes the connection between Lev 26:11–12 and Ezek 37:27 that Paul made in 2 Cor 6:16de. This is because formula (C) in Lev 26:12 points to the new covenant context in the prophetic books, to which we now turn our attention.

IV. *The Fear of God in the Context of the New Covenant*

In the biblical history of Israel, the people failed to observe God's commands (see, e.g., Ezek 20) and were sent into exile in 587 BCE.[110] However, as foreseen in Lev 26:40–42, God remembered his covenant with his people and once more promised to dwell among them and to reestablish a covenant relationship with them. In particular, Ezekiel declares that God will fulfill these promises in the eschaton (20:34; 36:24, 28; 37:27). God will grant the people a new heart and a new

---

the Exodus event. In Exod 6 God assures Moses that he will save the Israelites from the hands of Pharaoh, as has been promised by his covenant with the forefathers (v. 6; cf. Lev 26:13). Also, Rendtorff (*Covenant Formula*, 16) argues that both the use of the verb לקח ("to take") in the covenant formula of Exod 6:7, and the fact it follows God's promise of deliverance in v. 6, indicate that God initiates his act of deliverance so that Israel has become his people. This does not deny God's already existing covenant with the forefathers as expressed in vv. 4–5, but the first appearance of the bilateral form of the covenant formula connotes a shift or change in the former relationship with God through his deliverance at the Exodus, which requires the people to pursue a godly life in order to maintain this relationship. Cf. Milgrom, *Leviticus 23–27*, 2302, who argues therefore that the covenant formula in Lev 26:12 is Mosaic (Exod 6) and not Abrahamic. Similarly, Erhard Blum, *Studien zur Komposition des Pentateuch*, BZAW 189 (Berlin; New York: de Gruyter, 1990), 328.

109. See, e.g., ibid., 325–26; Rendtorff, *Covenant Formula*, 19–20; Milgrom, *Leviticus 23–27*, 2300–1. Moreover, the immediate context of Exod 34:43–4 entails God's promise and command regarding priestly consecration. In this way, the consecration becomes the grounds for God's promises of dwelling and covenant relationship: "So I will consecrate the tent of meeting and the altar and will consecrate Aaron and his sons to serve me as priests. *Then* I will dwell among the Israelites and be their God" (NIV, emphasis added).

110. Thomas Krüger, "Transformation of History in Ezekiel 20," in *Transforming Visions: Transformations of Text, Tradition, and Theology in Ezekiel*, ed. William A. Tooman and Michael A. Lyons (Cambridge: James Clarke, 2010), 161: "Ezekiel 20:5–29 recounts the history of Israel from its beginnings in Egypt up to the present."

spirit so that they will be able to keep his statutes and commands (36:26–27). As Paul's composite citation of Lev 26:11–12 and Ezek 37:27 in 2 Cor 6:16de shows, it is against this background that Paul argues that the promises of Lev 26:11–12 are now being fulfilled among the Corinthians as the beginning of the eschatological people of God. An examination of the Ezekiel passage will therefore shed further light on Paul's understanding of the function of the fear of God and his sanctuary in the fulfillment of the promises.

1. Ezekiel

William J. Webb lists six views on the cited scriptural text(s) of 2 Cor 6:16de: (1) only Lev 26:11–12 is cited; (2) Lev 26:11–12 is cited with influence from Ezek 37:27; (3) both Lev 26:11–12 and Ezek 37:27 are equally in view; (4) Ezek 37:27 is cited with influence from Lev 26:11–12; (5) Lev 26:12 and Ezek 37:27 are combined along with MT Exod 25:8 for ἐνοικήσω ἐν αὐτοῖς; and (6) Lev 26:12 and Ezek 37:27 are combined along with Jer 32:28.[111] Webb argues that 2 Cor 6:16de cites Ezek 37:27 with influence from Lev 26:11–12 for the following reasons: Ezek 37:27 (LXX) has "my dwelling place" (ἡ κατασκήνωσις μου), which is closer conceptually to "I will dwell among you" (ἐνοικήσω ἐν αὐτοῖς) in 2 Cor 6:16d than "my covenant" (τὴν διαθήκην μου) in Lev 26:11 (LXX); only Ezekiel has the third person (ἐν αὐτοῖς); and the eschatological context of Ezek 37 goes better with the catena and its eschatological promises in 2 Cor 6:16. Webb rightly highlights the importance of the new covenant theme ("second Exodus" in his terms) in 2 Cor 6:16de with regard to the eschatological, new temple context of the Ezekiel passage. However, his conclusion that both the form and context of 2 Cor 6:16de favor Ezek 37:27 over Lev 26:11–12 as the primary source fails to explain why Paul would conclude his OT citations of 2 Cor 6:16c–18 with "the fear of God" in 2 Cor 7:1, a motif that does *not* appear in the book of Ezekiel! On the other hand, Paul's reference to "the fear of God" in 7:1 picks up and relates directly to the motif of "the temple of the living God" in 6:16b in the light of Lev 26:2 as the introduction to the composite citation in 6:16de, in which Lev 26:11–12 is the lead and primary text. In this way, Paul frames his adaptation of Lev 26 with a reference to the temple on the one hand and the corresponding fear of God on the other. In other words, Webb's view overlooks the significance of the context of Leviticus for Paul's argument in 2 Cor 6:14–7:1 in that it is the presence of God among his people as his "temple" that evokes the fear of God among his people.

As argued above, the fear of God's sanctuary (מקדשׁי/τὰ ἅγιοι) signifies in Leviticus the proper response of God's people to God's manifestation of his presence and motivates them to keep his commandments (Lev 26:1–2). Conversely, the result of defiling the sanctuary due to a lack of this fear leads to God's severe, all-consuming judgment (20:3; cf. 26:14–39). Despite this command and warning,

---

111. Webb, *Returning Home*, 34–5. Cf. Scott, "Use of Scripture," 85–7; Beale, "Reconciliation," 238–9.

the people of God broke the covenant relationship by defiling God's promises and profaning his Sabbath (cf. Lev 26:1 with Ezek 23:38–9 cf. 5:11).

Nevertheless, in Ezek 37:26 God promises that he will establish a covenant of peace that will be also an "everlasting covenant," and that he will set "my sanctuary (מקדשי/τὰ ἅγιοι μου)" in their midst (cf. the promise of restoration in Lev 26:40–45). These promises are followed by the promises in v. 27 that Paul cites in 2 Cor 6:16de:

> I will make a *covenant of peace* with them; it shall be an *everlasting covenant* with them; and I will bless them and multiply them, and will set *my sanctuary* among them forever. My dwelling place shall be with them; and I will be their God, and they shall be my people
>
> Ezek 37:26–28, emphasis added.

As was clear in the context of Lev 26:1–2 and 11–12, the sanctuary that God will set in the midst of his people demands that the people fear his sanctuary as that which will motivate them to keep his commandments. So too in Ezek 37:14, 23–5, placing God's sanctuary in the midst of his people will lead to overcoming their idolatry and transgression (see below). In this way, the promises of restoration in Ezek 37 pick up the prior "new covenant" promise of Ezek 36:25–27, in which God places his Spirit within his people to overcome their idolatry and cause them to keep his statues and rules (cf. Lev 26:46 and the motif of overcoming the desolation of the land from Lev 26:40–5 that is picked up in the restoration prophecy of Ezek 36:29–35). It is therefore significant that Paul alludes to Ezek 36:25–7 in 2 Cor 3:3 as a corollary to his citation of Ezek 37:27 in 2 Cor 6:16de. It is against this background that Paul exhorts his believers to keep the commandment in the fear of God in 2 Cor 7:1, and only if one holds both Lev 26:11–12 and Ezek 37:27 in view does it become possible to understand Paul's argument in 2 Cor 6:14–7:1 with its emphasis on the church's freedom from idolatry as the temple of the living God (6:14–16).

Indeed, Elizabeth Hayes argues that Ezek 37 actually provides the most complete conceptual background for 2 Cor 6:14–7:1 as a whole because a number of themes in Ezek 37:15–24 stand out that are alluded to by the other OT passages quoted in 2 Cor 6:16c–18 in addition to Lev 26:11–12, such as 2 Sam 7 and Isa 52.[112] The themes include a single nation under one king in Ezek 37:22, 25 (cf. 2 Sam 7:8; Ezek 20:42), the promise that the people will no longer defile themselves with idols in Ezek 37:23 (cf. Lev 26:1; Ezek 20:41), the reference to God's servant, David, and the people's obeying God's laws and statutes in Ezek 37:24, 25 (cf. Lev 26:3; 2 Sam 7:14), the covenant of peace and the eternal covenant in Ezek 37:26 (cf. Lev 26:9,

---

112. Elizabeth R. Hayes, "The Influence of Ezekiel 37 on 2 Corinthians 6:14–7:1," in *The Book of Ezekiel and Its Influence*, ed. Henk Jan de Jonge and Johannes Tromp (Aldershot; Burlington, VT: Ashgate, 2007), 133–4.

42, 44, 45),[113] God's sanctuary and dwelling among his people in Ezek 37:27 (cf. Lev 26:11-12; 2 Sam 7:9), the covenant formula in Ezek 37:23, 27 (cf. Lev 26:12), and the nations' recognition that God sanctifies Israel in Ezek 37:28 (cf. Ezek 20:41; Isa 52:10-11).

Ezekiel 37 starts with the prophet's vision of the valley of dry bones (vv. 1-14) that concludes with God's promise of future deliverance as expressed in the restoration of the land (v. 12, 14b) and the presence of God's Spirit among his people (v. 14a).[114] The following section further describes God's future restoration when both Israel and Judah will become one nation (v. 22). At that time, God will take the initiative and make the people eligible for the establishment of the covenant relationship:

They shall never again defile themselves with their idols and their detestable things, or with any of their transgressions. I will save them from all the apostasies into which they have fallen, and I will cleanse them. Then they shall be my people, and I will be their God

v. 23.

God then mentions the Davidic covenant in vv. 24-5, with the declaration that his servant, David, shall be their leader forever. Then follows in v. 26 the establishment of the "covenant of peace" (ברית שלום/διαθήκη εἰρήνης; Ezek 34:25) with the people, which is an "everlasting covenant" (ברית עולם/διαθήκη αἰωνία; Ezek 16:60). In this covenant God will bless them by setting his sanctuary and his dwelling among them (vv. 26, 28) and by establishing a renewed covenant relationship with his people (v. 27). The result of God's deliverance is that the nations will know that the Lord sanctifies Israel when his sanctuary is among them forevermore (v. 28).[115]

---

113. Hayes does not mention Lev 26 for the covenant aspect, but lists only Ezek 37:26.

114. The spirit refers to the new Spirit in Ezek 36:26 that will be implanted in the people and will bring about conformance to God's laws (36:27). Moshe Greenberg, *Ezekiel 21–37: A New Translation with Introduction and Commentary*, AB 22A (New York: Doubleday, 1997), 746-7.

115. This work acknowledges the debate that Ezek 37 originally came after Ezek 39, as witnessed in Greek Papyrus 967 (late second to early third century CE). However, all Masoretic texts have the second thematic section of Ezek 37:15–28 as one sense division. Nevertheless, this text-critical issue is beyond the scope of this work, since its resolution most likely does not impact Paul's reading of the text. For a more detailed discussion of this issue, see Johan Lust, "Ezekiel 36–40 in the Oldest Greek Manuscript," *CBQ* 43 (1981): 517-33; Ashley S. Crane, *Israel's Restoration: A Textual-Comparative Exploration of Ezekiel 36–39*, VTSup 122 (Leiden; Boston: Brill, 2008), 207-64; Henk Leene, *Newness in Old Testament Prophecy: An Intertextual Study*, OTS 64 (Leiden; Boston: Brill, 2014), 172-82.

Hence, Ezekiel uses the conditional covenant blessings in Leviticus and turns them into descriptions of blessings that are guaranteed in a future restoration.[116] This is not because, however, there are no more covenant conditions in the new covenant. Rather, it is because under the new covenant God grants the people the renewed capacity to respond in obedience, including fearing him, which in turn leads to the fulfillment of God's promises of dwelling among his people and maintaining his covenant relationship with them (37:23, 26–27).[117] The command to fear God is still effective in that God's sanctuary will be set in the midst of the people.

In other words, in the new covenant context, God enables his people to keep his commands (Ezek 36:27; 37:23), which is the covenant stipulation required to receive God's promises (Ezek 36:28–30; 37:24–25; cf. Lev 26:3). Michael A. Lyons thus argues:

> Ezekiel's problem with the model of restoration found in Lev 26 is that it does not address the possibility that the people might not repent. Nor does it address the possibility that a repentant people might someday apostatize again. Ezekiel solves these problems in a very radical way. Instead of simply copying the covenant of Lev 26 and projecting it into the future, Ezekiel removes the punishments from the covenant and envisions a change that guarantees *the covenant stipulations will always be kept*. The change is one that God will perform in the hearts of the people.[118]

Whereas Leviticus demands that the people walk in God's statutes and observe

---

116. Michael A. Lyons, "Transformation of Law: Ezekiel's Use of the Holiness Code (Leviticus 17–26)," in *Transforming Visions: Transformations of Text, Tradition, and Theology in Ezekiel*, ed. William A. Tooman and Michael A. Lyons (Cambridge: James Clarke, 2010), 2. Lyons, 13, argues that Ezekiel's employment of Lev 17–26 falls into five categories. First, Ezekiel turns the positive and negative instructions into accusations. Second, Ezekiel turns the conditional covenant punishments of Lev 26 into descriptions of present or imminent judgment on Jerusalem. Third, Ezekiel takes the laws and appeals to them as authoritative standards for behavior. Fourth, Ezekiel turns the reference to the display of God's power in the Exodus (Lev 26:45) into an argument that the motivation for God's actions is concern for his reputation. Fifth, Ezekiel turns the conditional covenant blessings in Lev 26 into guaranteed covenant blessings in the future.

117. Given their history, Ezekiel believes that the people are incorrigible (Ezek 2:5, 6, 7, 8; 3:9, 26, 27; 12:2, 3, 9, 25; 16:44, 45; 17:12; 20:30; 24:3; 44:6), and hence the people can change only through God's intervention, i.e., by the divine gift of a new heart and new Spirit.

118. Lyons, "Transformation," 28, emphasis added. Scholars debate the literary relationship between Ezekiel and the Holiness Code (Lev 17–26). For the purposes of this work, it is unnecessary to determine the direction of dependence since this work focuses on *Paul's* conflating use of Lev 26 and Ezek 37. For a more detailed discussion of the issue of literary dependence, see ibid., 4–6.

his commands (Lev 26:3), Ezekiel argues that they *will* walk in God's statutes and observe his commands (Ezek 36:27). There is no lessening of the call to obey, hence the exhortations from God are still present. So the demands are still there in Ezekiel, but they are kept, for God's enablement of Israel is fulfilled through his granting of a new heart and a new Spirit (36:26–27; cf. 11:19–20; 18:31), both of which "refer to the same reality, namely the renewal of the moral will of the house of Israel by the outpouring of the dynamic power of Yahweh."[119] In Ezekiel this holy life under the new covenant of peace therefore takes place as the result of an inner renewal.[120] Again, this inner renewal will enable or cause the people to break away from the old pattern of rebellious behavior (cf. 20:8, 13, 21) and lead them to the observance of God's commands through righteous deeds. Thus, Henk Leene argues:

> According to Ezekiel, inner renewal *remains* an absolute requirement for admission to the people of God, even if it is YHWH who will eventually provide for the human fulfillment of this condition. Furthermore, this promise is the indispensable counterpart of the critical version of the nation's history in Ezek. 20:1–44.[121]

Moreover, not the people's initial effort, but only God's initiative brings this fulfillment: God will save the people from their apostasies and will cleanse their uncleanness (cf. Exod 26:45–46) solely for his own name's sake (Ezek 20:9, 14, 22; 36:22, 23; 39:7, 25).[122]

Ezekiel 37 is thus important for Paul's argument in 2 Cor 6:16de and its relationship to 7:1 because it points to the new covenant reality through which fallen Israel will once again obtain God's promises as summarized in the covenant formula of Lev 26:11–12 (cf. Ezek 36:28; 37:23). At the same time, the demand of the fear of God is still effective within the new covenant restoration in that God will set his sanctuary (מקדש/τά ἅγιοι) among his people (37:26). In response, and

---

119. Paul Joyce, *Divine Initiative and Human Response*, JSOTSup 51 (Sheffield: JSOT Press, 1989), 110–11.

120. Ezekiel describes the salvation of Israel in different terms, such as return (11:14), social restoration (11:18), and inner renewal (11:19). According to Henk Leene ("Ezekiel and Jeremiah: Promises of Inner Renewal in Diachronic Perspective," in *Past, Present, Future: The Deuteronomistic History and the Prophets*, ed. Harry F. van Rooy and Johannes Cornelis de Moor, OtSt 44 [Leiden; Boston; Kolun: Brill, 2000], 159), the same terms appear in Jeremiah, where God promises that the people will return (Jer 30:3), will be restored (31:27–30), and will be changed internally (31:31–4).

121. Leene, "Jeremiah," 154, original emphasis. Also idem, *Newness in Old Testament Prophecy: An Intertextual Study*, OTS 64 (Leiden; Boston: Brill, 2014), 166: "the inner change is not mentioned explicitly [in Ezek 37], but it is probably incorporated in the cleansing rite."

122. Leene, *Newness*, 171.

in view of their renewed heart and spirit, God exhorts the people to follow his ordinances and be careful to observe his statutes (37:24), showing that the covenant of peace, which is everlasting (v. 26), still requires the people to continue to pursue the holy life now enabled by God himself in order to inherit the covenant promises. Although Ezekiel does not mention the fear of God specifically in relationship to the reality of the everlasting covenant, one may assume that for Ezekiel too the fear of God associated with God's sanctuary continues to exist in the new covenant reality, motivating the people to observe God's commands.

Moreover, that Paul considered the fear of God to be a new covenant reality for Ezekiel, as it was for Isaiah and Leviticus, is further indicated by the judgment context of Ezek 20:34 that Paul will quote in 2 Cor 6:17d.[123] There God's promise to Israel that "I will bring you out from the peoples and gather you out of the countries where you were scattered" is followed by this warning:

> I will bring you into the wilderness of the peoples, and there I will enter into *judgment* with you face to face. As I entered into *judgment* with your ancestors in the wilderness of the land of Egypt, so I will enter into *judgment* with you
>
> vv. 35–6, emphasis added.

As scholars have recognized, God's "new covenant" promise in 20:34 therefore appears in the context of judgment.[124] For in Ezekiel, the future wilderness does not indicate a geographical place, but rather "an eschatological figure for the place of that judgment after which there will be no occasion of judgment."[125] It is also noteworthy that, as in the Egyptian wilderness, God will judge his *own* people (cf. 1 Cor 10:1-5). This will be done "face to face," which alludes to the original meeting on Mount Sinai when the people feared God (Deut 5:4–5, cf. Exod 20:20). The examination of the reality of the fear of God in the corresponding new covenant context of Jer 32:38–40 will further confirm that the judgment context of Ezek 20:34 likely provides an additional background for the fear of God in the new covenant context of Ezek 36–37, here too, as in Leviticus, identified with God's sanctuary.

2. Jeremiah

Ezekiel expresses the restoration of Israel in terms of the new heart and the new Spirit that will be given by God under an "everlasting covenant" (ברית עולם/διαθήκη

---

123. Thus, Jeffrey W. Aernie, *Is Paul also among the Prophets? An Examination of the Relationship between Paul and the Old Testament Prophetic Tradition in 2 Corinthians*, LNTS 467 (London: T&T Clark, 2012), 232. Moreover, this judgment context is further emphasized in 2 Sam 7:14, which Paul also quotes in 2 Cor 18a. In 2 Sam 7:14 God warns that "when he commits iniquity, I will punish him with a rod such as mortals use, with blows inflicted by human beings."

124. Moshe Greenberg, *Ezekiel 1-20: A New Translation with Introduction and Commentary*, AB 22 (New York: Doubleday, 1983), 372; Robert W. Jenson, *Ezekiel*, BTCB (Grand Rapids: Brazos, 2009), 162-3; Walther Eichrodt, *Ezekiel: A Commentary*, OTL (London: SCM, 1970), 276-81.

125. Jenson, *Ezekiel*, 162.

αἰωνία) in order to lead future Israel in the way of his statutes (Ezek 16:60; 36:36–37; 37:26). In Jeremiah this inner renewal also appears as part of a new covenant in which God will write his *Torah* upon the hearts of his people, which in turn will lead to a renewed covenant relationship (Jer 31:31–34 [38:31–34 LXX]; 32:36–40 [39:36–40 LXX]).[126] So both Ezekiel and Jeremiah clearly consider Israel's inner renewal to be an essential part of God's restoration of his people. Moreover, the promises used to describe this inner renewal in Jeremiah are similar to those of Ezekiel.[127] Jeremiah describes the promise of a new heart and a new Spirit in Ezekiel as a knowing heart (24:7), a seeking heart (29:13), as the law written upon the heart (31:33), and, of significance for our study, as the fear of God given in the heart (32:40). Moreover, as in Ezekiel, Jeremiah also indicates that this inner renewal leads the people to the observance of God's law and commands (cf. Jer 31:32).[128]

In this context, it is significant that Jeremiah describes Israel's inner renewal under an "everlasting covenant" (ברית עולם/διαθήκη αἰωνία) as God's putting *his fear* in the people's hearts, so that they may not turn from him (32:40). The comparison of Jeremiah's "new/everlasting covenant" in Jer 31:31–4; 32:36–40 with that of Ezekiel's promise of Israel's restoration under an "everlasting covenant" in Ezek 36–37 elucidates how the former can use the fear of God explicitly as the motivating characteristic of the obedient people of God described by the latter. In other words, for Ezekiel the necessity of the fear of God as an expression of the inner renewal of the people only appears *implicitly* through God's placing his sanctuary in the midst of his people, while in Jeremiah this aspect appears *explicitly* through God's placing his fear in the heart of his people. Paul does not quote Jeremiah's text specifically in 2 Cor 6:16c–18, but the new covenant motif from both Ezekiel and Jeremiah are explicitly brought together as mutually interpretive in 2 Cor 3:3–6, indicating that Paul saw these themes in the two prophets as interrelated.[129] It is not concluding too much, therefore, to suggest that Paul's use in our passage of Ezek 37:27 with Lev 26:11–12, given its own call for obedience (Ezek 37:24) and judgment context (cf. 20:35–36), may also provide part of the

---

126. Note the bilateral covenant formula in Jer 32:38. As Leene (*Newness*, 205) argues, "Jer 31:31–34 proposes a new covenant to replace Yhwh's covenant with Israel at the Exodus from Egypt. The new covenant does not differ from the old in its stipulations: both covenants insist on the human covenantal partner obeying the *torah*. Just this time Yhwh will write the *torah* on their hearts, so that everyone will be attuned to it."

127. Gerhard von Rad, *Old Testament Theology: The Theology of Israel's Prophetic Traditions*, vol. 2 (London: SCM, 1975), 235; Joyce, *Divine*, 117–20; Leene, "Jeremiah," 165; idem, *Newness*, 247.

128. Leene, "Jeremiah," 167.

129. For a more detailed argument on the extensive developments of this theme and the use of Ezek 36:26–7 and Jer 31:31–4 in 2 Cor 3:3 and 3:6 respectively, Scott J. Hafemann, *Paul, Moses, and the History of Israel: The Letter/Spirit Contrast and the Argument from Scripture in 2 Corinthians 3*, WUNT 2/81 (Tübingen: J. C. B. Mohr, 1995), 92–186; Aernie, *Paul*, 225–31.

Scriptural background for understanding why Paul concludes his exhortation to the Corinthians with the fear of God in 2 Cor 7:1.

V. Conclusion

Paul cites two promises in 2 Cor 6:16de: the promise of God's dwelling among his people and that of the establishment of a covenant relationship with them, the latter expressed in a bilateral covenant formula. The promises appear in Lev 26:11–12 and Ezek 37:27, but they function differently in each context: while Leviticus presents these promises as a consequence of keeping the covenant stipulations (cf. Lev 26:3), recognizing the potential of Israel's breaking the covenant (cf. Lev 26:14–39), Ezekiel presents the fulfillment of these promises as guaranteed in the future because God himself will enable and ensure that the covenant stipulations will be met. Nevertheless, it is significant for our study that, in spite of the different context of these promises, both Leviticus and Ezekiel express either explicitly or implicitly the essential role the fear of God plays within the covenant relationship, now expressed in terms of God's sanctuary. The command to fear God's sanctuary in Lev 26:2 is still effective in Ezek 37:26 when God places his sanctuary in the midst of his people. This new covenant reality is further highlighted in Jer 32:38–40, where in a parallel, new covenant passage God places the fear of him among the people's heart.

In Lev 26:1–2 the covenant stipulation that determines the covenant blessings, including the two promises in 2 Cor 6:16de, entails the fear of God, here expressed in the fear of God's sanctuary, which functions as a motivation for the people's holy life. The function of the fear of God's sanctuary as the expression of the fear of God in Lev 26:2 is therefore close to that of the fear of God in 2 Cor 6:16 and 7:1 in that it motivates the people's pursuit of a holy life as those among/in whom God now dwells as "the temple of the living God," and in doing so characterizes the people of God. This function of the fear of God from Lev 26:2 in relationship to the promises of Leviticus 26:11–12 is consequently a key to the transition of Paul's argument from 2 Cor 6:16 to 7:1, since within their own context the two promises in the context of Lev 26 naturally call to mind the need to fear God as his "temple," the renewed people of the new covenant (Cf. 2 Cor 3:6).

On the other hand, the new covenant context of Ezek 37:27 shows that, despite the promised certainty of inheriting the promises of the everlasting covenant of peace, the people of God are still required to respond properly to God's saving activity, which is expressed in terms of God's sanctuary having been placed among them. In Ezekiel, God promises to pour out his Spirit upon his people so that they will be able to meet the covenant stipulations by their obedience (36:27), which consequently leads to covenant blessings (36:28; 37:27). Thus, when Paul quotes God's two promises in 2 Cor 6:16de, he understands that the two promises in Lev 26:11–12 are now being fulfilled as a result of the establishment of the new, "everlasting covenant" anticipated in Ezek 37:27 (cf. 2 Cor 6:16b). These covenant blessings are being received only because God enabled the people to meet the covenant stipulations by pouring his Spirit on them. Under the realities of the new, "everlasting covenant" (Ezek 37:26; cf. Ezek 16:60; Jer 31:31; 32:40), the people of God can therefore now show the proper response to God's salvific acts, i.e., to fear God and pursue holiness as God's temple. Against these OT expectations and their fulfillment in the church as "the temple of the living God" (2 Cor 6:16bc), Paul naturally exhorts the Corinthians in 7:1 to cleanse themselves and thus complete holiness in the fear of God because, theologically, fearing God's judgment in response to his presence and the obedience it brings about are the proper attitude and actions characteristic of the new covenant people of God.

This function of the fear of God within the new covenant context is further emphasized by Paul's quotation of the commands from Isa 52:11 in 2 Cor 6:17ac. As we have seen, the context of Isa 50:4–52:11 shows once again, and even more directly, that the fear of God (50:10) derives from God's judgment (50:11) and motivates the people to show a proper response to God's redemptive acts, which includes keeping the commands quoted by Paul (cf. 51:17; 52:1, 11). Here too this OT backdrop leads Paul to exhort the Corinthians in 2 Cor 7:1 to cleanse themselves, thus completing holiness in the fear God. On the one hand, the fulfillment of the promises from Lev 26:11–12 and Ezek 37:27 lead to Paul's conclusion in 2 Cor 7:1 as the proper response to the covenant blessings already being experienced by the Corinthians. On the other hand, the commands of Isa 52:11 support Paul's exhortation in 2 Cor 7:1 for the Corinthians to cleanse themselves in view of the fear of God that is derived from an awareness of God's judgment. In both cases, Paul's reference to the fear of God as the means of completing holiness points to the necessity of keeping God's commandments in order to inherit God's promises.

Chapter 4

THE FEAR OF GOD WITHIN THE CONTEXT OF SECOND TEMPLE JUDAISM

We will now examine the theme of the fear of God within the larger context of Second Temple Judaism, which will show that Paul's view engages in a number of Jewish conversations concerning the fear of God as a motivation of the righteous.[1] As the following examinations of selected Second Temple documents suggest, Paul's use of the fear of God stands in proximity to the uses of this motif by other Jews in the Second Temple Period. Nevertheless, Paul's understanding of the fear of God is not identical to those Jewish voices, just as they disagree among themselves.

I. 2 Cor 6:14–7:1 Within the Context of Second Temple Judaism

Even though many scholars agree that 2 Cor 6:14–7:1 and Second Temple Jewish documents have similar traits, there is no consensus concerning the implications of these similarities.[2] In fact, the conclusions that scholars draw concerning the

---

1. The "Second Temple period" is here defined flexibly. Apart from the Testaments of the Twelve Patriarchs, the dating of which is disputed, all other chosen documents date from second century BCE to first century CE.
2. Joseph A. Fitzmyer, "Qumrân and the Interpolated Paragraph in 2 Cor 6:14–7:1," *CBQ* 23 (1961): 271–80; Joachim Gnilka, "2 Cor 6:14–7:1 in the Light of the Qumran Texts and the Testaments of the Twelve Patriarchs," in *Paul and Qumran: Studies in New Testament Exegesis*, ed. Jerome Murphy-O'Connor (London: G. Chapman, 1968), 48–68; Georg Klinzing, *Die Umdeutung des Kultus in der Qumrangemeinde und im Neuen Testament*, SUNT 7 (Göttingen: Vandenhoeck & Ruprecht, 1971), 172–82; Hans Dieter Betz, "2 Cor 6:14–7:1: An Anti-Pauline Fragment?" *JBL* 92 (1973): 88–108; Nils Alstrup Dahl, "A Fragment and Its Context: 2 Corinthians 6:14–7:1," in *Studies in Paul: Theology for the Early Christian Mission* (Minneapolis: Augsburg Fortress, 1977), 62–9; Jerome Murphy-O'Connor, "Philo and 2 Cor 6:14–7:1," *RB* 95 (1988): 55–69; George J. Brooke, *Exegesis at Qumran: 4QFlorilegium in Its Jewish Context*, JSOT 29 (Sheffield: JSOT Press, 1985), 211–19; idem, "2 Corinthians 6:14–7:1 Again: A Change in Perspective," in *The Dead Sea Scrolls and Pauline Literature*, STDJ 102 (Leiden: Brill, 2014), 1–16; James M. Scott, *Adoption as Sons of*

place of 2 Cor 6:14–7:1 within the context of Second Temple Judaism cover a wide spectrum. Some see the passage as a Christian redaction of original Jewish material,[3] an interpolation of a non-Pauline quotation,[4] or even an anti-Pauline argument.[5] We will discuss these views in more detail in the following chapter, but first, it is important to examine the motif of the fear of God in Second Temple Judaism itself. For despite the numerous studies on the relationship between 2 Cor 6:14–7:1 and other Second Temple Jewish documents, only a few have paid attention to the aspect of the fear of God in 7:1,[6] which, as we have seen, concludes (οὖν) the whole passage of 6:14–18.[7]

Therefore, just as we have examined the fear of God within the context of the scriptural passages Paul cites in 6:16c–18 in order to understand Paul's own argument against the backdrop from which it comes, it will be helpful to examine the theme of the fear of God in representative texts from Second Temple Judaism in order to place Paul's argument within the history of tradition within which Paul stands. Our task is thus to examine how Jewish writers handle the motif of the fear of God during the Second Temple Period in order to ask the following questions: "In what contexts does the fear of God appear?" and "What meaning and function does the fear of God have in these contexts?" Moreover, "What similarities and differences exist between the treatments of the fear of God in the Second Temple Jewish texts and its meaning and role in 2 Cor 6:14–7:1?" These questions will help us to understand Paul's use of the fear of God in 2 Cor 7:1 further by placing it within the spectrum of Second Temple Judaism.

God: An Exegetical Investigation into the Background of ΥΙΟΘΕΣΘΙΑ *in the Pauline Corpus*, WUNT 2/48 (Tübingen: J. C. B. Mohr, 1992), 188–220; William O. Walker Jr., *Interpolations in the Pauline Letters*, JSNT 213 (London: Sheffield Academic Press, 2001), 199–209; Albert L. A. Hogeterp, *Paul and God's Temple: A Historical Interpretation of Cultic Imagery in the Corinthian Correspondence*, BTAS 2 (Leuven; Dudley, MA: Peeters, 2006), 364–78.

3. E.g., Gnilka, "2 Cor 6:14–7:1."
4. E.g., Fitzmyer, "Qumrân"; Walker, *Interpolations*, 209.
5. E.g., Betz, "2 Cor 6:14–7:1."
6. For example, Gnilka ("2 Cor 6:14–7:1," 61), who argues that 2 Cor 6:14–7:1 belongs to a Christian (not Pauline) redaction in the Essene tradition, comments that the first and last parts of 7:1, including its mention of the fear of God, could be a *stylistic modification* or *addition of the author* to an originally non-Christian text, though they offer too weak a basis for a definite conclusion regarding its authorship. Most of the studies that compare 2 Cor 6:14–7:1 with the Second Temple Jewish documents have focused on the unusual vocabulary in 2 Cor 6:14–16 (including the hapax legomena), its dualistic ideas, its view of Belial, the reference to the temple, the covenant formula, the adoption formula, the command for separation, and several of the OT quotations in vv. 16–18.
7. Brooke ("Again," 9) thus argues, 7:1, as the conclusion to 6:14–7:1, "is no mere reiteration of the opening parenesis, but is a call to action in the light of the definitions of identity contained in the scriptural promises."

In order to gain an overview of the diverse ways in which Second Temple Judaism understood the fear of God, we have chosen to highlight four documents from Jewish pseudepigraphal writings which provide distinct voices about the fear of God: the Psalms of Solomon (Pss. Sol.), the Book of Jubilees (Jub.), 4 Ezra (in comparison to 6 Ezra), and the Testaments of the Twelve Patriarchs (T. 12 Patr.).[8] In the Psalms of Solomon the fear of God appears often and plays an important role regarding the redemption of the righteous. In contrast, though the Book of Jubilees contains the fear of God, it only appears a few times with a limited function; nevertheless, the assumed link between the fear of God and his judgment indicates that where judgment is given as the motivation, fearing God is also implied. The fear of God appears in 4 Ezra, but its function of motivating a righteous life in a way that is similar to 2 Cor 5:11 or 7:1 is expressed implicitly and becomes more apparent in 6 Ezra, which is a later Christian redaction. Similarly, the Testaments of the Twelve Patriarchs, which contain a mixed tradition of Jewish and Christian material, also show the way in which the fear of God functions within both Jewish and Christian contexts.

---

8. James R. Davila (*The Provenance of the Pseudepigrapha: Jewish, Christian, or Other?* JSJSup 105 [Leiden; Boston: Brill, 2005], 230) argues that nine documents are largely intact ancient Jewish Pseudepigrapha beyond a reasonable doubt: Aristeas to Philocrates, 2 Baruch, the Similitudes of Enoch, 4 Ezra, 3–4 Maccabees, the Latin Moses fragment (the Assumption/Testament of Moses), Pseudo-Philo's Biblical Antiquities, and the Psalms of Solomon. I do not claim that my four texts are the *only* representatives of the Jewish milieu from that period, but they are *sufficient* for us to map out the understanding in the fear of God in Second Temple Judaism. For the sake of argument, this work deliberately has also chosen Jewish documents that either include the aspect of the fear of God or share similarities with 2 Cor 6:14–7:1. One could certainly add other texts that include the fear of God, such as Sirach, where the fear of God is used "to combine the wisdom of Proverbs with the law of Moses" (see, for example, Sir 1:11, 12, 13, 14, 16, 18, 20, 27, 28, 30; 2:7, 8, 9, 15, 16, 17; 6:16, 17; 7:29, 31; 9:16; 10:19, 20, 22, 24; 15:1, 19; 17:8; 19:20; 21:11; 25:6, 10, 11; 26:3; 27:3; 34:14, 16, 17, etc.). Burton L. Mack, "Sirach," in *The HarperCollins Study Bible*, ed. Harold W. Attridge and Wayne A. Meeks, Revised ed. (San Francisco: Harper One, 2006), 1379. Additionally, there are also texts that are related to 2 Cor 6:14–7:1, such as 1 Enoch, which refers to "fear and trembling" regarding the final judgment (1 En. 1:5–7; 13:1–3; 14:13–14; 60:3–6; 101; 102:1–3), or 2 En. 34:1, which combines the commandment against idolatry and sexual immorality with the yoke motif (cf. 2 Cor 6:14a) and also with the fear of God. For the latter, see Francis I. Andersen ("2 Enoch," in *The Old Testament Pseudepigrapha Vol. 1*, ed. James H. Charlesworth, 3rd ed. [Peabody, MA: Hendrickson, 2013], 158), who comments that 2 En. 34 has affinity with 2 Cor 6:14–7:1. However, because of the limited space, this work has focused on the materials mentioned above. In addition, the present work will deal with the Qumran texts as they are related to the arguments presented by the other texts. All Qumran texts are quoted from Eibert J. C. Tigchelaar and Florentino García Martínez, eds., *The Dead Sea Scrolls Study Edition* (Leiden; New York; Grand Rapids: Brill; Eerdmans, 2000).

II. The Psalms of Solomon

The Psalms of Solomon are a collection of eighteen psalms that emerge from the tradition of a Jewish community in the first century CE.[9] The fear of God is interspersed throughout the document and appears seventeen times in ten psalms (Pss. Sol. 2:31 [2x]; 3:12; 4:21, 23; 5:18; 6:5; 12:4; 13:10; 15:13; 17:34, 40; 18:7, 8 [2x], 9, 11). As we will see, in these passages the fear of God characterizes the righteous, especially in relationship to God's judgment. Moreover, not only does the fear of God appear mostly in the context of divine judgment, it also shares a similar function of motivating a righteous life. Even though the judgment of God is primarily intended for the evil ones, the Psalms emphasize that this judgment will also be expanded to all Israelites, whom God will judge justly according to their deeds. Thus, the emphasis on the divine judgment of all people extends the fear of God, which derives from this judgment, to all nations, since all nations are consequently called to stand in fear before God. Moreover, the Psalms show that the fear of God due to his judgment will continue its function under the eschatological reign of the Messiah.

1. The Fear of God and the Theme of Judgment in the Psalms

The Psalms of Solomon might look similar to the psalter in the OT, but they differ in that the psalms in the Psalms of Solomon preserve specific, thinly veiled allusions to contemporary historical realities and therefore do not display "the patina which comes with repeated liturgical handling, the wearing away of specific historical allusions which allows the psalter's hymns to be meaningful in situations far removed from their original one."[10] Moreover, the Psalms of Solomon present an interesting intersection between various themes of biblical and Second Temple literature so that new constructs emerge.[11] In so doing, the authors of the Psalms reflect on their present desperate situation, such as the invasion and capture of Jerusalem by the Roman army under Pompey in the year 63 BCE and the siege of Jerusalem by Herod the Great and the Roman General Sosius in 37 BCE, while still maintaining a hopeful perspective toward the future.[12] Therefore, facing the

---

9. Robert B. Wright, ed., *Psalms of Solomon: A Critical Edition of the Greek Text*, JCTCRS 1 (London: T&T Clark, 2007), 2–7; idem, "Psalms of Solomon," in *The Old Testament Pseudepigrapha Vol. 2*, ed. James H. Charlesworth, 3rd ed. (Peabody, MA: Hendrickson, 2013), 640–41; Davila, *Provenance*, 159–64, 230–5. All passages of the Psalms of Solomon are quoted from Wright, "Psalms of Solomon," 639–70.

10. Wright, "Psalms of Solomon," 646.

11. Ibid: "the ethics and outlook of the Book of Proverbs are joined to apocalyptic expectation, the warranty of the Davidic covenant is fulfilled in the messianic hope, and the concept of the 'anointed one' becomes concretized in a specific expectation of an immediate consummation."

12. Wright, *Psalms of Solomon*, 1.

rise of enemies (4:1–5; 12:1–3; 17:5–6), the psalms present the punishment of the sinners (2:33; 3:11–12; 4:21–4; 12:4–6; 13:10–11; 15:4–13) on judgment day (15:12; 18:5) and the ultimate eschatological vindication of Israel (17:26–8; 18:5–9).[13] Furthermore, this motif of future judgment not only projects a hope for the future to the people, but it also exhorts them to live as the people of God in the present age (8:26; 9:7).

The judgment of God therefore functions in two ways in the Psalms of Solomon: it is first of all the *means* of eschatological vindication for the righteous in the future and, as such, provides a *motivation* for the righteous to pursue a godly life in the present. God is presented in the Psalms as the righteous judge (2:18; 4:24; 9:3) who will judge the sinners and evil ones according to their deeds who have rebelled against God and oppressed his people (2:33; 4:2; 9:5; 17:8–9). At the same time, the judgment of God also applies to the defiled "daughters of Jerusalem" (2:13), to "Israel" as a whole (8:26), to the "tribes of the people that have been made holy by the Lord their God" (17:26), to the "peoples in the assemblies, the tribes of the sanctified" (17:43), and even to the "peoples and nations" (17:3, 29), i.e., to the whole "earth" (8:24; 15:12) and the whole "world" (18:3). However, unlike the judgment on the evil ones that brings destruction, the judgment on the people of God is intended for their discipline (8:26) and leads them to repentance (9:7). These two functions of God's judgment do not signify that there are two kinds of judgment that apply differently to believers and unbelievers respectively, but rather that the difference lies in whether one possesses the fear of God in the present that derives from the eschatological judgment to come. In other words, it is not the judgment of God per se, but the existence of the fear of God among God's people that distinguishes the righteous from the wicked.

In this regard, the judgment of God and the fear of God are closely connected, but they are not identical. First, as mentioned above, the judgment of God applies to all people, but the fear of God functions as a characteristic only of believers (the righteous), whose fate contrasts with that of unbelievers (the wicked), who do not respond to the call to fear God. Therefore, while God's salvation will be experienced by those who fear him, those who do not fear God will be condemned under God's judgment:

> They have not remembered God, *nor have they feared God* in all these things; but they have angered God, and provoked him. May *he banish them* from the earth for they defrauded innocent people by pretense. Blessed are those who *fear God* in their innocence; the Lord shall save them from deceitful and sinful people and save us from every evil snare
>
> 4:21–3, emphasis added.[14]

---

13. Davila, *Provenance*, 161; George W. E. Nickelsburg, *Resurrection, Immortality, and Eternal Life in Intertestamental Judaism and Early Christianity*, expanded ed., HTS 56 (Cambridge, MA; London: Harvard University Press, 2006), 163–7.

14. Also, see Pss. Sol. 2:33; 3:11–12; 12:4–6; 13:11–12; 15:12–13 (cf. 5:18; 6:5).

Second, the reign of the Messiah or future king in the eschaton is a time in which the fear of God will continue to characterize his people. Since the fear of God is a defining characteristic of the righteous, it continues to play an important role in the eschaton as an essential means by which the Messiah will rule over his people (18:7–8), by which the people will live in the days of mercy (18:9), and by which even nature will abide (18:11). A closer examination of Ps. Sol. 17 will further shed light on the role of the fear of God during the eschatological reign of the Messiah.

2. The Fear of God in Ps. Sol. 17

Psalm of Solomon 17, which is the longest psalm in the collection and stands strategically as the next to the last,[15] contains both a description of the evil that characterizes the present and an apocalyptic fervor that shifts the scene "from historical recital to eschatological entreaty."[16] In particular, the author expresses his hope for an eternal king from the line of David (17:4) who will establish a kingdom that will endure forever (v. 3). In order to accomplish this, the king will fight (vv. 22–4, 35–6), rule (vv. 21, 26, 36), and judge (vv. 25–6, 29, 36, 43) against Israel's enemies (vv. 5–6, 11–20).[17] In vv. 8–10, the judgment of the future king against these enemies stands in parallel to the judgment of God:

> You rewarded them, O God, according to their sins; it happened to them according to their actions. According to their actions, God showed no mercy to them; he hunted down their descendants, and did not let even one of them go. The Lord is faithful in all his judgments which he makes in the world.

Like God, the future, messianic king will judge sinners according to their deeds (vv. 25, 36), but his judgment will also extend to the "tribes of the people that have been made holy by the Lord their God" (v. 26), the "peoples in the assemblies, the tribes of the sanctified" (v. 43), as well as to "the peoples and nations" (v. 29). Thus, as with God's judgment (8:26), the king will also "judge the Israelites" (17:26).

In Ps. Sol. 17 the role of the future king as the judge is thus closely related to the fear of God. First, the fear of God functions as a virtue of the king himself, "[who is] mighty in his actions and strong in the fear of God" (v. 40),[18] as well as describing the attitude that all nations should hold before the king, since he shall "be

---

15. Joseph L. Trafton, "What Would David Do? Messianic Expectation and Surprise in Ps. Sol. 17," in *The Psalms of Solomon: Language, History, Theology*, ed. Eberhard Bons and Patrick Pouchelle, SBLEJL 40 (Atlanta: SBL Press, 2015), 162.

16. Wright, "Psalms of Solomon," 665.

17. Trafton ("What Would David Do?" 163–5) argues for four actions (these three plus "shepherding" in v. 40) as the Jewish expectations for the coming Davidic king.

18. According to Trafton (ibid., 171), this belongs to the qualities of the anticipated king as also found in Isa 11:1–5.

compassionate to all the nations that fearfully stand before him" (v. 34).[19] Psalm of Solomon 18:7–9 further emphasizes this point, in which the fear of God functions as the decree of the Lord Messiah:

> [the coming generation under the reign of Messiah] (which will be) under the rod of discipline of the Lord Messiah, in *the fear of his God*, in wisdom of spirit, and of righteousness and of strength, to direct people in righteous acts, in *the fear of God*, to set them all in *the fear of the Lord*; A good generation (living) in *the fear of God*, in the days of mercy. (emphasis added)

The fact that the king will bring to the nations his judgment and fear at the same time indicates that the fear derives from the judgment, and that it becomes the appropriate attribute that the people (including both the Israelites and the redeemed nations) must acquire under the reign of the future king.[20] Thus, the fear of God also functions as a characteristic of the righteous, and describes the reign

---

19. "Ἐνώπιον αὐτοῦ ἐν φόβῳ," following Wright, *Psalms of Solomon*, 194–5, who renders the phrase differently in his later edition: "(who) reverently (stand) before him," Wright, "Psalms of Solomon," 668.

20. Trafton, "What Would David Do?" 169: "Given the generally negative view of the nations in the psalm (vv. 3, 7, 11–15, 22, 24–5, 30), this action can only come as a surprise." These features of the fear of God also appear in the poetic Qumran writings, where the fear of God often marks the righteous in the context of God's judgment. For example, 1QH[a] XX, 3 states that the author will praise God's name "among those who fear him." (Likewise, "those who fear God keep her [Wisdom's] paths and walk in her laws" in 4Q525 4, 9.) The eschatological hymn of 4QPs[f] (4Q88) IX describes the righteous as "those who fear God" (line 14) when God "comes to judge all things to obliterate evil-doers from the earth" (lines 5–6) and "[the sons] of wickedness will find no [rest]." The judgment context of the fear of God is also apparent in 11QPsAp[a] (11Q11) II, 10–11, where "God [will judge them] and they will fear that great [punishment (?)]." The fear of God as an eschatological characteristic appears in the prayer of the king of Judah in 4Q381 31, where the author proclaims that he "will narrate before those who fear you" (line 4) in the presence of his enemies (line 5), whom God will "humiliate," (line 5) "overturn" (line 5), and "destroy" (line 6) on the "day of wrath" (line 7). The author continues that he "will sing and rejoice in you in the presence of those who fear God" (4Q381 33, 5) for God will *judge his servants* in his justice according to his compassion (line 6). The "servants" refer to the people of God in the previous lines, "But you, my God will send your spirit and [have pity] on the son of your maidservants, and compassion on the servant who approaches you" (lines 4–5); thus, God's judgment will be upon his own people and will bring the fear of God among his people. Furthermore, the fear of God motivates the people to act righteously: "I shall fear you and purify myself from all the abominations that I am aware of. And I shall humble my soul in your presence" (4Q381 45, 1–2). While the unclean people will be rejected before God, those who fear God will be before him forever (4Q381 46, 6). In this regard, the author of 4QShir[b] (4Q511) 35 declares that he will "spread the fear of God in the ages of my generations to exalt the name" (line 6)

of the future king in the eschaton when God's vindication of Israel will be fulfilled.[21] The fear of God will remain and function as a norm for the people of God who will "be under the rod of disciple of the Lord Messiah" (18:7) so that God will "direct people in righteous acts, in the fear of God to set them all in the fear of the Lord" (18:8) and eventually the generation "will be living in the fear of God" (19:9).

3. The Psalms as Background for the Fear of God in 2 Cor 7:1

These features of the fear of God outlined above stand in parallel to the usage of the fear of God in 2 Cor 7:1, where the fear of God is also a motivation for the righteous, who have already experienced their restoration that has begun (cf. 6:16b, "we are the temple of the living God"), but are still waiting for its future consummation (cf. 7:1a, "having these promises"). Furthermore, although the judgment context is not directly apparent in the immediate context of 7:1, the previous chapters have shown that the judgment theme (with regard to the fear of God) is present both in the context of 2 Corinthians (cf. 5:10–11) and in the OT contexts of the Scriptures that Paul quotes in 6:16c–18.

III. The Book of Jubilees

The next document to be examined is the Book of Jubilees, a Jewish document composed in Palestine around the second century BCE.[22] Scholars have observed remarkable similarities between 2 Cor 6:14–7:1 and Jub. 1: the reference to God's "sanctuary" in their midst (Jub. 1:17, 27, 29), the Covenant Formula as given in

---

in the context of "God's judgment of vengeance to exterminate wickedness" (line 1) and "the rage of God's wrath" (line 2). The fear of God also functions as a means to subjugate the evil spirits (line 7) and as a norm among the holy people of God whom God made holy for himself like an everlasting sanctuary (lines 3–4).

21. God's judgment upon his own people will be for their "discipline" (8:26), and will lead to their "repentance" (9:7), so that "any person who knows wickedness shall not live among his people" (17:27) and God will make the people know that "they are all children of their God" (17:27).

22. James C. VanderKam, "Recent Scholarship on the Book of Jubilees," *CurBR* 6, (2008): 405; idem, *The Book of Jubilees*, GAP (Sheffield: Sheffield Academic Press, 2001), 11, 17–21; O. S. Wintermute, "Jubilees," in *The Old Testament Pseudepigrapha Vol. 2*, ed. James H. Charlesworth, 3rd ed. (Peabody, MA: Hendrickson, 2013), 43–5; Michael Segal, *The Book of Jubilees: Rewritten Bible, Redaction, Ideology and Theology*, JSJSup 117 (Leiden; Boston: Brill, 2007), 35; Davila, *Provenance*, 13, 71, 163. The text of Jubilees is preserved in highly fragmentary manuscripts among the Judean Desert manuscripts, but complete in later primary or secondary translations (Ethiopic text) (Davila, *Provenance*, 13). All Jubilees passages are quoted from James C. VanderKam, *The Book of Jubilees: A Critical Text*, CSCO 87, 88 (Leuven: Peeters, 1989), unless otherwise noted.

Lev 26:12 (Jub. 1:17), the pluralized Adoption Formula of 2 Sam 7:14 (Jub. 1:24), the Exodus typology (Jub. 1 as a whole), the reference to "Belial" being opposed to "righteousness" (Jub. 1:20), the themes of purification (Jub. 1:23), "the living God" (Jub. 1:25), and idolatry (Jub. 1:8, 9, 11), and the exhortation in Isa 52:11 (Jub. 22:16).[23] Furthermore, as in the Psalms of Solomon, in Jubilees divine judgment is the fate of the evil ones who did not obey God's commandments, the awareness of which functions as a motivation for the righteous to pursue a godly life. However, even though the function of the judgment of God is very similar to that in the Psalms of Solomon, the fear of God does not appear in Jubilees as frequently as in the Psalms. Nor does Jubilees show the connection between the fear of God and the judgment as explicitly as it occurs in the Psalms.

1. The Similarities between Jubilees and 2 Cor 6:14–7:1

Before getting into the differences between Jubilees and 2 Cor 6:14–7:1, it is appropriate to compare the similarities between two documents. As mentioned above, Jubilees and 2 Cor 6:14–7:1 have not only certain themes and language in common, but they also allude to the same OT passages for support. For our study, the following are the most significant. First, the beginning of Jubilees mentions the promises of God's dwelling in the midst of his people and the establishment of the covenant relationship, which also appear in 2 Cor 6:16de, as well as sharing the same reference to Lev 26:11–12: "I will build my temple among them and will live with them; I will become their God and they will become my true and righteous people" (Jub. 1:17).[24] Inasmuch as Jub. 1 serves as the introduction to the narrative and thereby "implies that the perspective presented in it is one that the author wished to impress upon his readers,"[25] the fulfillment of God's promises in the future to dwell in a covenant relationship with his people (1:17) becomes one of the main themes in Jubilees.[26] The restoration of

---

23. So, e.g., Betz, "2 Cor 6:14–7:1," 94–95; Scott, *Adoption*, 210n104; David I. Starling, *Not My People: Gentiles as Exiles in Pauline Hermeneutics*, BZNW 184 (Berlin; New York: de Gruyter, 2011), 88–93.

24. Wintermute ("Jubilees," 53) acknowledges the allusions to Lev 26. Likewise, Scott, (*Adoption*, 200) argues that in Jub. 1:17 the covenant formula in Lev 26:12 is combined with Zech 8:8 to refer to the new covenant situation, as the continuation of Jub. 1:15–18 shows.

25. VanderKam, *Jubilees*, 132.

26. Contra VanderKam (ibid.), who argues that eschatology is not a dominant concern in Jubilees. According to VanderKamn, only two passages, Jub. 1:7–29 and 23:11–31, focus on this subject. However, Segal (*Jubilees*, 137–9) argues that in the Watchers Story in Jub. 5 there is an additional literary motif from 1 En. 10:12, which describes the final judgment ("the great day"), and thus reinterprets the flood narrative eschatologically. According to Segal, 141, the topic of God as a righteous judge points to "a connection between Jub. 5:13–18 and the legal passages that are interspersed throughout the entire book." Therefore, as we will see, God's role as the one who executes judgment on the eschatological day of judgment (as in 23:31), which appears several times throughout Jubilees (cf. 21:4; 33:18), takes an important role in the book.

God's relationship with his people as expressed in this covenant formula is then promised once more in 2:19.

Second, the restoration theme in Jubilees has similarities with the new covenant theme in 2 Cor 6:14–7:1. The author of Jubilees knows that the Israelites will break the covenant and will be sent into exile (Jub. 1:9–14); but, nevertheless, he expects that at the time of restoration there will be repentance and restoration (1:15), since God promises the people that he "will cut away the foreskins of their minds and the foreskins of their descendants' minds" and will "create a holy spirit for them, and will purify them in order that they may not turn away from me from that time forever" (1:23). Consequently, the people's "souls will adhere to God and to all his commandments and perform his commandments" (1:24). These features of purification, creation of a holy spirit, obedience to God's commandments, and the description of God's relationship with his people in terms of the covenant formula allude to God's restoration in Ezek 36:25–8; 37:23–4, which is the background of the two promises of restoration in Ezek 37:27 quoted by Paul in 2 Cor 6:16de. Furthermore, the related adoption formula that follows in Jub. 1:24 is similar to that in 2 Cor 6:18 (cf. Jub. 1:25, 28; 19:29),[27] and the resultant description of the

---

27. Scott (*Adoption*, 105–17) demonstrates in detail the use of the adoption formula of 2 Sam 7:14 in the Second Temple Period. According to Scott, 104, Jewish tradition applies 2 Sam 7:14 eschatologically either to the Messiah (4Q174 I, 11), or to Israel (Jub. 1:24), or to both (T. Jud. 24:3). Scott, 106–9, argues that in doing so Jub. 1:24 subsumes the promise under the new covenant that is to be instituted at the eschatological restoration. In this regard, the fact that the adoption formula of 2 Sam 7:14 applies to believers in 2 Cor 6:18 shows the approximation of 2 Cor 6:18 to Jubilees. For the relationship between 4Q174 and 2 Cor 6:14–7:1, see further Brooke (*Exegesis at Qumran*, 211–19), who compares the four former studies by Fitzmyer, "Qumrân"; Gnilka, "2 Cor 6:14–7:1"; Bertil Gärtner, *The Temple and the Community in Qumran and the New Testament*, SNTSMS 1 (Cambridge: Cambridge University Press, 1965), 49–56; and Klinzing, *Umdeutung*, 175–82, and argues that 4Q174 and 2 Cor 6:14–7:1 have many similarities, such as the adoption formula of 2 Sam 7:14, the allusion to Ezek 37:23 (4Q174 I, 16–17), the motif of the community as the temple of God (4Q174 1:4–9), the separation from all impurity (4Q174 I, 3–4), and Belial (4Q174 I, 8–9). Brooke, 217, thus concludes that both 4Q174 and 2 Cor 6:14–7:1 are "heirs of a common tradition concerning the eschatological community." Recently, observations regarding the similarities between 4Q174 and 2 Cor 6:14–7:1 are made by Timothy H. Lim, *Holy Scripture in the Qumran Commentaries and Pauline Letters* (Oxford; New York: Clarendon; Oxford University Press, 1997), 157–58, and Peter J. Tomson, "Christ, Belial, and Women: 2 Cor 6:14–7:1 Compared with Ancient Judaism and with the Pauline Corpus," in *Second Corinthians in the Perspective of Late Second Temple Judaism*, ed. R. Bieringer et al., CORINT 14 (Leiden; Boston: Brill, 2014), 115–16. Besides the different correspondence of the adoption formula in 4Q174 and 2 Cor 6:18, 4Q174 I, 8–9 describes Belial and his followers and then briefly mentions the judgment against them, but the function of judgment as the motivation for the righteous or the fear of God that derives from judgment do not appear in this Qumran text.

people as "sons of the living God" (Jub. 1:25, cf. 21:4) resembles Paul's statement that believers are "the temple of the living God" (2 Cor 6:16b).

Third, Jub. 22:16 contains the same command from Isa 52:11 that Paul quotes in 2 Cor 6:17:

> Now you, my son Jacob, remember what I say and keep the commandments of your father Abraham. *Separate from* the nations, and do not eat with them. Do not act as they do, and do not become their companion, for their actions are something that is impure, and all their ways are defiled and something abominable and detestable (emphasis added).[28]

In Jub. 22:11–23 Abraham consequently exhorts Jacob to beware of the gentiles, who are idol worshippers (vv. 17–18) and act maliciously (v.19). This kind of exhortation against the Gentiles as evil ones who stand in opposition to God and his people appears throughout Jubilees. Moreover, as part of this opposition, Jubilees introduces a host of angels and demons between God and man, by means of which he tries to deal with the problem of evil in the present world.[29] This observation leads to the next similarity between Jubilees and 2 Cor 6:14–7:1.

Fourth, the name "Belial" (בליעל) appears in both Jubilees and 2 Cor 6:15a, forming a contrast with God/Christ. In Paul's argument, Belial is contrasted with Christ as part of a chain of contrasts, and, similarly, in Jubilees Belial appears as part of a number of contrasts, such as "the spirit of Belial" against "the upright spirit" (1:20),[30] and "the sons of Belial" (15:33)[31] against "the sons of Israel," who will be called "sons of the living God" (1:25).[32] Michael Segal thus comments that in Jewish literature of the Second Temple period:

> Belial was transformed into a proper noun, as the personal name of the head of the demonic, evil forces in the world, who stands in opposition to God and the righteous heavenly forces. The viewpoint expressed in these compositions is dualistic: the evil axis in the world is in constant struggle against justice and its adherents.[33]

---

28. Wintermute ("Jubilees," 98) acknowledges the allusion to Isa 52:11 in this passage.

29. Ibid., 47. Wintermute argues that the author of Jubilees teaches the following things about evil: (1) it is superhuman; (2) but it is not caused by God; (3) therefore, it comes from the angelic world, which has suffered a breach from God's good order. In response, instead of the continuous effect of the initial sin of Adam, Jubilees focuses on the helplessness of mankind.

30. Following Wintermute, "Jubilees," 53. VanderKam (*Jubilees*, 5) takes the phrase as "the just spirit."

31. Following Wintermute, "Jubilees," 87. VanderKam (*Jubilees*, 94) takes the phrase as "people of Belial."

32. VanderKam, (*Jubilees*, 127–8) argues that, as in the Hebrew Bible, "Belial" may have a meaning of "worthlessness," "ruin," "destruction" (cf. 1 Sam 25:5).

33. Segal, *Jubilees*, 251–2.

As a result, in Jubilees Belial comes to designate a demonic power and refers to Satan.[34] Belial or Satan represent the evil power that opposes God and performs only negative functions, such as accusing people (1:20), misleading them into destruction (7:27; 10:1, 3, 5, 8), causing diseases (10:12–13), and even killing people (10:2; 49:2).[35] As the corollary to this demonic action, the "dualism of the angelic world was reflected in the world of men"[36] is for the author of Jubilees the answer to the problem of evil in the present age. Wicked angels, like Belial, were, "for the author of Jubilees along with other Jews of this period, a constant source of danger; they could infiltrate people's minds, leading them astray or even driving them mad."[37] In addition, Belial is also replaced by "(the Prince of) Mastema,"[38] whose will is carried out by evil, savage spirits or demons (11:5).[39] Similarly, the spirits of

---

34. Wintermute, "Jubilees," 53.

35. VanderKam, *Jubilees*, 131.

36. Wintermute, "Jubilees," 48.

37. James L. Kugel, *A Walk through Jubilees: Studies in the Book of Jubilees and the World of Its Creation*, JSJSup 156 (Leiden; Boston: Brill, 2012), 25.

38. In Jubilees Matsema appears several times in the place of Belial (11:5; 17:16; 20:28–9; 48:1–4, 9–19; 49:2). Mastema plays the role of the leading figure of the evil forces from the period of Noah to the Exodus, and afterwards Belial takes over his role in the context of the Israelites' future (15:33) and redemption (1:20). In the Hebrew Bible "Mastema" means "animosity," "hostility" (Hos 9:7–8) and in Jubilees it represents "a proper name for the chief demonic power that has jurisdiction over a contingent of evil spirits"; Loren T. Stuckenbruck, "The Demonic World of the Dead Sea Scrolls," in *Evil and the Devil*, ed. Ida Fröhlich and Erkki Koskenniemi, ISCO 481 (London: Bloomsbury T&T Clark, 2013), 64. There is, however, a debate among scholars about the relationship in Jubilees between Belial, Mastema and Satan. For example, Stuckenbruck, 64–8, is hesitant to identify Mastema and Belial and rather claims that the appearance of the two names in Jubilees shows the mix of different traditions. Similarly, Devorah Dimant ("Between Qumran Sectarian and Non-Sectarian Texts: The Case of Belial and Mastema," in *Dead Sea Scrolls and Contemporary Culture: Proceedings of the International Conference Held at the Israel Museum, Jerusalem [July 6–8, 2008]* [Leiden: Brill, 2011], 235–6) argues that Belial belongs to a lower rank than Mastema and the two cannot be identified. On the other hand, however, scholars like VanderKam (*Jubilees*, 127), Wintermute ("Jubilees," 46–8), Kugel (*Jubilees*, 25, 83), and Segal (*Jubilees*, 10, 251–6) argue that Mastema and Belial in Jubilees portray the same figure. Derek R. Brown (*The God of This Age: Satan in the Churches and Letters of the Apostle Paul*, WUNT 2/409 [Tübingen: Mohr Siebeck, 2015], 31) thus argues that "*Jubilees* portrays the figure of Satan, typically called (the prince of) Mastema or Belial, as ruling over both evil spirits and various human beings." According to Brown, 33n38, Satan and Mastema "are actually likely meant to be viewed as one and the same, even though the relationship between Satan and the price [sic] of the spirits in *Jubilees* is at times confusing." We will deal with Belial more in detail in our treatment of the Testaments of the Twelve Patriarchs.

39. VanderKam, *Jubilees*, 131. Segal (*Jubilees*, 99) argues that the original tradition about Prince Mastema embedded in chs 17–18, 48 shows that he acted alone against God and his council, but this tradition has been expanded as passages in which Mastema is mentioned now also include the spirits or demons as assistants.

the children of the "Watchers," who were originally good angels (4:15), but fell into sin (5:6–11), wander the earth as demons who are subjected to Satan (10:11) and lead the people astray (10:1) until the judgment day.[40] Together with the demons under the authority of Mastema and/or Belial they form an opposing force against God, so that the people of God should take heed. Therefore, Noah warns against "the demons" (7:27)[41] and "Watchers" (10:5–6),[42] and Abraham (Abram) prays to God to save him from the hands of "evil spirits" (12:20) and to save Jacob and his seed from "the spirit of Mastema" (20:28).

Of significance for our study, therefore, is that in Jubilees the people are continuously warned to beware of the evil spirits and those who follow them because they too are in danger of being doomed together with these evil ones at the last judgment. For example, Noah warns his sons about the day of judgment, "on which the Lord God will punish them with the sword and fire because of all the evil impurity of their errors by which they have filled the earth with wickedness, impurity, fornication, and sin" (9:15). Abraham also foretells the end of the sons of Belial in his prediction of the future of the people of Israel:

> And now I shall announce to you that the sons of Israel will deny this ordinance and they will not circumcise their sons according to all of this law because some of the flesh of their circumcision they will leave in the circumcision of their sons. And all of the sons of Belial will leave their sons without circumcising just as they were born. And great wrath from the Lord will be upon the sons of Israel because they have left his covenant and have turned aside from his words
>
> 15:33–4.[43]

Moreover, the theme of judgment in Jubilees functions not only to motivate God's people to resist the evil powers, but also to pursue righteousness. For example, Abraham's delineation of the judgments of the giants and of the people of Sodom who had been judged on account of their evil deeds in 20:5–6 is followed by his exhortation to "love the God of heaven, and hold fast to all his commandments" in v. 7.

2. The Theme of Judgment in Jubilees

The theme of judgment itself appears throughout Jubilees (2:29; 4:6, 19, 23–4; 5:10–16; 7:29; 9:15; 10:5–6, 22; 16:6, 9; 20:5–6; 21:4; 22:22; 23:11, 22, 31; 24:33; 40:6), especially in terms of "the day of judgment," when the people "will come before the Lord and they will make known all of the sins which occur in heaven and earth and which are in the light or in the darkness or in any place"

---

40. Wintermute, "Jubilees," 47; VanderKam, *Jubilees*, 34–5; Segal, *Jubilees*, 10.

41. Kugel (*Jubilees*, 72–3) thus comments that for the author of Jubilees, "demons and wicked angels are a constant danger, since they can enter the mind and mislead people."

42. There are allusions to Num 16:22; 27:16. Ibid., 82.

43. Following Wintermute, "Jubilees," 87.

(4:6).⁴⁴ The judgment will be executed upon all of those "who corrupted their ways and their actions before the Lord" (5:10), and since "the judgment of them all has been ordained and written on the heavenly tablets, there is no injustice. (As for) all who transgress from their way in which it was ordained for them to go—if they do not go in it, judgment has been written down for each creature and for each kind" (5:13). God is thus a righteous judge (5:16)⁴⁵ and everyone will be subjected to his judgment, "each one according with his way" (5:15).⁴⁶ Even though Jub. 5 identifies the great day of judgment with the flood,⁴⁷ Jubilees shows throughout the entire book that this day refers to "the day on which evildoers will be punished, at the time of the transition from this world to the eschatological era (cf. 4:19; 9:15; 10:17, 22; 22:21; 23:11; 24:30, 33)."⁴⁸ VanderKam thus comments regarding God's judgment in the future that:

> *Jubilees* contains a number of stories which illustrate divine justice (e.g. the expulsion from Eden, the flood, Sodom and Gomorrah) but it also adds comments emphasizing that God was the one behind the punishment (see 16:5-6, 8-9; 30:5-22) and that he will punish in the future (see 23:22).⁴⁹

44. Following Wintermute, "Jubilees," 61. Regarding the day of judgment, the role of Enoch becomes important as the one who "is there writing condemnation and judgment of the world, and all of the evils of the children of men ... until the day of judgment" (4:23-4; cf. 4:19; 10:17). VanderKam argues that the mention of the heavenly tablets on which Enoch records his condemnation derives from the Enochian literature. For a more detailed discussion about the heavenly tablets and the connection of Jubilees to Enochian literature, see VanderKam, *Jubilees*, 89-0; Kugel, *Jubilees*, 11-14; and especially Segal, *Jubilees*, 26, who argues that the heavenly tablets contain the Torah and *te'udah*, and *te'udah* should be understood as "stipulations of the covenant" by which the people will be rewarded or punished in the judgment. For a more detailed discussion, see Segal (ibid., 282-316).

45. Thus, Segal, *Jubilees*, 140: "Since YHWH serves as a judge, it is incumbent upon all people to behave in accordance with the regulations that are in force for them. The Watchers story in *Jub.* 5 ... rather calls on all people to behave according to 'their way in which it was ordained for them to go,' and thus to obey God's command."

46. Segal (ibid., 109-18) argues that the judgment theme in Jub. 5 lies parallel to 1 En. 10-11 because the author of Jubilees used 1 En. 10-11 as a source to rewrite the Watchers story in Jub. 5. Segal, 138, argues that Jub. 5 (esp. vv. 13-18) takes the Watchers story as a paradigm for the lesson of reward and punishment, and by presenting God as a judge calls for the obligation of each one to follow God's commandments (similar to Jub. 7:20-39; 20:5). According to Segal, 142, this redaction, enabling the author to combine the rewritten stories and the legal passages, "is one of the most prominent characteristics of *Jubilees*."

47. Note the similar description of the people standing in judgment in Jub. 5:10 and Gen 6:12.

48. Segal, *Jubilees*, 133.

49. VanderKam, *Jubilees*, 122. Kugel (*Jubilees*, 55-6) argues that after the flood, "with human nature retooled, each and every sin committed would automatically be punished with the full force of the law." In this context, Kugel interprets the judgment on the Heavenly Tablets (5:13) as "punishment."

Here too the significance for our study is the fact that this theme of judgment, so central to Jubilees and which is seen to apply to everyone according to his/her deeds, becomes the *motivation* for the people to follow God's commandments. Hence, Jub. 2:29 states that the judgment of God should be made known and recounted to the children of Israel so that they will "keep the Sabbath thereon and not forsake it in the error of their heart." So as Segal argues, "the idea of God as a righteous judge appears as a reason for the composition of the entire book"[50] in that the themes of the final judgment and of God as a judge serve to induce the observance of God's commandments by warning the readers of the punishment awaiting anyone who fails to make the proper choice.[51] This role of judgment as motivation is clearly exemplified through the figure of Joseph in 39:6, who did not surrender himself because he remembered that there is a "judgment of death"[52] which has been decreed for him in heaven before the Lord Most High.

3. The Fear of God in Jubilees

However, while the theme of judgment functions as the motivation for the people of God, Jubilees makes no explicit reference to the fear of God in the context of judgment. For example, in Jub. 22:11–23 Abraham warns Jacob of the destiny of the idol worshippers who bow down to demons and act maliciously that their end will be "the place of judgment" (cf. 22:17, 19). Then Abraham exhorts Jacob to beware of the Gentiles, but in this context there is no admonition to fear of God; on the contrary, Abraham exhorts him not to fear other people, "*Do not fear*, my son, Jacob, and *do not be in terror*, O son of Abraham" (v. 23, emphasis added).[53]

Fear regarding God appears five times in Jubilees (18:9, 11; 30:26; 36:7 and 43:10),[54] but the judgment of God is only implied in these passages. The first two occurrences appear at the end of the test of Abraham. God commands his angel to stop Abraham from killing Isaac because God knows "that he is the one who fears the Lord" (cf. Gen 22:12). It is noticeable that unlike the Genesis narrative, where God initiates the testing of Abraham, in Jubilees Prince Mastema is presented as the one who opposes Abraham and puts him to the test (Jub. 17:15–18). Moreover, in the end, Mastema is put to shame because of Abraham's faithfulness (18:12). In other words, the context shows that fearing God is related to "not falling into

---

50. Segal, *Jubilees*, 141n99.

51. Ibid., 143.

52. Following Wintermute ("Jubilees," 129). VanderKam (*Jubilees*, 257) renders this phrase as "penalty of death."

53. Following Wintermute ("Jubilees," 99). VanderKam (*Jubilees*, 133) renders this as "Do not be afraid ... and do not be upset."

54. There is a reference to fear in the establishment of the covenant with Abram in 14:13, but it is not clear from the context that this fear refers to the fear of God. VanderKam (*Critical Text*, 85) comments that the construction indicates the phrase is to be taken as a "fear of great darkness."

Mastema's test," which is an act of obedience, but the relation between fear and divine judgment (of Mastema or Abraham), that is, the former derives from the latter, is only implied.

The next occurrence of the fear of God in Jub. 30:26 describes the situation after Levi and Simeon take vengeance on the Shechemites (cf. Gen 34–5, especially 35:5): "A *fear of the Lord* was in all the cities which were around Shechem. They did not set out to pursue Jacob's sons because *fear* had fallen on them" (emphasis added). The vengeance on Shechem is described as God's judgment since "the Lord handed them over to Jacob's sons for them to uproot them with the sword and to effect punishment against them" (Jub. 30:6). Once again there is an implicit connection between the fear of God and his judgment in that fear appears as a result of God's action in having given the Shechemites over to Jacob's sons. What is more interesting is the fact that God uses this incident as a warning to Israel:

> For there will be plague upon plague and curse upon curse, and *every judgment*, and plague, and curse will come. And if he does this thing [of marriage with foreigners], or if he blinds his eyes from those who cause defilement and from those who defile the sanctuary of the Lord and from those who profane his holy name, (then) all of the people *will be judged* together on account of all of the defilement and the profaning of this one
>
> 30:15, emphasis added.[55]

Hence, as this text makes clear, the fear of God among the Shechemites derives from his judgment and this judgment is not limited to the Gentiles, but is an example of what also applies to the Israelites. Therefore, albeit not explicitly expressed, the fear of God (deriving from God's judgment) is required of the Israelites as the judgment functions as a motivation for them to pursue a holy life.

In Isaac's farewell advice to his two sons (Jub. 36), fearing God appears in conjunction with worshipping him:

> Now I will make you swear with the great oath ... that you will continue to *fear and worship him*, as each loves his brother kindly and properly. One is not to desire what is bad for his brother now and forever, throughout your entire lifetime, so that you may be prosperous in everything that you do and *not be destroyed*
>
> 36:7–8, emphasis added.

The text shows that fearing God and worshipping him are expressed in the love of one's brother. Moreover, Isaac warns his sons that they will be destroyed if they fail to fear and worship God in this way, thus linking the fear of God to the threat of divine judgment. The passage then goes on to stress that if either of them seeks

---

55. Following Wintermute ("Jubilees," 113). VanderKam (*Jubilees*, 196) renders judgment as "punishment."

evil against the other, God's judgment will be upon him (vv. 9–11). Here the link between the fear of God and divine judgment, though still implied, is virtually direct. Two additional aspects are notable about God's judgment in this context. First, Isaac warns that God's judgment will be like that on Sodom (v. 10), which, in other passages, exemplifies God's judgment on all evil ones (16:6, 9; 20:5, 22:22). Second, this judgment is executed "on the day of turmoil and execration and indignation and wrath" (v. 10), which alludes to the last judgment, especially given the reference to the "Book of Life" in this context ("He will be erased from the disciplinary book of mankind. He will not be entered in the book of life but in the one that will be destroyed" cf. 4:19–25; 5:13–16; 40:6). The warning is therefore clear: if the people (of God) do not follow a righteous path, God's judgment on the last day will be upon them as upon the evil ones. Thus, divine judgment functions in 36:7–11 as a motivation for righteous life that is characterized as fearing God and worshipping him. For although the relation between the themes of God's judgment theme and the fear of God as a motivation for living righteously is not explicitly expressed in this context, the link is unmistakable.

The last appearance of the fear of God in Jubilees is in Joseph's address to his brothers: "As for me, I fear the Lord. As for you, go to your houses, but your brother is to be enslaved because you have done something evil . . ." (43:10). Although other Jewish documents, like the T. Benj. 3:3–4, describe Joseph as a person who is motivated by his fear of God, in Jubilees it is God's judgment that motivates Joseph to act righteously (40:6), while the corresponding fear of God is only implied in the context in that it is a "judgment of death which is decreed for him in heaven before the Lord Most High" (cf. Gen 42:18).[56]

4. Jubilees as Background for the Fear of God in 2 Cor 7:1

Through the cumulative observations above, one can glimpse in Jubilees the connection between the fear of God and the theme of judgment, as well as the function of the fear of God as a motivation for the righteous, although they are mostly embedded in the context and not expressed explicitly. Rather, it is the judgment theme in Jubilees that functions as the explicit motivation for the righteous, though of course the judgment in view is ultimately God's. In this regard, Jubilees demonstrates that, within the spectrum of Jewish understanding of the fear of God, even when only judgment is explicitly mentioned as the motivation for a righteous life, the assumed link between the fear of God and his judgment makes it clear that where judgment is given as the motivation, fearing God is also implied.

---

56. For a more detailed study on the role of Joseph, see Harm W. Hollander, *Joseph as an Ethical Model in the Testaments of the Twelve Patriarchs*, SVTP 6 (Leiden: Brill, 1981), 94; Robert A. Kugler, *The Testaments of the Twelve Patriarchs*, GAP 10 (Sheffield: Sheffield Academic Press, 2001), 19.

IV. 4 Ezra and 6 Ezra

Fourth Ezra, which dates from the end of the first century CE, is one of the most profound theological reflections in the Second Temple Period on Israel's past and present situation, as well as on Jewish expectations for the future.[57] In regard to the latter, in "4 Ezra" 16:67 the fear of God that derives from divine judgment appears as the motivation for the righteous life: "Behold, *God is the judge, fear him!* Cease from your sins, and forget your iniquities, never to commit them again; so God will lead you forth and deliver you from all tribulation" (emphasis added). This exhortation is similar to what we saw in the Psalms of Solomon in that here too the fear of God's judgment functions as the explicit motivation for a righteous life, and also to 2 Cor 7:1, where people are exhorted to pursue holiness "in the fear of God" as the corollary to the fear of God's judgment in 2 Cor 5:11 (cf., e.g., Pss. Sol. 2:33; 3:12; 4:23–25; 13:12; 15:12–13). However, the evidence in 4 Ezra 16:67 is not appropriate for mapping out the conceptual background to Paul's argument in 2 Cor 7:1 because of the scholarly consensus that chs 15–16 of 4 Ezra, also known as 6 Ezra,[58] belong to a Christian redaction which dates relatively later than chs 3–14.[59]

---

57. Bruce W. Longenecker, *2 Esdras*, GAP (Sheffield: Sheffield Academic Press, 1995), 13–15. This work will follow the text of Bruce Manning Metzger, "4 Ezra," in *The Old Testament Pseudepigrapha Vol. 1*, ed. James H. Charlesworth, 3rd ed. (Peabody, MA: Hendrickson, 2013), 517–9, which includes 5 Ezra as chs 1–2 and 6 Ezra as chs 15–16. Also, following Metzger ("4 Ezra," 518–19), a bracket marks the text of Codex Ambianensis, which contains the "missing" section 7:[36]–[105] in Codex Sangermanensis. Consensus has been reached among scholars about the Jewish background of 4 Ezra 3–14. Michael Edward Stone, *Fourth Ezra: A Commentary on the Book of Fourth Ezra*, Hermeneia (Minneapolis: Fortress, 1990), 9–10; Davila, *Provenance*, 137–41.

58. The text of *6 Ezra* consists of two parts: a prophecy in 15:1–16:34 that evil will strike the world as a punishment against human sin and an encouragement amid persecutions in 16:35–78 for a group called God's servants or chosen ones. Theodore A. Bergren, "Prophetic Rhetoric in 6 Ezra," in *For a Later Generation: The Transformation of Tradition in Israel, Early Judaism, and Early Christianity*, ed. Randal A. Argall, Beverly A. Bow, and Rodney Alan Werline (Harrisburg: Trinity Press International, 2000), 25. This work will use 6 Ezra for 4 Ezra 15–16 from now on.

59. Longenecker, *2 Esdras*, 110–14; Metzger, "4 Ezra," 517–18; Theodore A. Bergren, "Fifth Ezra: A New Translation and Introduction" and "Sixth Ezra: A New Translation and Introduction," in *Old Testament Pseudepigrapha: More Noncanonical Scriptures*, ed. Richard Bauckham, James R. Davila, and Alexander Panayotov, vol. 1 (Grand Rapids; Cambridge: Eerdmans, 2013), 467–75, 483–90. After an examination of the transmission history of the individual components of 4, 5, and 6 Ezra, Bergren concludes that 4 Ezra is clearly Jewish while 5 and 6 Ezra are both probably Christian and that the process of accretion almost certainly took place in a Christian context. Bergren's assertion of the Christian authorship of 6 Ezra relies on two main factors: the author seems to allude to the Book of Revelation and the descriptions of the persecution in 6 Ezra seem to predict the pagan persecutions of Christians in the second and third centuries. Theodore A. Bergren, "Christian Influence on

Sixth Ezra shows, however, that Paul's thought in 2 Cor 5:11 and 7:1 is part of a trajectory of thought that continues on in both Jewish and Christian contexts. For 6 Ezra represents the argument of 4 Ezra on the one hand, while at the same time representing its acceptance within Christian circles on the other. Moreover, the clear distinction between the Jewish and Christian origins of 4 Ezra and 6 Ezra respectively enables us to compare the understanding of the fear of God within its early Jewish and Christian backgrounds, which often cannot easily be distinguished, especially in a text such as the Testament of the Twelve Patriarchs (see below).

1. 4 Ezra and 6 Ezra

The comparison of 4 and 6 Ezra regarding their notions of the fear of God is possible because they share the same practical purpose of explaining how to live in the present age. Nevertheless, comparing the features of the fear of God in these documents does not presuppose that they share an identical eschatology. In 4 Ezra 7:28–[44] God's son, the Messiah, will be revealed and will rule over the temporary kingdom for 400 years.[60] On his death, the world will be turned back to primeval silence for seven days, and then the general resurrection and final judgment will follow immediately. In contrast, the eschatology of 6 Ezra "is rather simple and primitive in form. There is no complex eschatological timetable or elaborate apocalyptic scenario."[61] Moreover, James R. Davila, who argues for the Jewish composition of 4 Ezra 3–14 based on the fact that it is replete with Jewish signature features, sees the eschatology of 4 Ezra as being inconsistent with that of early Christianity, especially with regard to the messianic scenario in 7:28–[44].[62] However, it should also be kept in mind that 4 Ezra "was not concerned with logical consistency in his eschatological descriptions, but used various eschatological ideas simply to support different points of argument at different places in his presentation."[63] Thus, 4 Ezra describes the eschatological process as "a

---

the Transmission History of 4, 5, and 6 Ezra," in *The Jewish Apocalyptic Heritage in Early Christianity*, ed. James C. VanderKam and William Adler, CRINT 4 (Minneapolis; Assen: Fortress; Van Gorcum, 1996), 126–27; *Sixth Ezra: The Text and Origin* (New York; Oxford: Oxford University Press, 1998), 103–15. The original Jewish document of 4 Ezra [2 Esdras chs 3–14] was composed between 90 and 100 CE, while 6 Ezra can be dated to the third century CE. Bergren, "Christian Influence," 102–3; idem, *Sixth Ezra*, 116–32; Michael E. Stone, "2 Esdras," in *The HarperCollins Study Bible*, ed. Harold W. Attridge and Wayne A. Meeks, Revised ed. (San Francisco: Harper One, 2006), 1588–9; Metzger, "4 Ezra," 520.

60. While the Latin versions and Arabic 1 versions of *4 Ezra* have "four hundred years," the Syriac version has "thirty years," Arabic 2 version has "one thousand years," and the Ethiopic and Armenian versions omit the duration.

61. Longenecker, *2 Esdras*, 25.

62. Davila, *Provenance*, 137–41: "This inconsistency with Christian eschatology is obviously due to the fact that the author of *4 Ezra* sees the advent and death of the Messiah as still in the future" (p. 140).

63. Longenecker, *2 Esdras*, 23.

coherent and consecutive structure of events," rather than in consistency.[64] As a result, the eschatological ideas in 4 Ezra do not aim to provide the readers/audience with a comprehensive explanation of eschatology, but rather to give them practical instructions about the present age from an eschatological perspective.[65]

In this regard, despite the differences in their eschatology, both 4 and 6 Ezra are using the fear of God in similar ways to address their own people. In particular, the focus of both 4 and 6 Ezra is on an eschatologically driven exhortation regarding ethical issues and individual salvation.[66] For our purposes, therefore, we do not aim to compare the Jewish and Christian eschatology of 4 and 6 Ezra, but rather 1) to examine how their respective eschatological understandings meet their purposes of addressing how to live in the present age, especially regarding their respective understandings of the fear of God in relationship to the judgment of God, and then 2) to compare the fear of God in 4 and 6 Ezra with the way it is understood in 2 Cor 7:1.

2. The Fear of God and the Theme of Judgment in 4 Ezra

In 4 Ezra the fear of God appears in relationship to God's final judgment, which is treated in chs 7–8; 12; 14. There, Ezra is told by the angel Uriel in chs 7–8 and by God in chs 12, 14 about the day of judgment that will come at the end of time (7:26, [38], 43; 8:61; 12:34). On that day the Most High will be revealed upon the seat of judgment in order to judge both the righteous and the unrighteous according to their deeds (7:33, 35, [105]; 8:33; 12:33; 14:32, 35).[67] As a result, two different destinies for the human race are presented in that God (or the Messiah who is sent by God as the agent of judgment cf. 12:32-4) will destroy the unrighteous ones who scorned his law (7:24, [72], [79]–[87]; 8:56; 12:33), but deliver in mercy the remnant of his people (7:[88]–[99]; 12:34). Fourth Ezra 7:[45]–[48] declares as a consequence that "nearly all humanity" who transgressed the law, including Jews and Gentiles, will be condemned under the judgment of God (7:[37]–[8], [72]–[3], [79]–[81], 130–1; 8:55–8; 9:11–12), a position that Ezra formerly thought to be Gentiles' alone.[68] In 4 Ezra the responsibility for this

---

64. Stone, *Fourth Ezra*, 206. Similarly, Longenecker, *2 Esdras*, 21.

65. Stone, *Fourth Ezra*, 204–7. Stone, 206, gives an example of two major groupings of associated eschatological ideas: the last generation and the increase of evil until its consummation, which is to be followed by the messianic kingdom, and ideas such as resurrection, judgment, reward, and punishment.

66. Longenecker, *2 Esdras*, 27.

67. Nickelsburg (*Resurrection*, 173) thus argues that, "[The wicked and the righteous] receive reward or punishment [on the judgment day] for their obedience and disobedience to God's law."

68. Longenecker, *2 Esdras*, 48. Nickelsburg (*Resurrection*, 214) makes a similar argument that the judgment motif in 4 Ezra is universal in that it becomes the means by which final rewards and punishments can be dispensed to everyone.

annihilation rests solely on those who will be destroyed because it results from their own wrong doing, since they had the choice either to follow or to abandon God's law (7:[72], 127–31; 8:55–6; 9:11).[69] Thus, salvation will be granted only to the few who have stored up a treasure of good works with the Most High on account of their faith (7:[77]; 9:7).

The fear of God in 4 Ezra appears in accordance with this eschatological perspective regarding God's judgment. In anticipation of the final judgment, the fear of God functions as a description of the righteous in contrast to the unrighteous (7:[79]; 8:28), and thus characterizes the law abiding life of the righteous that will lead to their redemption on the day of judgment (7:[87], [98]). For example, in 7:[79]–[87] Uriel explains to Ezra the seven ways in which judgment will fall upon the unrighteous, who "have shown scorn and have not kept the way of the Most High, and who have despised his Law, and who have hated *those who fear God*" (7:[79], emphasis added). The hostility of the unrighteous against the righteous is then described in 8:57: "Moreover they [who perish] have even trampled upon his righteous ones," which furthers the clear reference of the righteous as "those who fear God" in 7:[79]. Again in 8:28 Ezra implores God to show mercy to his creation, pleading that God should "think not on those who have lived wickedly, in your sight; but remember those who have willingly acknowledged that *you are to be feared*" (emphasis added). Ezra contrasts two ways of life in ch. 8: the life of the wicked (vv. 27, 28), which is characterized by its sins (v. 26) and compared to the ways of cattle (vv. 29, 30), and the life of the righteous, who serve God in truth (v. 26), keep his covenants amid afflictions (v. 27), willingly acknowledge that God is to be feared (v. 28), and have gloriously taught God's law (v. 29), putting their trust in God's glory (v. 30).

Furthermore, the fear of God characterizes the life of the righteous in that fearing God stands parallel to keeping God's law (7:[89], [94]), which determines one's redemption on the day of judgment. On that day, the righteous ones, who fear God, who "laboriously served the Most High" and who "withstood danger every hour to keep the Law of the Lawgiver perfectly" (7:[89]), "shall rejoice with boldness" without the fear of their destruction, "for they hasten to behold the face of him whom they served in life and from whom they are to receive their reward when glorified" (7:[98]). Those who fear God in the present, as manifest in their keeping of the law, will not fear God on the day of judgment. In contrast, the stance of the unrighteous ones, who did not fear God, but "have hated those who fear God," "have shown scorn and have not kept the way of the Most High," and "have despised his Law" (7:[79]), will be just the opposite:

---

69. Longenecker, *2 Esdras*, 49–50. According to Longenecker, 50, the view that the transgressors of the law will be condemned to torment and destruction was shared in the most traditional patterns of Jewish thought and piety, but the revelation of Uriel in 4 Ezra differs in that the transgressors do not have recourse to divine assistance to redeem their doom.

They shall utterly waste way in confusion and be consumed with shame, and shall wither *with fear at seeing the glory of the Most High* before whom they sinned while they were alive, and *before whom they are to be judged in the last times*

7:[87], emphasis added.

Once again, those who do not fear God in the present, as manifest in their despising the law, will fear God on the day of judgment.

Moreover, the fact that fear before the judgment seat of God characterizes the righteous now and the unrighteous on the day of judgment (cf. 12:33) once more emphasizes that fear derives from God's final judgment, whether in the present or at the end of this age. In 4 Ezra the last judgment thereby provides a motivating fear for the people to pursue a righteous life now in order to avoid fearing God in the future. To that end, the nearness of the last judgment is emphasized (8:18, 61), along with the fact that at the last judgment everyone is held accountable for his or her own righteous or unrighteous deeds (7:[105]; 8:33). In so doing, Ezra instructs the people to adopt the eschatological frame of reference by looking to the future, rather than focusing on the present in order to forsake evil and pursue righteous deeds (cf. 7:16):[70]

Then land was given but you and your fathers committed iniquity and did not keep the ways which the Most High commanded you. And because he is *a righteous judge*, in due time he took from you what he had given ... If you, then, will rule over your minds and discipline your hearts, you shall be kept alive, and after death you shall obtain mercy. For after death *the judgment will come*, when we shall live again; and then the names of the righteous will become manifest, and the deeds of the ungodly will be disclosed

14:31–5, emphasis added.

It is this acknowledgment of the coming last judgment and of the accountability of everyone for their own deeds that motivates the people to leave their fathers' iniquity and to keep God's commands. For this reason, the fear of God, because it derives from God's judgment, not only characterizes the righteous, but also functions as a motivation for the righteous life.[71]

---

70. Ibid., 46.

71. As Longenecker (ibid., 104–7) argues, 4 Ezra resembles other popular Jewish perspectives in that it shares the same expectation for the vindication of the righteous in the future. For example, 1QWar Scroll (1QM) eagerly expects that the righteous will take part in the eschatological battle of the Sons of Light against the Sons of Darkness and eventually establish the reign of God. As in 4 Ezra, the judgment of God is thus also an important theme in 1QM, where the salvation of the people of God is brought about through the destruction of the evil ones (1QM XI, 13–14; XII, 5; XIII, 15; XIV, 7), who are described as the Sons/lot of Darkness (1QM I, 1, 10, 11, 16; XIII, 5, 16; XIV, 17) and as the army/lot/angels of Belial (1QM I, 1, 5, 13, 15; XI, 8; XIII, 2, 11–12; XIV, 9–10; XV, 2–3; XVIII, 1, 3). Nevertheless, 4 Ezra stands in marked contrast with 1QM in that the former stresses that the triumph of the righteous comes exclusively by means of divine initiative and is not assisted in any way by their own actions.

In this regard, 6 Ezra bears some obvious resemblances to 4 Ezra.[72] They are both written in a time of crisis, they both aim to explain the present tragic events, they both project the eschatological vindication of God, and they both exhort the addressees to persevere in the face of extreme suffering. In fact, the first command in 6 Ezra does not introduce a new audience, but is intended to be addressed to the people of 4 Ezra 14.[73] In this way, the author of 6 Ezra appropriates the motifs of 4 Ezra as addressed to the Jewish community of the late first century CE and applies them to the Christian community in the late third century CE.[74] In this regard, the exhortation of the Christian redactor in 16:67, "Behold, God is the judge, fear him! Cease from your sins, and forget your iniquities, never to commit them again; so God will lead you forth and deliver you from all tribulation," stands in continuity with the same motifs in 4 Ezra. It summarizes the significance of the fear of God as a characteristic of the righteous deriving from final judgment, and its function of motivating the righteous life that were already present in the Jewish text.[75]

According to Longenecker, 105, 4 Ezra "wants to encourage quiet living among the people, whose sights should be set not on the reversal of their portion in the present age of evil but on the hope that they will be among those who are judged worthy to inherit the next world of marvel." In contrast, 1QM describes the vindication of God's people as an overthrow of evil and the establishment of justice which is accomplished through an organized rebellion and war against the army of Belial, in which the righteous themselves lend assistance or play a part (1QM I, 5; XII, 5). This battle is further described in 1QM II, 10–14; XIX, 4 as a war (of God's people) against other nations. In this regard, it is noteworthy that 1QM does not contain any explicit references to the fear of God; references to fear only appear in exhortations not to fear the enemy, so, e.g., "Listen Israel, those of you approaching for battle against your enemies. *Do not be afraid*, and may your hearts not fail; *do not fear* and *do not tremble* in front of them, for your God goes with you to do battle for you against your enemies to save you" (1QM X, 3–4, emphasis added); "*Do not be afraid* or [tremble, may your hearts not weaken], do not be startled, or hesitate in front of them" (1QM XV, 8, emphasis added). Several scholars, such as Fitzmyer ("Qumrân," 273-7), Gnilka ("2 Cor 6:14–7:1," 54–61), and Klinzing (*Umdeutung*, 172-5), claim 1QM to be one of the backgrounds of 2 Cor 6:14–7:1 based on its reference to Belial and the text's dualism, but they fail to recognize that in respect to the role of the fear of God in eschatological redemption the two documents differ as much as they are alike.

72. Longenecker, *2 Esdras*, 114.

73. Ibid., 112.

74. Ibid., 113. Longenecker, 113–14, lists the brutal experiences that the community faces, the exhortation to the community to endurance, God's deliverance of the righteous, and the commandment to obey God's law as the overlapping themes of 4 Ezra and 6 Ezra. Longenecker, 114, mentions the call to fear God's judgment as a theme in 6 Ezra, but does not make a connection to 4 Ezra.

75. Bergren (*Sixth Ezra*, 23) argues that the exhortation in 16:67 is not directed toward the persecutors outside the community as depicted in 16:68–70, but "[r]ather the intended objects of this advice seem to be individuals within the author's own community." In other words, the exhortation functions as ethical and moral instruction toward the people within the community.

3. 4 Ezra as Background for the Fear of God in 2 Cor 7:1

As Bruce W. Longenecker comments, "*4 Ezra* might best be described as an affirmation of God's justice and sovereignty."[76] As an expression of this divine justice God's future vindication of the righteous appears together with God's condemnation of the evil ones and, as a result, God's judgment becomes a motivation for the people of God to pursue a righteous life. The fear of God in 4 Ezra, which appears in the judgment context, functions as a characteristic of the righteous and their law-abiding life. Moreover, 4 Ezra shows that those who fear God in the present, as manifest in their keeping of the law, will not fear God on the day of judgment (7:[98]). In contrast, the stance of the unrighteous ones, who did not fear God in the present and despised his law will fear God on the day of judgment (7:[87]). Again, there are not two kinds of "fear," but only one fear, that derives from the final judgment of God and functions differently in relationship to two types of persons and times in which this fear is experienced. The motivational feature of the fear of God is more deliberately expressed in 6 Ezra, which shares not only the same conviction concerning God's sovereignty in the eschaton, but also the same practical intention toward the community. It is thus appropriate to argue that the understanding of the fear of God and its function in 4 Ezra is continued on in the understanding of the fear of God in 6 Ezra, as summarized in 16:67: the fear of God derives from the last judgment and becomes a motivation to pursue a righteous life.[77] Fourth and Sixth Ezra thus add to our map of the Second Temple Jewish understanding of the fear of God in that they show how the fear of God's judgment is consistently portrayed as a motivation for obedience among the righteous in both Jewish and Christian traditions. Our examination of the Testaments of the Twelve Patriarchs will further support this observation.

V. *The Testaments of the Twelve Patriarchs*

The last text this work will explore is the Testaments of the Twelve Patriarchs, which also share many similarities with 2 Cor 6:14–7:1.[78] The fear of God occurs 18 times

---

76. Longenecker, *2 Esdras*, 94.

77. In addition, another similarity between 4 Ezra and 2 Cor 6:14–7:1 appears besides the fear of God. The exhortation in 4 Ezra 7:[76], "do not be associated with those who have shown scorn, nor number yourself among those who are tormented," shows a strong similarity to Paul's exhortation in 2 Cor 6:14–16a. "Those who have shown scorn" alludes back to the description of the wicked ones in 4 Ezra 7:22–24, (cf. 7:[79], [81]) and "those who are tormented" alludes back to the description of the wicked ones in 7:[72] (cf. 7:[80], [84], [86]; 8:59; 9:9).

78. For example, Gnilka ("2 Cor 6:14–7:1," 61) argues that the author of 2 Cor 6:14–7:1 is a Christian who "has been considerably influenced by traditions which are active in Qumran and the *Test. XII Patr.*, as is proved by a number of parallel concepts and ideas." Gnilka does not include the fear of God as one of the parallel concepts between the two

in the Testaments, mostly in the paraenetic sections, in which each patriarch exhorts his children to avoid sin and to exemplify various virtues (see T. Reub. 4:1; T. Sim. 3:4 [2x]; T. Levi 13:1, 7; T. Jud. 16:2 [2x]; T. Zeb. 10:5; T. Dan 6:1; T. Gad 3:2; 5:4; T. Jos. 2:4; 5:2; 11:1; T. Benj. 3:3, 4 [2x]; 10:10).[79] The fear of God is significant in the Testaments in that it not only appears mostly in the paraenetic parts, where the emphasis of the Testaments lies,[80] but also functions as a substitute for the love of God in the twofold commandment that encapsulates the ethics of the Testaments.[81]

1. The Jewish and Christian Backgrounds of the Testaments

One important issue that needs to be addressed prior to the examination of the fear of God is the question of whether the Testaments are a Jewish document

---

documents, however, but regards it as a stylistic modification of the redactor. Also Tomson ("Christ, Belial, and Women," 113) argues that Paul's contrast between Belial and Christ in 2 Cor 6:15a directly recalls T. Lev 19:1. All passages from the Testaments of the Twelve Patriarchs are quoted from H. C. Kee, "Testaments of the Twelve Patriarchs: A New Translation and Introduction," in *The Old Testament Pseudepigrapha Vol. 1*, ed. James H. Charlesworth, 3rd ed. (Peabody, MA: Hendrickson, 2013), 775–828.

79. According to Kugler (*Testaments*, 12–15), each testament contains all or part of a standard introduction, which includes a statement of the patriarch's final words, an announcement of his impending death, and a statement of his age at the time of death. Afterwards there are three parts to the main body: the patriarch's biographical account (hagiography); the patriarch's commandments and exhortations to his audience (ethics); and the patriarch's prediction of the future of Israel (eschatology). In conclusion, there is a description of the patriarch's death and burial. The amount of material devoted to each part varies, but the general pattern appears in all of the Testaments. Cf. H. Balz ("φοβέω, φοβέομαι, φόβος, δέος," *TDNT* 9:205) argues that the Testaments develops the OT theme of the fear of God in many formula-like expressions.

80. Hollander, *Joseph*, 6. Hollander, 6–7, argues that, in contrast to the paraenesis sections in the Testaments, eschatology is not their focal point since eschatological verses are few and do not play an important role in the documents, but rather the ethical commandment is the focus of the author. So too Harm W. Hollander and Marinus de Jonge, *The Testaments of the Twelve Patriarchs: A Commentary*, SVTP 8 (Leiden: Brill, 1985), 32: "the Testaments have to be regarded as a collection of exhortatory writings, and that the ethical section forms the centre of the individual testaments." However, because the context of the Testaments shows that the fear of God, which lies at the heart of the ethical exhortations, derives from the eschatological judgment and functions as motivation for ethical teaching, Hollander's argument that eschatology is not the focal point in the Testaments is less plausible. As we will see, in the Testaments, the ethical commandments are inextricably linked to eschatology by means of the motif of the fear of God.

81. Hollander and de Jonge, *Twelve Patriarchs*, 32: "The final exhortations are concerned with God's commandments, often summed up under the two headings of fear of the Lord and love to one's neighbour."

from the second century BCE that contains later Christian interpolations,[82] or a Christian product from about CE 200 that retains Jewish influences.[83] Although much ink has been spilled on this issue, scholars have not reached an agreement, mainly because of the difficulty of distinguishing between the Jewish and Christian traditions in the text without the aid of any comparative textual evidence from an outside Christian circle.[84] Moreover, because the Jewish and Christian traditions are so closely interwoven in the text, any conclusions based solely on a literary analysis remain merely a matter of *probability* rather than *certainty*. In this regard, Marinus de Jonge, who argues that one should take a literature-critical approach to the problem instead of a text-critical one, concludes as follows:

> We are not able to prove that the *Testaments* were *composed* in Christian circles in the second half of the second century; they may also be the outcome of a thorough and to a considerable degree consistent redaction of an earlier Jewish writing. But it is extremely difficult to find convincing proof for the existence of such a document, nor are we in a position to determine its contents.[85]

Therefore the aim of our work is not to determine the origin of the current text, nor to detect Christian interpolations in the text, nor to reconstruct an original Jewish *Vorlage*.[86] Instead, based on the mixture of Jewish and Christian traditions in the document, the present work attempts to understand the *function of the fear of God* in the paraenetic sections of the Testaments in their current form and to compare it with that of the fear of God in 2 Cor 7:1.[87]

---

82. Jürgen Becker, *Die Testamente der Zwölf Patriarchen*, JSHRZ 1 (Gütersloh: Mohn, 1974), 25; Kee, "Testaments," 777–8.

83. Hollander and de Jonge, *Twelve Patriarchs*, 82–85; Marinus de Jonge, *Pseudepigrapha of the Old Testament as Part of Christian Literature: The Case of the Testaments of the Twelve Patriarchs and the Greek Life of Adam and Eve*, SVTP 18 (Leiden: Brill, 2003), 84–106.

84. Marinus de Jonge, "The Two Great Commandments in the Testaments of the Twelve Patriarchs," *NT* 44, (2002): 372.

85. Marinus de Jonge, "The Testaments of the Twelve Patriarchs: Christian and Jewish. A Hundred Years after Friedrich Schnapp," in *Jewish Eschatology, Early Christian Christology, and the Testaments of the Twelve Patriarchs: Collected Essays of Marinus de Jonge*, NovTSup 63 (Leiden: Brill, 1991), 41, original emphasis.

86. For a more detailed summary of arguments regarding the date and origin of the Testaments of the Twelve Patriarchs, see Kugler, *Testaments*, 31–8 and James R. Davila, "Testaments of the Twelve Patriarchs," *Old Testament Pseudepigrapha—School of Divinity, University of St Andrews*, February 1997, [accessed 1 February 2016] https://www.st-andrews.ac.uk/divinity/rt/otp/abstracts/testoftwelve/.

87. See too now, Yulin Liu (*Temple Purity in 1–2 Corinthians*, WUNT 2/343 [Tübingen: Mohr Siebeck, 2013], 52–3), who includes the Testaments in his examination of the Second Temple context of the theme of temple purity in 1, 2 Corinthians.

Despite their dissension about their origin, most scholars agree that the paraenesis of the Testaments, like the document as a whole, contains *both Jewish and Christian traits*.[88] This mixed character of the paraenesis thus serves as a bridge that connects early Jewish and Christian ethics.[89] In this regard, de Jonge, who argues that the Testaments are a Christian product, acknowledges the continuity between the Hellenistic-Jewish and Christian paraenesis.[90] In other words, albeit without maintaining that the Testaments consist solely of Jewish documents, one should not deny the Jewish character of their paraenesis. Therefore, the fear of God, which plays an essential role in the paraenesis of the Testaments, is also an important aspect of both Jewish and Christian tradition.

2. Ethics and the Fear of God in the Testaments

The ethics of the Testaments, to which the notion of the fear of God is related, are encapsulated in what is called the "double" or twofold commandment in the Testament of Naphtali:

> The commandments of the Lord are *double*, and they are to be fulfilled with regularity
>
> 8:7, emphasis added.

---

88. R. Travers Herford, *Talmud and Apocrypha: A Comparative Study of the Jewish Ethical Teaching in the Rabbinical and Non-Rabbinical Sources in the Early Centuries* (London: Soncino, 1933), 238-40; de Jonge, *Pseudepigrapha*, 102-5; Kugler, *Testaments*, 17, 23; Hollander, *Joseph*, 9.

89. Likewise, R. H. Charles (*The Greek Versions of the Testaments of the Twelve Patriarchs: Edited from Nine Mss.: Together with the Variants of the Armenian and Slavonic Versions and some Hebrew Fragments* [Oxford: Clarendon, 1908], xvii) argues that the ethical teachings in the Testaments help to bridge the chasm between the ethics of the OT and the NT.

90. De Jonge, *Pseudepigrapha*, 103. De Jonge, 103-4, argues that the ethical pronouncements of the Testaments might have received their present form at the final molding of the document in Christian circles, but because of the overlapping features between Jewish and Christian ethics, it is hard to distinguish the two traditions within the mixed nature of the paraenesis. So too, idem, "Christian and Jewish," 241-3; idem, "The Main Issues in the Study of the Testaments of the Twelve Patriarchs," in *Jewish Eschatology, Early Christian Christology, and the Testaments of the Twelve Patriarchs: Collected Essays of Marinus de Jonge*, NovTSup 63 (Leiden: Brill, 1991), 160-3; Kugler, *Testaments*, 37-9; Davila, *Provenance*, 2-4. As Hollander and de Jonge (*Twelve Patriarchs*, 47) argue, "It is not easy (and probably impossible) to determine the actual 'Sitz im Leben' of the material or the situation for which the author wrote more precisely." This work will therefore focus on the overlapping characteristics of Jewish and Christian features that appear in the paraenetic sections of the Testaments and which, as we will see, are related to and summarized by the motif of the fear of God.

> And there are the *two* commandments: Unless they are performed in proper sequence they leave one open to the greatest sin. It is the same with the other commandments
>
> 8:9, emphasis added.

Regarding the content of the twofold commandment in the Testament of Naphtali, H. C. Kee comments:

> No indication is given as to which are the "two" commandments, and thus what the correct sequence of obeying them is. One might infer from 8:1–8 that they are (1) loving God and (2) loving neighbor. This sequence would then mean to give obligation to God priority over responsibility to fellow humans.[91]

In view of this assumption regarding the content of the twofold commandments, de Jonge argues that the Testaments integrate the patriarchs' ethical instruction together with the fulfillment of the double commandment to love God and neighbor (Deut 6:5), as seen elsewhere in the Testaments:[92]

> Keep the Law of God, my children; achieve integrity; live without malice, not tinkering with God's commands or your neighbor's affairs. *Love the Lord and your neighbor*; be compassionate toward poverty and sickness
>
> T. Iss. 5:1–2, emphasis added.[93]

It is noteworthy that the fear of God can also appear in the context of this twofold commandment as a substitution for the commandment to love God:

> *Fear the Lord and love your neighbor.* Even if the spirits of Belial[94] seek to derange you with all sorts of wicked oppression, they will not dominate you, any more than they dominated Joseph, my brother. For the person *who fears God and loves his neighbor* cannot be plagued by the spirit of Belial since he is sheltered by the fear of God
>
> T. Benj. 3:3–4, emphasis added.[95]

---

91. Kee, "Testaments," 814n8c.

92. De Jonge, *Pseudepigrapha*, 18. Kugler, *Testaments*, 15. These commandments also occur separately throughout the Testaments: to love (fear) God (T. Levi 13:1; T. Zeb. 10:5; T. Dan 6:1 (cf. T. Gad 3:2; 5:2, 4; T. Benj. 10:10); to love one's neighbor (T. Reub. 6:9; T. Sim. 4:7; T. Zeb. 8:5; T. Gad 6:1, 3; 7:7; T. Jos. 17:2).

93. Also see T. Iss. 7:6–7; T. Dan 5:1–3.

94. Kee ("Testaments") uses "Beliar" in his text, but for the sake of continuity within our argument, we will use "Belial" unless otherwise noted (Theodore J. Lewis, "Belial," *ABD* 1:654–6).

95. Also, see T. Jos. 11:1, which Kugler (*Testaments*, 18) regards as an example of the twofold commandment.

In these passages two features indicate that the fear of God substitutes for the traditional first command of the twofold commandment, i.e., to love God, as its conceptual and interchangeable parallel. First, here too, as in T. Iss. 5:1 (see above) and T. Dan 5:1, the twofold commandment, now including the command to fear God, once again functions as a summary of what it means to keep God's law.[96] Likewise, in T. Jos. 11:1 to fear God is equated with "one's doing the Law of the Lord." Second, in T. Benj. 3:3–4 fearing God as part of the twofold commandment is given as the antidote to being persecuted by Belial. This parallels the fact that in the Testaments the patriarchs explain that Belial will flee when their audience follows the patriarchs' example of piety and truth by loving God and other people (T. Iss. 7:6–7) and of observing the Lord's commandments by loving God and others (T. Dan 5:1–3).

As the texts above indicate, the role of Belial is particularly important in the Testaments with regard to its ethics since Belial forms the dualistic counterpart to God, so that the patriarchs repeatedly exhort their audience to make a choice between keeping God's commandments and siding with Belial.[97] For example, this

---

96. Hollander (*Joseph*, 93) comments that the first command, to love God, is put into practice by keeping God's moral commandments.

97. In the Qumran literature, Belial continued to be used as a reference to humanity's wickedness and death in relationship to a general sense of "evil" (cf. 1QH^a XII, 10, 12–13; XIV, 21–2; XV, 3–4), but was also transformed into the personal name of the head of the demonic, evil forces in the world who stands over against God and his righteous heavenly forces (cf. 1QM I, 1; XIII, 10–12; 1QS I, 18, 23–4; II, 5, 19; III, 20–5; CD IV, 13, 15; V, 17–19; VIII, 2; XII, 2–3). Although the specific function of Belial differs slightly according to each document (e.g., Belial functions in the War Scroll as the head of the army who will be in the final war against the sons of light, whereas in the Damascus Document Belial takes on a role as an agent of God's punishment against evildoers), the fate of Belial remains nevertheless uncontested. Belial rules only for a limited duration and the final judgment will bring Belial and his force to an end (Lewis, *ABD* 1:654–6; Michael Mach, "Demons," *EDSS* 1:189–92; Segal, *Jubilees*, 251–6; Ryan E. Stokes, "Belial," *EDEJ* 435–6; Annette Steudel, "God and Belial," in *The Dead Sea Scrolls Fifty Years After Their Discovery: Proceedings of the Jerusalem Congress, July 20–5, 1997*, ed. Lawrence H. Schiffman et al. [Jerusalem: Israel Exploration Society in cooperation with the Shrine of the Book, Israel Museum, 2000], 334–40). Thus, Steudel ("God and Belial," 335) argues that the Qumran community understood their own present time as being part of the last period of history, which underlies the rule of Belial (1QS I, 18, 23; 4Q174 III, 8; CD XII, 2). Segal (*Jubilees*, 253) also points out, in Qumran literature human beings are unable to choose between good and evil, and anybody who is under the "dominion of Belial," is by definition a sinner (e.g., 1QM XIV, 9; XVIII, 1; 1QS I, 18, 24; II, 18; III, 21–3). This notion shows a difference from that of the Testaments, where the audience is continuously exhorted to make the right decision against Belial and his forces (T. Levi 19:1; T. Iss. 6:1; 7:6–7; T. Dan 5:1; T. Benj. 3:3–4). In other words, even though the Testaments and the Qumran literature share similar dualistic views, their understanding of human responsibility differs. In this regard, as we have noted already, the fear of God does

dualism appears in the choices between "light or darkness, the Law of the Lord or the works of Belial" (T. Levi 19:1); "the spirit of truth or the spirit of error" (T. Jud. 20:1); "abandoning the commands of the Lord or allying themselves with Belial" (T. Iss. 6:1); "fearing the Lord or [siding with] Satan" (T. Dan 6:1); "the Law of the Lord or the law of Belial" (T. Naph. 2:6); the decision "to hold fast God's will or [to hold fast] the will of Belial" (T. Naph. 3:1); "to perform justice and every law of the Most High or to be led astray by the spirit of hatred" (T. Gad 3:1); "keeping the Law of the Lord or paying attention to evil" (T. Ash 6:3);[98] and "fearing God or being plagued by the spirit of Belial" (T. Benj. 3:4). Furthermore, the choice between these dual forces is crucial because it determines one's destiny in the eschatological judgment. The patriarchs warn those who ally with Belial and act according to the spirits of error that they will face condemnation in the end: "In the second [heaven] are the armies arrayed for the day of judgment to work vengeance on the spirits of error and of Belial" (T. Levi 3:3); "There shall no more be Belial's spirit of error, because he will be thrown into eternal fire" (T. Jud. 25:3). Therefore, in the Testaments "what is now real and valid for those who fear the Lord and obey him completely will become full reality in the future when Belial and his spirits will suffer a final defeat."[99]

In addition to its function as a summary of keeping God's commandments, the fact that the exhortations to the righteous are closely connected to the warnings against Belial and the evil spirits,[100] and that Belial is linked to the motif of condemnation, serve to elucidate the same two features of the fear of God in the Testaments that we have seen in the other Second Temple texts: first, the fear of God derives from the eschatological judgment, by which Belial (and those who ally with him) will be destroyed;[101] second, the people have to choose sides between

---

not play a significant part in the Qumran passages here and those mentioned above (cf. note 71), while it is essential in the Testaments. Therefore, the fear of God is significant in the ethics of the Testaments (even on a par with loving God in the great, double commandment!) since it motivates the people to righteous life and thus brings about the *actual, decisive* difference in the eschatological judgment.

98. In the Testament of Asher, "to pay attention to evil" (6:3) is linked to "to imitate the spirits of error" (6:2), which refers back to T. Asher 1:8–9: "But if the mind is disposed toward evil, all of its deeds are wicked; driving out the good, it accepts the evil and is overmastered by *Belial*, who, even when good is undertaken, presses the struggle so as to make the aim of his action into *evil*, since the *devil's* storehouse is filled with the venom of the *evil spirit*" (emphasis added).

99. Hollander and de Jonge, *Twelve Patriarchs*, 45.

100. Ibid.

101. Testament of Levi 3:9 further supports this connection between the fear of God and judgment, "So when the Lord looks upon us we all *tremble*, Even the heavens and earth and the abysses tremble before the presence of his majesty" (emphasis added). Kee ("Testaments," 789n3) comments that this passage alludes to Isa 13:9–13, where the shaking occurs on the day of the Lord, i.e., the day of judgment.

God and Belial, and the fear of God functions as the motivation for them to make the right choice.[102] These features of the fear of God are well summarized in the Testament of Benjamin, to which we now turn our attention.

3. The Fear of God in the Testament of Benjamin

The Testament of Benjamin, as the last of the testaments in the sequence, is important with regard to the ethics of the whole, because it "gives a résumé of the

---

102. It is appropriate to mention the works of Philo at this point because Philo shows similarities with the Testaments in his understanding of the fear of God. Philo refers to fear in a negative emotional sense as related to threats, dangers, etc. (e.g., *Unchangeable* 64; 71; *Creation* 142; *Alleg. Interp.* 2. 8; 3. 37, 113; *Heir* 23; etc.), but he also uses it in a positive sense, in which case the fear of God functions similarly to the Testaments of the Twelve Patriarchs. For example, in *Unchangeable* 69 fear functions as one of the two essential exhortations of the law in parallel to the love of God: "And therefore it seems to me that with the two aforesaid maxims, 'God is a man,' and 'God is not as a man,' he has linked two other principles closely connected and consequent on them, namely *fear and love*. For I observe that all the exhortations to piety in the law refer either to *our loving or our fearing the Existent*. And thus to love Him is the most suitable for those into whose conception of the Existent no thought of human parts or passions enters, who pay Him the honour meet for God for His own sake only. *To fear* is most suitable to the others" (emphasis added). Here, fear and love show one's proper response to God, but different from the Testaments, for Philo "fear" is a lesser response to God than "love." Fear also appears in a similar context in *Migration* 21, which is a comment on Gen 42:18, but here too fearing God describes a stage of a man "who is not yet capable of loving God." Of interest too is the fact that both Jerome Murphy-O'Connor ("Philo and 2 Cor 6:14–7:1," in *Keys to Second Corinthians: Revisiting the Major Issues* [Oxford; New York: Oxford University Press, 2010], 121–39) and Betz ("2 Cor 6:14–7:1," 93–4) observe similar features between Philo and 2 Cor 6:14–7:1, such as dualistic concepts, the reference to Lev 26:12, and the concept of God's dwelling among his people. Murphy-O'Connor argues that because there is no evidence that the Qumran materials, which parallel 2 Cor 6:14–7:1, were in circulation outside of the Essene movement, it is less plausible that the passage carries Essene influence; rather, the parallels point to an influence by the Hellenistic Judaism represented by Philo. For according to Murphy-O'Connor, the parallels to Philo in 2 Cor 6:14–7:1 indicate that the language and ideas of 6:14–7:1 are perfectly at home in Hellenistic Judaism and therefore the passage contains a significant number of Pauline elements (contra Betz, who makes a similar observation but concludes that the passage is anti-Pauline). Neither Murphy-O'Connor nor Betz mention the fear of God in their arguments. Nevertheless, the parallels between 2 Cor 6:14–7:1 and Philo do not exclude the parallels between 2 Cor 6:14–7:1 and Qumran texts, or *vice versa*. On the contrary, Paul's use of notions and features that overlap with other Second Temple Jewish documents indicates that he was in conversation with the same constellation of concepts, rather than with one particular document or stream of the tradition. All the works of Philo are quoted from Philo, *Philo*, trans. F. H. Colson and G. H. Whitaker, Loeb Classical Library 226–7, 247, 261, 275, 289, 320, 341, 363, 379 (Cambridge, MA: Harvard University Press, 2014).

author's ethical ideas and of his ideas about the future of Israel and the Gentiles, elements which are found throughout the preceding testaments."[103] As we have seen above, in T. Benj. 3:3–4 the fear of God appears twice, both times as part of the twofold commandment, the keeping of which is promised to provide protection against Belial:

> *Fear the Lord* and *love your neighbor*. Even if the spirits of *Belial* seek to derange you with all sorts of wicked oppression, they will not dominate you, any more than they dominated Joseph, my brother. For the person *who fears God* and *loves his neighbor* cannot be plagued by the spirit of *Belial* since he is sheltered by *the fear of God* (emphasis added).

Conversely, the author emphasizes that God's condemnation is the consequence for those who align themselves with Belial. For example, the author exhorts the people to "flee from the evil of Belial" (7:1), and presents Cain as the example of someone who obeys Belial (7:3–4). Then the author warns that those who are like Cain in obeying Belial in their moral corruption and in their hate for their brother will "be punished with a similar judgment [as Cain]" (7:5), and that this judgment will be upon all people (10:9). In the last chapter of the testament the author consequently exhorts the people to "keep the Law of the Lord and his commandments" (10:3), which are exemplified in "doing truth to one's neighbor" (10:2).[104] In this context the author once again mentions the judgment that will be upon Israel and all the nations in the last days, when the Lord first "judges Israel" for the wrong she has committed (10:8) and then does the same for all the nations (10:9). In this regard, de Jonge comments that T. Benj. 10:

> not only characterizes and summarizes the ethical teaching of the *Testaments*, it also establishes a clear connection between obedience to the teaching of the patriarchs and receiving, together with them, a share in the salvation that God 'will reveal to all the nations.'[105]

This future judgment thus becomes a motivation for the audience as the author exhorts them to be with "those who fear the Lord" on the day of judgment (10:10).

As this text illustrates, and as we have noted above, it is difficult to describe the Testaments as "Jewish" or "Christian" based on the commandments in the

---

103. Hollander and de Jonge, *Twelve Patriarchs*, 411.

104. "According to the Testaments, love for one's neighbour is the summing up of the demands of the law, which is first of all understood as a collection of ethical commands" Ibid., 418.

105. De Jonge, "Commandments," 381. De Jonge argues that the final testamentary chapter in the T. Benj. is clearly Christian, but also admits that it is hard to remove the clearly Christian passages from the text as an interpolation.

paraenesis because the ethical instructions and exhortations in the Testaments are not quoted directly from the Torah, but are rather a general paraenesis intended to indicate "how God's will, as manifested in the Torah, should be done in concrete, everyday circumstances."[106] Instead, the paraenesis is to be seen as an overlapping bridge between the Jewish and Christian traditions embedded in the texts.[107] It is all the more significant, therefore, that the fear of God lies at the heart of these overlapping ethical instructions and functions as a summary and essence of the paraenesis that is equally valid for both traditions.

4. The Testaments as Background for the Fear of God in 2 Cor 7:1

De Jonge argues that, given its interwoven Jewish and Christian elements, the ethics of the Testaments are important for an understanding of both traditions in that they show:

> that the *Testaments of the Twelve Patriarchs* tell a fascinating story about the struggle within early Christianity to understand the relevance of those parts of the Jewish scriptures dealing with the period of the patriarchs (and of Jewish interpretations of Genesis) for Christians.[108]

From this perspective, the twofold commandment, which is "the most adequate expression of the law of God,"[109] rightfully summarizes the ethics of the Testaments and in so doing functions as a characteristic of both its Jewish and Christian backgrounds. For the purpose of our study, it is therefore significant that the fear of God lies at the heart of the twofold commandment and functions as an example

---

106. Ibid., 380n15; cf. 385, 389. Kugler (*Testaments*, 17) argues that the twofold commandment to love God and neighbor is the summary of the law given through both the teaching of Moses and the teachings and life of Jesus. Kugler, 19, thus argues that, in this sense, Joseph is described in the Testaments as the role model who accomplishes God's commandment perfectly, and is thus portrayed like Jesus in the Testaments (see T. Zeb. 2:2; 3:3; T. Gad 2:3; T. Benj. 3:8). For a more detailed argument on this issue, see Hollander, *Joseph*. Hollander, 94, argues that Joseph as the figure in the ethical passages (such as, T. Reub. 4:8–10; T. Zeb. 8:4–5; T. Sim. 4:3–7; 5:1; T. Lev. 13; T. Benj. 3:1–6; 4:1–5; 5:1–5; 6:1–7; 7:1–8:3) shows the dependence of the Testaments on the OT/LXX and also reflects the typical Hellenistic background of the Testaments. Hollander, 97, thus concludes that, "In any case, the question whether the Testaments are originally Christian and Jewish will have to be studied also in the context of the analysis of early Christian paraenesis in its interplay with Hellenistic and Jewish ethics."

107. Kugler, *Testaments*, 17: "Patriarchal moral instruction is implicitly identified with Hellenistic (and Hellenistic-Jewish and Christian) ethical norms."

108. De Jonge, "Commandments," 391.

109. Ibid., 383. De Jonge argues that Gen 49:14–15 LXX influenced the author in this passage.

of and motivation for a righteous life. Paul's argument in 2 Cor 7:1 and its context clearly fit within the trajectory of this Jewish and Christian tradition. Moreover, the fear of God and the righteous life, which the fear of God motivates, are contrasted with the evil life that is allied to Belial, just as Paul's admonition in 7:1 forms a counterpart to his exhortation to flee Belial in 6:15.[110] For the fear of God derives from the judgment that will be upon not only Belial and the wicked,[111] but also upon all nations, including Israel, and, as a result, functions as the motivation for the people to pursue a righteous life (cf. 2 Cor 5:10–11). These features regarding the fear of God, in addition to the dualistic view of Belial and God, are thus conceptually parallel to Paul's argument in 2 Cor 6:14–7:1.

VI. *The Fear of God within the Spectrum of Second Temple Judaism*

Our studies of the fear of God in these representative Second Temple Jewish documents lead to an important cumulative result. Our sample by no means represents a complete range of Jewish perspectives in the Second Temple Period, but it is sufficient to map out the spectrum of both similarity and diversity that existed in the Jewish understanding and use of the motif of the fear of God at the time.

The Psalms of Solomon show that the fear of God functions as a characteristic of the righteous in this age and derives from the awareness of the judgment that will be the fate of the wicked. At the same time, the fear of God in the Psalms of Solomon also functions as the characteristic of the eschatological reign of the Messiah and applies to all people (including the nations), motivating them to pursue righteousness. Jubilees, on the other hand, maps out the other pole on the spectrum, in which the fear of God is not expressed explicitly with regard to motivating or characterizing the life of the righteous. Instead, the judgment motif functions in Jubilees as a motivation for the righteous. Jubilees demonstrates that, even when only judgment is explicitly mentioned as the motivation for a righteous life, the assumed link between the fear of God and his judgment indicates that the judgment context implies the fear of God. Between these two poles, 4 Ezra, like the Psalms of Solomon, refers to the fear of God that derives from God's judgment and thereby functions as the motivation for the people; but, as in Jubilees, its function is only expressed implicitly. Nevertheless, 4 Ezra shows that those who fear God in the present will not fear God on the day of judgment, but those who do not fear God in the present will fear God on that day. This observation further supports

---

110. Thus, Hollander and de Jonge, *Twelve Patriarchs*, 47: "The dualistic elements in the exhortation stress the importance of making fundamental decisions in choosing between good and evil, God and Beliar."

111. In the Testaments, "Beliar's defeat is connected with Jesus' coming on earth as well as with his parousia, both aspects of God's final intervention in the future as seen from the standpoint of the patriarchs." Ibid., 45.

that there are not two kinds of "fear," but only one fear that derives from the final judgment of God and functions differently in relationship to two types of person and times in which this fear is experienced. The motivational function of the fear of God was more directly expressed in 6 Ezra, which enabled us to see the way in which the Christian redactor used the fear of God more deliberately as the motivation for the righteous. Lastly, the Testaments of the Twelve Patriarchs show that the understanding of the fear of God, as a summary of what it means to keep God's law, in its connection to the judgment of God, and regarding its function as the motivation for a righteous life in opposition to the temptations and rule of Belial are constituent aspects of the fear of God within both Jewish and Christian traditions. The fear of God in Second Temple Judaism thus consistently appears in the context of God's judgment and often functions as the motivation for a righteous life. Furthermore, the Christian redaction of the Jewish documents of 4 Ezra and 6 Ezra, as well as the Christian adaption of the Testaments of the Twelve Patriarchs, implies that the function of fear as a motivation for the righteous might appear more explicitly in later Christian redaction.

As this examination also highlights, and as will become clear as we turn back to 2 Cor 6:14–7:1, Paul, too, participates in these ongoing Jewish conversations concerning the function of the fear of God in the life of the righteous. For as an extension of what George J. Brooke rightly argues concerning the parallels between Paul and the Qumran literature, the close parallels between 2 Cor 6:14–7:1 and the Second Temple Jewish literature:

> should not be read as indicating a direct or indirect line of tradition; rather, it is better to suppose that such parallels demonstrate most closely how both sets of literature ... are part of a broad spectrum of Jewish literature of the Graeco-Roman world.[112]

These documents therefore provide the continuing conceptual, history-of-tradition context, which began with the OT itself, into which Paul's understanding of the fear of God can be placed. Paul's exhortation in 2 Cor 7:1 to the Corinthians to cleanse themselves "in the fear of God" and its function within his argument are not unfamiliar when read within their Second Temple Jewish context. The texts we examined from within Second Temple Judaism demonstrated that the features and function of the fear of God we encountered in the Law and the Prophets continued on in Paul's Jewish tradition, but as in Paul's own argument, 6 Ezra and the Testaments of the Twelve Patriarchs seem to indicate that the function of the fear of God as a motivation for the righteous is expressed more explicitly in later Christian documents. Moreover, and of particular significance, is the way in which these texts underscored the fact established in the OT traditions that there are not two kinds of "fear," one positive and one negative, but that the same fear functions differently in relationship to two types of persons and times in which this fear is

---

112. Brooke, "Again," 15.

experienced. This was especially evident in 4 Ezra, where it shows that those who fear God in the present, as manifest in their keeping of the law, will not fear God on the day of judgment (7:[98]). In contrast, those who did not fear God in the present, as manifest in their despising of the law, will fear God on the day of judgment.

Hence, Paul's argument in 2 Cor 6:14–7:1 within its own context is in conversation with the contemporary Jewish conceptions of his age regarding the fear of God as they developed the OT tradition in which, as we have seen, the fear of God functioned in similar ways. Against this backdrop, it becomes clear that the meaning and function of the fear of God in Paul's argument in 2 Cor 6:14–7:1 constitute an important example of Paul's use of the OT within its ongoing Jewish tradition, as well as anticipating its later Christian reception. We now turn to investigate the way in which the use and development of the motif of the fear of God in the OT and Second Temple Jewish literature inform our understanding of 2 Cor 6:14–7:1.

Chapter 5

THE FEAR OF GOD WITHIN PAUL'S ESCHATOLOGY

Following Chapter Three's examination of the fear of God in its relevant OT context, and its Second Temple Jewish setting in Chapter Four, this chapter revisits 2 Cor 6:14–7:1. The examination so far has shown that the reference to the fear of God in 5:11 and 7:1 is consistent with the OT both in terms of its meaning and role within the context of judgment and its function of motivating a life of righteousness in view of this divine judgment. These features of the fear of God also appear with different emphases within the spectrum of Second Temple Jewish documents. Against this interpretive backdrop, the task of this chapter is to show how Paul's use of the fear of God reflects his eschatology and, in so doing, reshapes our understanding of his exhortation in 2 Cor 7:1 in light of the immediate context of 6:14–7:1 and contributes to an understanding of the wider argument of the epistle.

I. *The Fear of God and the Integrity of 2 Cor 7:1*

Despite the numerous discussions of the meaning and provenance of 2 Cor 6:14–7:1, very few scholars have addressed the significance of the reference to the fear of God in 7:1, even though its place within the argument of 7:1 plays a decisive rhetorical role in the passage.[1] Moreover, the meaning and significance of the fear

---

1. E.g., Hans Dieter Betz ("2 Cor 6:14–7:1: An Anti-Pauline Fragment?" *JBL* 92 [1973]: 99n78) regards the phrase ἐν φόβῳ θεοῦ as "a non-Pauline phrase, pointing, as in Judaism, to the eschatological judgment," but does not further explain its function or why it must be non-Pauline if it points to the eschatological judgment. Likewise, William J. Webb (*Returning Home: New Covenant and Second Exodus as the Context for 2 Corinthians 6.14–7.1*, JSNTSup 85 [Sheffield: JSOT Press, 1993], 66) recognizes the connection of the fear of God with the new covenant context, but does not further explain the connection. And although William O. Walker Jr. (*Interpolations in the Pauline Letters*, JSNTSup 213 [London: Sheffield Academic Press, 2001], 203–7) examines the other central motifs in 7:1 (i.e., the references to being beloved, the promises, cleansings, defilement, body and spirit, and completing holiness), he does not deal with the fear of God.

of God within 7:1 shed light on the debates surrounding 6:14–7:1 by helping to answer the questions regarding both the *content* and *context* of 2 Cor 6:14–7:1, and hence of its *origin* as well.[2] Before turning to these matters directly, however, it is first necessary to examine how a recognition of the importance of the fear of God in 6:14–7:1 relates to the two main approaches to the text in recent scholarship, i.e., those positing "interpolation theories" and those employing a "salvation-historical hermeneutic."

1. Interpolation Theories

As is well known, many scholars have advocated interpolation theories that regard 2 Cor 6:14–7:1 as deriving from a Pauline or non-Pauline source which has been inserted into Paul's argument with varying degrees of successful integration into its surrounding context. Reimund Bieringer divides the positions regarding 2 Cor 6:14–7:1 into five main categories based on their opinions of the text's *authenticity* (regarding its content) and *integrity* (regarding its fit in the present context): (1) neither authenticity nor integrity; (2) no authenticity but integrity; (3) authenticity but no integrity; (4) authenticity and integrity; and (5) those holding an indecisive position.[3] Other scholars provide different categories for understanding the scholarly positions on 2 Cor 6:14–7:1,[4] but theirs are not far

---

2. James M. Scott ("The Use of Scripture in 2 Corinthians 6.16c–18 and Paul's Restoration Theology," *JSNT* 56 [1994]: 74) lists three categories of ongoing debate regarding 2 Cor 6:14–7:1: its origin, its place in the context, and its interpretation.

3. Reimund Bieringer, "2 Korinther 6,14–7,1 im Kontext des 2. Korintherbriefes. Forschungsüberblick und Versuch eines eigenes Zugangs," in *Studies on 2 Corinthians*, ed. Reimund Bieringer and Jan Lambrecht, BETL 122 (Leuven: Leuven University Press; Peeters, 1994), 551–70. Bieringer, 559, maps out the scholarly positions up to 1994 on a chart that is later updated by Emmanuel Nathan, "Fragmented Theology in 2 Corinthians: The Unsolved Puzzle of 6:14–7:1," in *Theologizing in the Corinthian Conflict: Studies in the Exegesis and Theology of 2 Corinthians*, ed. Bieringer, Reimund et al., BTAS 16 (Leuven: Peeters, 2013), 211–28 (updated chart on p. 222).

4. For example, Walker (*Interpolations*, 199) proposes four categories: (1) composed by Paul specifically for inclusion in its present location in 2 Corinthians, (2) composed by Paul for some other occasion but subsequently included in its present location either by Paul or by someone else, (3) composed by someone other than Paul but included in its present location by Paul, (4) both composed by someone other than Paul and included in its present location by someone other than Paul (not necessarily the same person). Nathan ("Fragmented Theology," 213) categorizes them in a similar way. See too Christoph Heil ("Die Sprache der Absonderung in 2 Kor 6,17 und bei Paulus," in *The Corinthian Correspondence* [Leuven: Leuven University Press, 1996], 718–21) for the same categories. By comparison, Webb (*Returning Home*, 159) argues for three categories: (1) interpolation theories, (2) non-contextual integration theories, (3) contextual integration theories. Webb, 159, thus argues that, "each of these categories suggests a degree of contextual compatibility, ranging from absolutely no contextual integration, an extremely limited integration, to a significant level of integration."

from Bieringer's in that the criteria for their categories can also be condensed into two essential questions, one regarding its *content* ("Who wrote it?") and the other its *context* ("Does it belong in its present location?") of 2 Cor 6:14–7:1.[5] Both questions focus on the internal evidence of the passage since all of the early text witnesses include 2 Cor 6:14–7:1 in its present position.[6] Moreover, William J. Webb has shown that the dominant interpolation theories for 2 Cor 6:14–7:1 have evolved historically from those advocating a Pauline source for the interpolation

---

5. Thus, Nathan, "Fragmented Theology," 213.

6. Despite the numerous debates on 2 Cor 6:14–7:1, the textual evidence shows significant consistency. Gordon D. Fee, "II Corinthians vi. 14–vii. 1 and Food Offered to Idols," *NTS* 23 (1977): 143; Nathan, "Fragmented Theology," 223–4. According to NA[28], the variants of the passage are limited to minor wording differences, and only 6:16b shows phrasal variants, which do not alter the meaning of the text. In 6:16b, there are variants between ὑμεῖς γὰρ ναὸς θεοῦ ἐστε ("for you are the temple of God") in P[46], C, D², F, G, K, Ψ, 630, 1241, 1505; ἡμεῖς γὰρ ναὸς ἐστε θεοῦ ("for we are the temple of God") in ℵ², 0209 (ἐστε ναός); ἡμεῖς γὰρ ναοὶ θεοῦ ἐσμεν ("for we are the temples of God") in ℵ (original reading of a correction), 0243, 1739; ἡμεῖς γὰρ ναὸς θεοῦ ἐσμεν ("for we are the temple of God") in B, D (original reading of a correction), L, P, 6, 33, 81, (104), 326, 365, 1175, 1881, 2464. Albert L. A. Hogeterp (*Paul and God's Temple: A Historical Interpretation of Cultic Imagery in the Corinthian Correspondence*, BTAS 2 [Leuven; Dudley, MA: Peeters, 2006], 374–5) provides three possibilities for these variants: (1) Paul implies and doubly emphasizes a contrast between "we" believers as God's Temple, and "they" the unbelievers who persist in moral impurity; (2) Paul emphasizes his relation and solidarity with the Corinthians as "we" against "they," who are the opponents of Paul's gospel mission; (3) Paul contrasts "we," the Christian believers as God's Temple, and "they," the Israelites of the old covenant who worship God in the Jerusalem Temple cult. Hogeterp argues that Paul does not oppose the Israelites in general but the unbelievers who boast of their Jewish descent, and he thus concludes that the "we" of 6:16 and 7:1, "links the apostle firmly with the addressees of his mission, thereby implicitly countering the claims of Jewish descent of Paul's opponents ... Paul's notion of the community as Temple should be understood in contrast to unbelief from the part of Gentiles, Jews, and opponents of Paul alike" (p. 377). We will deal with the cultic temple purity and the concept of unbelievers below. More significantly, the OT passages in 2 Cor 6:16–18 show no textual variants except for μου and μοι in v. 16e, which do not affect the meaning. Therefore, Walker (*Interpolations*, 200), who argues for an interpolation of the passage, concludes that, "Only in conjunction with other compelling arguments, however, could these textual variants be seen as possible indications of interpolation." Regarding 2 Cor 7:1, P[46] has πνεύματι for πνεύματος, ἁγιωσύνης for ἁγιωσύνην, and ἀγάπῃ for φόβῳ. The last change of the "love of God" for the "fear of God" in P[46] seems to reflect the close conceptual link between the love of God and the fear of God in biblical and Jewish thought, which is also apparent in the Testaments of the Twelve Patriarchs (see Chapter Four), but needs further examination. Walker's argument (ibid.) that the change in P[46] "may reflect an attempt to make the passage more 'Pauline' in tone" is invalid since Paul also mentions both love and fear in the same context in 2 Cor 5:11 and 14.

to a non-Pauline source.[7] For our purposes, since we are interested in the meaning of 7:1 within its immediate context, this work will focus primarily on two representative examples of interpolation theories that posit a non-Pauline or anti-Pauline *content* of the interpolation, regardless of its presumed connection with the larger *context* of Paul's argument.[8] Our work on the relationship between 5:11 and 7:1, however, will also address the second concern.

One frequently cited proposal of a non-Pauline interpolation is that of Joseph A. Fitzmyer.[9] Fitzmyer presents five features of 2 Cor 6:14–7:1 as evidence of its "significant Qumran background": (1) the triple dualism of uprightness and iniquity, light and darkness, Christ and Belial; (2) the opposition to idols; (3) the concept of the temple of God; (4) the separation from impurity; and (5) the concatenation of Old Testament quotations. From an examination of its content, Fitzmyer concludes that 2 Cor 6:14–7:1 is an Essene paragraph that was interpolated into the Pauline letter through Christian reworking.[10] Fitzmyer's argument focuses on the content of 2 Cor 6:14–7:1, but falls short in explaining its role, if any, within the larger context of the passage: "when the total Qumrân influence is considered along with the other reasons (the interrupted sequence of the surrounding context, the self-contained unit and the strange vocabulary), the evidence seems to total up."[11]

---

7. Webb, *Returning Home*, 160. According to Webb, the source of the (written) interpolation was attributed to: (1) the lost previous letter mentioned in 1 Cor 5:9; (2) some dislocated part of 1 Corinthians (originally belonging before 1 Cor 5:9, before 6:3, after 6:20, or after 10:22); (3) some other part of his correspondence with the Corinthian church. For a more detailed discussion of these arguments and the scholars who propose them, see ibid., 160–1. Webb, 161, points out that Pauline interpolation theories cannot explain the issue of unbelievers in 2 Cor 6:14, nor can it explain the different foci of 2 Cor 6:14–7:1 and the "previous letter" regarding sexual immorality; he therefore concludes that these Pauline interpolation theories tend to create more problems than they solve. Likewise, David I. Starling, *Not My People: Gentiles as Exiles in Pauline Hermeneutics*, BZNW 184 (Berlin; New York: de Gruyter, 2011), 77: "arguments of this kind [an interpolation of a Pauline material] are not driven by the allegedly non-Pauline or anti-Pauline content of the paragraph but by questions to do with its (mis)placement in this present context in 2 Corinthians."

8. For other surveys, see Webb, *Returning Home*, 159–75; Heil, "Sprache," 718–21; James D. H. Amador, "Revisiting 2 Corinthians: Rhetoric and the Case for Unity," *NTS* 46 (2000): 92–111; Starling, *Not My People*, 76–87; Ralph P. Martin, *2 Corinthians*, 2nd rev., WBC 40 (Grand Rapids: Zondervan, 2014), 352–60; George J. Brooke, "2 Corinthians 6:14–7:1 Again: A Change in Perspective," in *The Dead Sea Scrolls and Pauline Literature*, STDJ 102 (Leiden: Brill, 2014), 1–16. These sources have contributed to the discussion below.

9. Joseph A. Fitzmyer, "Qumrân and the Interpolated Paragraph in 2 Cor 6,14–7,1," *CBQ* 23 (1961): 271–80.

10. Ibid., 279–80.

11. Ibid., 279.

While Fitzmyer argued mostly about the *content* of 2 Cor 6:14–7:1 vis-à-vis the Qumran materials, a half a century after Fitzmyer, William O. Walker, Jr. expands the interpolation theory on the basis of the *context* of the passage.[12] Walker argues that 2 Cor 6:14–7:1 is an interpolation of Qumran material that was introduced into Paul's epistle.[13] However, because there is no significant text-critical evidence for an interpolation, Walker's argument rests heavily on evidence from the passage's *context* (i.e., its motivational and locational function) and *content* (i.e., its linguistic, ideational, and comparative nature).[14] Regarding the content of the passage, Walker does not present more evidence than Fitzmyer, but rather argues that 6:14–7:1 is not related in any meaningful way to its immediate context, mainly because without it Paul's argument flows smoothly both syntactically and logically from 6:11–13 to 7:2–3.[15]

As these two examples illustrate, interpolation theories stress the apparent distinctiveness of the content of 6:14–7:1 and its seeming abruptness within its context. They also provide suggestions for its origin, but feel no need to explain the function or purpose of the interpolation within its present location.[16] As to the motivation for the interpolation of the passage, Walker follows the explanation of Robert Jewett that the passage was inserted due to the subsequent competition of Christian groups castigating each other as heretical.[17]

---

12. Walker, *Interpolations*, 199–209.

13. Ibid., 199. Walker, 207, argues that the numerous affinities between 2 Cor 6:14–7:1 and the Qumran material do not guarantee that the passage was not introduced by Paul himself, who "might have included Qumran-like materials in one of his own letters or, indeed, have been influenced by such materials." Nevertheless, since the passage appears closer in content to the post-Pauline writings (e.g., in its use of certain vocabulary), it seems more probable that Paul did not introduce this passage into the present location.

14. In this light, Walker's argument corresponds to Webb's description of interpolation theories eight years earlier: "[Those who argue that 2 Cor 6:14–7:1 is a non-Pauline interpolation], their conclusions are based upon two points of evidence: the lack of contextual compatibility and the non-Pauline content of the fragment." Webb, *Returning Home*, 162.

15. Walker, *Interpolations*, 201. Walker, 202, furthers his argument by pointing out that 6:11–13 and 7:2–3 would form a perfect chiasmus without 6:14–7:1. For a more discussion of this proposal, see idem, "2 Cor 6.14–7.1 and the Chiastic Structure of 6.11–13; 7.2–3," *NTS* 48 (2002): 142–4.

16. Amador, "Revisiting," 101n27: "while parallels [between 2 Cor 6:14–7:1 and manuscript fragments from Qumran] appear to exist, no reasonable thesis has been put forward regarding how, but more importantly *why*, such an insertion would make its way into the argument at this point, if it were a free-floating fragment. The question of *invention* and argumentative function is simply ignored" (original emphasis).

17. Walker, *Interpolations*, 209, quoting Robert Jewett, *The Redaction of I Corinthians and the Trajectory of the Pauline School*, JAARSup 44 (Missoula, MT: American Academy of Religion, 1978), 395. Betz ("2 Cor 6:14–7:1," 108) concludes that 2 Cor 6:14–7:1 conveys a

2. The Salvation-Historical Hermeneutic

In contrast to the interpolation theories, those advocating a salvation-historical hermeneutic read 2 Cor 6:14–7:1 in continuity with the epistle as a whole through a lens in which both Paul and the Corinthians are experiencing the eschatological fulfillment of the OT promises of redemption.[18] From this perspective, both the *content* and *context* of the passage function within the consistent flow of the salvation-historical narrative running throughout the epistle. This approach takes the OT citations in 6:16c–18 as the *crux interpretum* indicating that Paul understands these OT promises (presented in v. 16de and vv. 17d–18a) as now being fulfilled in the lives of the Corinthians (v. 16bc; cf. 1:1, 20; 3:2–3, 18; 5:17; 7:4).[19]

As a prime proponent of this approach, G. K. Beale argues that in 2 Corinthians Paul advocates that the realities of the "new creation" and "reconciliation in Christ" take place through his own ministry (cf. 5:14–21) and indicate the "inaugurated

theology that is not only non-Pauline, but anti-Pauline: "Paul must have been the embodiment of everything that the Christians speaking in 2 Cor 6:14–7:1 warned against." Betz, like Fitzmyer, argues based on internal content features, such as the address to the Corinthians, the promise(s), the exhortation for separation and purification, etc. Betz thus concludes that, "the redactor of the Pauline corpus, for reasons unknown to us, has transmitted a document among Paul's letters which in fact goes back to the movement to which Paul's opponents in Galatia belonged" (p. 108). Heil ("Sprache," 723-6) similarly argues that the passage is an interpolation mainly because the command to separate "ἀφορίζειν" in 6:17a, cannot be reconciled with Paul's negative use of the word elsewhere (cf. Gal 2:12).

18. Following Starling (*Not My People*, 85-7), who defines a salvation-historical hermeneutic as Paul's reading of the Scripture in relation to the broader salvation-historical narrative in which the texts (that Paul cites) are embedded. Besides the interpolation theories and salvation-historical hermeneutic, Starling also adds the approach of the "pesher exegesis" that grants the Pauline authorship of 2 Cor 6:14–7:1 and explains the OT quotations in 6:16c–18 as an instance of Paul's charismatic pesher exegesis (pp. 81-5). Likewise, Martin (*2 Corinthians*, 368) argues that Paul's OT citations in 6:16c–18 reflect his use of the pesher method. However, as Starling (*Not My People*, 82) argues, this approach is problematic because "there are the difficulties in determining whether the use of the term 'pesher' and the phenomena of Scripture citation and commentary in the Qumran literature are sufficient evidence for us to speak of a 'genre' of midrash pesher, and the additional difficulties in sustaining an argument that the existence of parallel phenomena in some of Paul's letters can be explained by the hypothesis that he was following the conventions of this genre."

19. For a detailed argument that Paul's use of "promise(s)" in texts, such as Rom 9:4; 15:8; 2 Cor 1:20; Gal 3:14–29; 4:28, refer to the fulfillment of OT promises, see David I. Starling, "The Yes to All God's Promises: Jesus, Israel and the Promises of God in Paul's Letters," *RTR* 71 (2012): 185–204, especially 187–9; Kevin P. Conway, *The Promises of God: The Background of Paul's Exclusive Use of "epangelia" for the Divine Pledge*, BZNW 211 (Berlin; Munich; Boston: de Gruyter, 2014), 207–12.

fulfillment of Isaiah's and the prophets' promises."[20] As such, these realities serve Paul's purpose throughout the epistle of demonstrating the authenticity of his divine apostleship against those who are questioning it.[21] In this context, 2 Cor 6:14–7:1 functions as an essential, logical link that reinforces Paul's as an *intended* interruption of Paul's final appeal for reconciliation beginning in 6:11–13, which is a repetition of his initial appeal in 5:20–6:2.[22] Thus, the OT quotations in 6:16c–18 are not later interpolations, but references within their OT contexts to God's promise to restore his people, which Paul now applies to the church in Corinth.[23] Paul utilizes these OT backgrounds to enforce his argument that the Corinthians need to be reconciled with him (and ultimately with God) by accepting his apostleship, thereby "'making complete' their profession to be partakers of the Old Testament promises of restoration."[24]

Other scholars argue similarly under the rubric of a salvation-historical hermeneutic, though with slightly different foci. For example, in his interpretation of 2 Cor 6:14–7:1 Webb builds on Beale's proposal and further argues that Paul continues his discussion of the new covenant ministry in 5:11–7:4 by drawing upon "Exodus/return traditions" and applying them to the Corinthians.[25] James M. Scott also argues that the OT quotations in 6:16c–18 show the promise of the new covenant to be in conscious continuity with the Sinai covenant and its fulfillment to take place in the establishment of a reciprocal, new covenant relationship between God and his people.[26] In this regard, Paul cites Isa 52:11 because it fits the Exodus typology of the new covenant that now applies to the Corinthians. Thus, Isa 52:11 in 2 Cor 6:17 should be interpreted in the context of a second-Exodus redemption in which the returning exiles, now identified with the Corinthians, are exhorted to separate themselves.[27] According to Scott, not only the exhortation in

---

20. G. K. Beale, "The Old Testament Background of Reconciliation in 2 Corinthians 5–7 and Its Bearing on the Literary Problem of 2 Corinthians 6:14–7:1," in *The Right Doctrine from the Wrong Texts? Essays on the Use of the Old Testament in the New* (Grand Rapids: Baker Books, 1994), 217–47. According to Beale, 213, reconciliation in Christ is "Paul's way of explaining that Isaiah's promises of 'restoration' from the alienation of exile have begun to be fulfilled by the atonement and forgiveness of sins in Christ."

21. Ibid., 219.

22. Ibid., 234. Similarly, Paul Barnett, *The Second Epistle to the Corinthians*, NICNT (Grand Rapids: Eerdmans, 1997), 355: "Indeed, the whole parenesis 6:14–7:1 is the end point and climax of the appeal [Paul] began at 5:20."

23. Beale, "Reconciliation," 235.

24. Ibid., 230.

25. Webb, *Returning Home*, 154. For Webb's explanation of the difference between his approach and Beale's, see ibid., 27–8 and 180–1.

26. Scott, "Use of Scripture," 88: "the citation combination constitutes not just a haphazard collection of scriptural prooftexts, but rather a highly integrated composition, replete with a unifying theme and inner coherence which can be fully appreciated only on the basis of the OT/Jewish background."

27. Ibid., 84.

6:17, but also all the exhortations in 6:14–7:1 show the Corinthians the implications of the reality of the new covenant for their sanctification.[28] Scott J. Hafemann similarly concludes that, "Paul's argument throughout 2 Corinthians is best understood within a *history-of-redemption perspective* focused on the restoration of God's people in Christ under the new covenant."[29] According to Hafemann, the theme of reconciliation with God through Christ (5:18–21), which is the beginning of the new creation and the eschatological redemption of the world (5:17), alludes to the theme of Israel's restoration as a "second Exodus" in Isa 40–66. This restoration is now fulfilled through the Spirit (cf. the use of Isa 49:8 in 2 Cor 6:2), and, as a result, the Corinthians are exhorted to take part in God's salvation of the world.[30] In this context, Hafemann argues that 2 Cor 6:14–7:1 is not an interpolation:

> but a fitting application of Paul's covenantal perspective. The call to separate oneself from unbelievers in obedience and cultic purity (6:14–15 and 7:2–4), like the calls to reaffirm allegiance to Paul and his ministry that frame them (6:11–13 and 7:2–4), are grounded in the covenant formulas and their implications quoted in 6:16–18.[31]

3. *The Fear of God and the Past Approaches to 2 Cor 6:14–7:1*

Although understanding the meaning and role of the fear of God within the argument of 2 Cor 6:14–7:1 cannot on its own settle the debate regarding these different approaches to this passage, a closer examination of its function within Paul's eschatology adds more weight to the salvation-historical hermeneutic approach.

On the one hand, regarding the *content* of the passage, the existence of the fear of God motif in 7:1 cannot serve as conclusive evidence for either Pauline or non-Pauline authorship of the passage. For, as already observed in Chapters Three and Four, the theme of the fear of God appears both in the contexts of the OT passages cited in 6:16c–18 and in other Jewish documents that are contemporaneous with Paul. Hence, the reference to "the fear of God" could be motivated by these OT texts and/or other Jewish traditions regardless of whether Paul or someone else wrote this passage. However, the fact that the reference to the fear of God in 7:1 derives from the OT quotations in 6:16c–18 corresponds to Paul's mode of

---

28. Ibid.

29. Scott J. Hafemann, "Paul's Use of the Old Testament in 2 Corinthians," *Int* 52 (1998): 252, emphasis added. Likewise, idem, "Paul's Argument from the Old Testament and Christology in 2 Cor 1–9," in *The Corinthian Correspondence*, ed. Reimund Bieringer, BETL 125 (Leuven: Leuven University Press; Peeters, 1994), 300: "Paul's argument throughout 2 Cor 1–9 appears best understood within a *salvation-history framework* which focuses on the restoration of God's people in Christ" (emphasis added).

30. Hafemann, "Old Testament in 2 Corinthians," 252.

31. Ibid., 252–3.

argumentation throughout 2 Cor 1–7 and hence tips the scale in favor of its Pauline authorship. Moreover, as the salvation-historical hermeneutic has emphasized, this is confirmed by the eschatological, new covenant content of the OT quotations themselves, which further supports Paul's understanding of its fulfillment among the Corinthians (cf. 6:16b and 7:1a with 3:6–18 and 6:1–2).

On the other hand, with regard to the question of the integrity of 2 Cor 6:14–7:1, the reference to the fear of God in 7:1 is not foreign within 2 Corinthians. Paul repeatedly uses the same motif implicitly and explicitly in the wider context of the letter, and above all in 5:11, which functions together with 7:1 to frame the intervening argument.[32] As observed in Chapter Two, in 5:10–11 "the fear of the Lord" derives from considering the eschatological reality of the judgment seat of Christ and thus motivates Paul's ministry of reconciliation given by God (5:18), who desires to reconcile the world to himself through Christ (5:19–20). As the ambassador of Christ, Paul therefore exhorts those Corinthians who are still in rebellion against Paul's ministry to be reconciled with God by accepting Paul and his gospel (6:13; 7:2). Paul consequently warns the Corinthians not to "accept the grace of God in vain" (6:1) by refusing him (and ultimately God) and exhorts them to take part in his ministry (cf. 5:17; 6:2). However, participating in Paul's ministry requires that the Corinthians depart from "unbelievers." Hence, Paul's exhortation "not to be mismatched with unbelievers" (6:14) has the same intention as his call for them to "open your hearts" (6:13; 7:2).

Contextually, 2 Cor 6:14–7:1 thus supports Paul's explicit and implicit exhortations throughout 5:10–7:2 by reminding the Corinthians of how God's promises from the Scriptures are being and will be fulfilled among them through his own ministry. By establishing this eschatological framework for Paul's ministry and consequent admonitions, 6:16c–18 also sets forth the eschatological grounds and means for fulfilling Paul's specific call to reconciliation in 5:20 and 6:1: namely, "by cleansing yourselves and in this way completing holiness in the fear of God" (7:1). Following the exhortation in 7:1 is the way in which one is reconciled to God (5:20) by not accepting his grace in vain (6:1). Hence, just as the fear of God motivates Paul in his ministry (5:11), Paul also wants it to motivate the Corinthians in their pursuit of holiness (7:1).[33] Moreover, the conceptual unity between 6:14–7:1 and Paul's argument in its larger context is matched by the conceptual unity within 6:14–7:1 itself, to which we now turn our attention.

II. *The Argument of 2 Cor 7:1*

As proposed in Chapter Two, 2 Cor 7:1 functions as the concluding summary of the preceding paragraph in 6:14–18. The conjunction (οὖν) indicates an inferential

---

32. For the explicit references, cf. 2 Cor 7:5, 11, 15; 11:1–3; 12:19–21. This work will deal with these passages in the conclusion. Implicitly, cf. our discussion of the content of Paul's fear in 6:1 in Chapter Two.

33. Thus, Hafemann, "Paul's Argument," 300.

syntactical connection between 7:1 and 6:14–18 and the similar doublet structure of promise-command in both 6:16c–18 and 7:1—not only in its form, but also in its content—reflects a close semantic and theological relationship between 7:1 and the preceding catena of Scripture (6:16c–18).[34] Just as God's commands in v. 17ac are based on the fulfillment of God's promises in v. 16de, and, at the same time condition the fulfillment of God's promises in the future in vv. 17d–18a, so too the same twofold relationship between promise and command exists in 7:1. The command, "let us cleanse ourselves from every defilement of flesh and spirit" (7:1b), is based on the adverbial participle clause, "having these promises" (7:1a), but at the same time the fulfillment of these promises is contingent on keeping this command.[35] This relationship is further unpacked by the second adverbial participle clause, "completing holiness in the fear of God," the themes of which appear to be Paul's own commentary on the preceding admonition from Scripture. This second adverbial participle clause clarifies Paul's admonition in view of his own understanding of the OT commands and thus becomes the key to understanding the command in 7:1 and the argument of 6:14–7:1 as a whole.[36] Hence, a close reading of 7:1 becomes essential for understanding Paul's argument in the preceding text. We will deal with 7:1 according to its own four syntactical sections, each of which comprises a separate theme:

7:1a   [Therefore, beloved ones] having these promises,
1b   let us cleanse ourselves from every defilement of flesh and spirit,
1c   completing holiness
1d   in the fear of God.

1. Having These Promises

The conjunction, οὖν, indicates that Paul's exhortation in 7:1b is based on the previous argument in 6:16c–18, the first aspect of which is summarized in 7:1a. Hence, as mentioned above, the specific ground for Paul's exhortation in 7:1b from

---

34. The demonstrative ταύτας in 7:1a refers back to the promises in 6:16d–18b and both commands in 6:17ac and 7:1b deal with cleansing and purification.

35. Webb (*Returning Home*, 33) overlooks this doublet of promise and command in 7:1 when he argues that the catena may have been molded in view of the appeals of both 6:14a and 7:1b. Webb argues that 6:14a aligns with the imperatives in the OT catena, while 7:1 picks up *only* the promises. Webb overlooks the hortative in 7:1b, which resembles the imperatives in 6:17a and 6:17c, and he does not unpack the double implication of the promises (fulfilled and unfulfilled) in 7:1a.

36. The comment of Steven E. Runge (*Discourse Grammar of the Greek New Testament: A Practical Introduction for Teaching and Exegesis* [Peabody, MA: Hendrickson, 2010], 129) is insightful: "Participles that precede the main verb have the effect of backgrounding the action with respect to the main verb of the clause, while most participles that follow the main verb elaborate the main verbal action."

the previous argument is given in the present tense, adverbial participle clause, "having these promises."[37] The demonstrative pronoun, ταύτας, indicates that, from within the previous argument, the command of 7:1b is based specifically on the promises set forth in the previous OT quotations, i.e., the promise of God's presence (6:16d, 17d), the establishment of a covenant relationship as encapsulated in the covenant formula (v. 16e), and the creation of their identity as God's sons and daughters as stated in the adoption formula (v. 18a). It is notable that the reference to the promises in 7:1a does not specifically distinguish between, but rather includes the promises of *both* 6:16de and 6:17d–18a, which, as we have observed in Chapter Two, denote the fulfilled and unfulfilled aspects of God's eschatological blessings. Therefore, "having these promises" implies *both* the already state of having received a fulfillment of the promises as the *foundation* for the commands *and* also the yet-to-come state of their future fulfillment as *contingent* upon these same commands.[38]

On the one hand, Paul claims in 6:16b that he and the Corinthians *are* (cf. ἐσμεν) the temple of the living God, indicating that they are already experiencing God's presence in accordance with the promise of v. 16de (cf. καθὼς εἶπεν ὁ θεὸς in v. 16c). The OT promises in v. 16de serve to attest that the covenant promise *is now a reality for believers* in Christ.[39] Specifically, the new identity that both Paul and the Corinthians share is given to them in fulfillment of the covenant formula from Lev 26:11–12 and Ezek 37:27, which is also reflected in the fact that God anointed the Corinthian community as a messianic people (2 Cor 1:18–22).[40] Even Hans Dieter Betz, who argues 6:14–7:1 to be an anti-Pauline interpolation, still agrees that in 6:16b a general ontological possibility of religious existence is now being claimed as a reality in the Christian congregation.[41] In this regard, the fulfillment of the promises does not lie totally in the future, but includes the reality that has *already* been fulfilled between Paul and the Corinthians.[42]

On the other hand, these promises also have a future dimension. As discussed in Chapter Two, within the argument of 2 Cor 6:14–18 inheriting God's promise of

---

37. Thus, Jan Lambrecht, *Second Corinthians*, SP 8 (Collegeville, MN: Liturgical Press, 1999), 119; Murray J. Harris, *The Second Epistle to the Corinthians: A Commentary on the Greek Text*, NIGTC (Grand Rapids; Milton Keynes: Eerdmans; Paternoster, 2005), 511.

38. Thus, Margaret E. Thrall, *A Critical and Exegetical Commentary on the Second Epistle to the Corinthians: Introduction and Commentary on II Corinthians I–VII*, vol. 1, ICC (Edinburgh: T&T Clark, 1994), 480.

39. David E. Garland, *2 Corinthians*, NAC 29 (Nashville: Broadman & Holman, 1999), 338; Frank J. Matera, *II Corinthians: A Commentary*, NTL (Louisville; London: Westminster John Knox, 2003), 164. Also, in 1 Cor 3:16–17 Paul had already identified the Corinthians, as the believing community, with the temple of God. For a more detailed discussion of this relationship, see Hogeterp, *God's Temple*, 365–85.

40. Barnett, *Second Corinthians*, 351.

41. Betz, "2 Cor 6:14–7:1," 92.

42. Thus, Lambrecht, *Second Corinthians*, 119; Barnett, *Second Corinthians*, 356.

his presence in v. 17d and of the reality of adoption in v. 18a are both contingent upon obedience to his preceding commands in v. 17c. What is striking is the fact that even though the promises in v. 16de are already fulfilled (v. 16b), Paul treats them equally as the promises that, together with the promises in vv. 17d–18a, will reach final fulfillment in the future, since they all appear in the future tense in the quotations from the OT in v. 16de and vv. 17d–18a. Moreover, in 7:1a Paul still considers them to be "promises" that have not yet reached their final fulfillment in that ἔχοντες, being a present-tense participle, indicates an ongoing action that is contemporaneous to the exhortation, καθαρίσωμεν.[43] In short, they are still "promises"!

Another feature of the passage that shows Paul's treatment of the promises to be both fulfilled and unfulfilled at the same time is the difficulty of drawing a distinction between the content of the promises that appear as fulfilled and function as the basis of God's commands (i.e., those regarding God's presence among his people in v. 16d and his acceptance of them as his people in v. 16e), and the promises that are contingent on keeping the commands (i.e., those regarding God's acceptance in v. 17d and his acceptance of them as his sons and daughters in v. 18a).[44] Hence, the same promises are presented as *both* fulfilled *and* unfulfilled, as *both* an accomplished reality upon which obedience is based and a reality that is contingent upon their obedience to God's commands for its future fulfillment. As the references in 2 Cor 6:16c–18 to the covenant relationship in Lev 26:12, Ezek 37:27, and 2 Sam 7:14 all attest, this twofold nature of the promises corresponds to the structure of the covenant itself. Within the covenant relationship, the call to obedience in the present, by which the covenant is maintained, is based on God's saving actions in the past in fulfillment of his promises, by which the covenant relationship is established. In turn, God's promised deliverance in the future, which consummates the covenant, is dependent on the keeping of the commands in the present.[45]

---

43. Daniel B. Wallace, *Greek Grammar beyond the Basics: An Exegetical Syntax of the New Testament* (Grand Rapids: Zondervan, 1996), 614, 25.

44. Contra, e.g., Furnish (*II Corinthians*, 375), who argues that there is a clear distinction between the promises, stating that the promises in 7:1 consist of those already fulfilled in v. 16de and of those yet to be fulfilled in vv. 17d–18a.

45. In the same context, Starling ("Promises," 188) argues regarding the "promises" in 2 Cor 1:20: "The 'yes' that is spoken by God, then, is not the fulfilment of all the promises within the Christ event itself, as if the content of the promises were no longer live and pending; it is the partial fulfilment in Christ and in the pouring out of his Spirit on his people, as a 'first instalment' and a guarantee of the remainder." Similarly, Conway, *Promises*, 209–11: "As the recipients of God's covenantal love, which is demonstrated by their inheritance of the future completion of the promises, they should return such love with Spirit-empowered obedience to the new covenant" (p. 211). Insightful in this regard is Hafemann's "threefold covenant structure" of the covenant relationship between God and his people: God's unconditional acts of provision in the past lead to the covenant stipulations

In this regard, both Paul and the Corinthians are already experiencing the promised realities of God's presence among them as his covenant people, while at the same time holding on to these promises for the future. In 7:1, their "having these promises," with their dual "already" and "yet-to-come" aspects, thus provides both the basis and motivation for the exhortation that follows.

2. Let Us Cleanse Ourselves from Every Defilement of Flesh and Spirit

The main verbal assertion in the sentence is stated in the hortatory command of 7:1b: "let us cleanse ourselves." This is the only instance in the undisputed Pauline letters of the use of the verb, "to cleanse" (καθαρίζω), to refer to the believers' own action with regard to themselves, and it is used in this way nowhere else in the NT. Elsewhere it always implies the activity of God or the Spirit with regard to believers.[46] As scholars have noted, the verb in its present context connotes ritual cleansing,[47] which is further emphasized by its combination with "defilement" (μολυσμός), which does not occur elsewhere in the NT, but in LXX is always related to the defilement caused by idols.[48] As such, Paul's command in 7:1 recalls his rejection in 6:16a of any commonality between the church as the temple of God and idolatry. In addition, this connotation of defilement caused by idolatry is further signified by the corresponding verb form, "to defile" (μολύνω), which appears three times in the NT (1 Cor 8:7; Rev 3:4; 14:4). In 1 Cor 8:7 and Rev 14:4 the verb explicitly signifies idol worship, which resonates with LXX use of the verb (cf., e.g., Isa 59:3; 65:4; Jer 23:11).[49] The connection between the defilement of clothes in Rev 3:4 and ritual impurity might not be immediately clear,[50] but similar

---

in the present, upon which the covenant relationship is maintained, that will lead to the consummation of the covenant promises or curses in the future. Scott J. Hafemann, "The Covenant Relationship," in *Central Themes in Biblical Theology: Mapping Unity in Diversity*, eds. Scott J. Hafemann and Paul R. House (Nottingham, England: Apollos, 2007), 20–65, especially 34–40.

46. E.g., Eph 5:26; Tit 2:14; Heb 9:14, 22, 23; 10:2.

47. E.g., Barnett, *Second Corinthians*, 356; Hogeterp, *God's Temple*, 376–77; Yulin Liu, *Temple Purity in 1–2 Corinthians*, WUNT 2/343 (Tübingen: Mohr Siebeck, 2013), 231–32; Martin, *2 Corinthians*, 373.

48. The instances in which the noun is used in LXX (cf., e.g., Jer 23:15; cf. 1 Esd 8:80; 2 Macc 5:27) show how closely it could be associated with defilement resulting from pagan idolatry. Furnish, *II Corinthians*, 365; Barnett, *Second Corinthians*, 356; Harris, *Second Corinthians*, 512.

49. Rev 14:4 describes "those who did not defile themselves with women," but as in Rev 17–18 such a defilement with a woman is closely associated with idol worship (cf. Rev 2:20).

50. Scholars' opinions differ on the interpretation of the term, ἐμόλυναν τὰ ἱμάτια αὐτῶν. Suggestions include: "Martyrdom," as G. B. Caird, *The Revelation of Saint John*, BNTC (Peabody, MA: Hendrickson, 1966), 49. "Soiled clothes that disqualified the worshipper and dishonored the god," Robert H. Mounce, *The Book of Revelation*, NICNT (Grand Rapids:

uses in LXX point to ritual defilement as the meaning of this defilement as well (cf. Gen 37:31; Song 5:3; Lam 4:14).[51]

The following qualifying expression "of flesh and spirit" (σαρκὸς καὶ πνεύματος) should be approached carefully. Given the cultic context of ritual defilement signified by the command, Paul's reference to "flesh and spirit" should not be read in terms of the theological contrast between flesh/spirit characteristic of Paul's writings elsewhere.[52] Rather, the expression is a nontechnical description of humanity, as Paul uses it in other places (cf. 1 Cor 7:34; 1 Thess 5:23).[53] That is, Paul uses the expression, "flesh and spirit," to refer to his *holistic* view of humanity as the object of the cleansing, i.e., of what can be defiled.[54] Together with his emphasis on the entirety of the person, Paul's focus is therefore also on "every" (παντός), i.e., on

---

Eerdmans, 1977), 112; Grant R. Osborne, *Revelation*, BECNT (Grand Rapids: Baker Academic, 2002), 178; and Leon Morris, *Revelation*, TNTC 20 (Downers Grove, IL: InterVarsity Press, 2009), 77. Similarly, J. Ramsey Michaels (*Revelation*, IVPNTC 20 [Downers Grove, IL: InterVarsity Press, 1997], 82) focuses on impurity when he comments that, "Soiled or disheveled clothing, or no clothing at all, [in the book of Revelation] is a symbol of religious and moral impurity and shame." My position is close to that of G. K. Beale (*The Book of Revelation: A Commentary on the Greek Text*, NIGTC [Grand Rapids: Carlisle: Eerdmans; Paternoster, 1999], 276): "That a context of idolatry is in mind is apparent from the use of μολύνω ('stain'), which is used elsewhere of the threat of being 'stained' with the pollution of idolatry."

51. However, this ritual cleansing should not be identified with baptism, contra those who treat 2 Cor 6:14–7:1 as a paraenetic baptismal tradition; see, e.g., Georg Klinzing, *Die Umdeutung des Kultus in der Qumrangemeinde und im Neuen Testament*, SUNT 7 (Göttingen: Vandenhoeck & Ruprecht, 1971), 180–2; Thrall, *Second Corinthians*, 1:34n224. Contrary to 1 Cor 6:11 and Eph 5:26, where specific allusions are made to baptism, 2 Cor 6:14–7:1 does not mention water or evoke the image of the act of washing with water. Thus, Albert L. A. Hogeterp, "Community as a Temple in Paul's Letters: The Case of Cultic Terms in 2 Corinthians 6:14–7:1," in *Anthropology and Biblical Studies: Avenues of Approach* (Leiderdorp: Deo, 2004), 282–3.

52. E.g., Rom 8:5–11; 1 Cor 5:5; Gal 3:3; 4:29; 5:16–26; 6:8. Because Paul often sets flesh in opposition to spirit, the meaning of the combined expression, "of flesh and spirit" in 2 Cor 7:1, has been controversial among scholars. In 7:1, we are taking σάρξ to be a reference to the body as a whole rather than to some part of the body or as a reference to a sinful reality in contrast to the Holy Spirit. Likewise, Furnish (*II Corinthians*, 365) comments that "the combination *flesh and spirit* refers either to the totality of human existence or to its outward and inward aspect"; for this latter view, see too Harris, *Second Corinthians*, 512. Also, Garland, *2 Corinthians*, 342: "Defilement 'of body and spirit' means that the entire person, externally and internally, is corrupted by idolatrous practices." For further discussions about Paul's use of the expression "body and spirit," see Thrall, *Second Corinthians*, 1:30–1.

53. Barnett, *Second Corinthians*, 356n71; Matera, *II Corinthians*, 168.

54. Thus, Martin, *2 Corinthians*, 375.

the fact that *every* kind of defilement on *every* part of a person should be cleansed.[55] Since Paul views the church as God's temple, he uses the corresponding ritual purity language to refer to ethical and moral disobedience as that which now defiles the believer (cf. Paul's use of the motif of the church as God's temple in the context of his warning against profaning it in 1 Cor 3:9–17; 5:6–8; 6:18–20). As Paul's next statement about holiness indicates, "cleansing from every defilement" signifies the Corinthians' pursuit of a life of moral purity, in accordance with the essential character of God, which is expressed in obedience (cf. 2 Cor 7:15).

3. Completing Holiness

The second adverbial participle clause, "completing holiness" (ἐπιτελοῦντες ἁγιωσύνην), being employed in the present tense, denotes a contemporaneous, imperfective or continuous aspect that is required of believers in their cleansing. As such, it functions as a syntactical parallel to the present tense participle ἔχοντες in v. 1a in that both modify καθαρίσωμεν. However, it functions differently from the first participle logically in that, while "having these promises" functions as a ground clause for the main verb, "completing holiness" indicates the result or effect of "cleansing oneself."[56]

Paul uses the verb, ἐπιτελέω ("to complete") seven times in his writings.[57] When using this verb, Paul consistently points to the future consummation of what is presently being undertaken, as is indicated by his use of contrasting terms that indicate the beginning of the process in the same context.[58] For example, Paul uses

---

55. Thus, Barnett, *Second Corinthians*, 356; Harris, *Second Corinthians*, 512; C. K. Barrett, *A Commentary on the Second Epistle to the Corinthians*, BNTC (London: Black, 1973), 202.

56. Contra Harris (*Second Corinthians*, 513n104), who takes "completing holiness" as a subsequent exhortation or imperative in addition to "let us cleanse." According to Wallace (*Beyond the Basics*, 650), the cases in which participles function independently as either indicatives or imperatives are "extremely rare." And in this case, the participle is not isolated, but there is an appropriate independent verb to which the participle can belong syntactically and logically. Also, see the excursus on "Imperatival Use of Participles in 1 Peter" in Paul J. Achtemeier, *1 Peter: A Commentary on First Peter*, ed. Eldon Jay Epp, Hermeneia (Minneapolis: Augsburg Fortress, 1996), 117: "[Identifying participles as imperatives] cannot be said to have been normal practice in Hellenistic Greek."

57. E.g., Rom 15:28; 2 Cor 7:1; 8:6; 8:11 (2x); Gal 3:3; Phil 1:6. According to BDAG, 383, ἐπιτελέω means "to finish, to bring to an end," "to complete, to accomplish," or "to fulfill." BDAG lists 2 Cor 7:1 under the section, "to bring about a result according to plan or objective, *complete, accomplish, perform, bring about*" and suggests that the phrase in this context means "*bring about sanctification.*"

58. Rom 15:28 does not include a contrasting term, but even here, the future aspect is implied in the verb: "When therefore I *have completed* this and have delivered to them what has been collected, I will leave for Spain by way of you" (ESV, emphasis added).

προενάρχομαι ("to begin with already")⁵⁹ in 2 Cor 8:6, 10 and ἐνάρχομαι ("to begin with")⁶⁰ in Gal 3:3 and Phil 1:6, as the counterpart in these passages to the verb. Thus, based on Paul's other uses, this verb indicates an active process that has been started in the past, but is to be fulfilled in the future.

The object of this completion or fulfillment, ἁγιωσύνη ("holiness"), appears three times in the Pauline corpus (Rom 1:4; 2 Cor 7:1; 1 Thess 3:13) and occurs the same number of times in LXX (Ps 29:5 [MT 30:5]; 95:6 [MT 96:6]; 97:12 [MT 96:12]). It is notable that in all three LXX occurrences "holiness" describes *God's* holiness and not that of his people. Given this use of the word in LXX, one might expect that Paul, too, would always use "holiness" to refer to God's holiness rather than to that of his people. In fact, Paul uses "holiness" in Rom 1:4 to describe the Holy Spirit (πνεῦμα ἁγιωσύνης), which is close to LXX use of the word.⁶¹ However, in 2 Cor 7:1 and 1 Thess 3:13 Paul uses "holiness" with reference to God's people. Therefore, an examination of its parallel use in 1 Thess 3:13 helps to clarify Paul's distinct use of ἁγιωσύνη over against its use in Rom 1:4 and LXX:

> Now may our God and father himself, and our Lord Jesus, direct our way unto you. And may the Lord make you to increase and abound in love to one another and to all men, just as we also to you, in order that your heart might be firmly strengthened, *blameless in holiness* (ἀμέμπτους ἐν ἁγιωσύνῃ), before our God and Father at the coming of our Lord Jesus with all his saints
>
> 1 Thess 3:11–13, emphasis added.

Three things are worthy of note regarding the use of "holiness" in this text in comparison with 2 Cor 7:1. First, it appears, both as a present state defined by the love for others to be brought about by the Lord in the lives of his people, and as a future eschatological reality in that the believers' state of holiness will be firmly established by God "at the coming of our Lord Jesus with all his saints," which clearly refers to God's coming judgment at Christ's parousia.⁶² Second, the way in

---

59. BDAG 868: "*begin (beforehand)* so that the beginning lies in the past as contrasted w. the present."

60. BDAG 331, "*begin.*" Ἐνάρχομαι has the same root and a very similar meaning to προενάρχομαι.

61. Maximilian Zerwick, *Biblical Greek: Illustrated by Examples*, Scripta Pontificii Instituti Biblici 114 (Rome: Scripta Pontificii Instituti Biblici, 1963), §40, analyzes it as a "Hebrew Genitive." C. E. B. Cranfield (*A Critical and Exegetical Commentary on the Epistle to the Romans*, 6th ed., ICC [Edinburgh: T&T Clark, 1975], 63–4) argues that πνεῦμα ἁγιωσύνης simply reflects the Hebrew expression that is found in the OT and Jewish literature (Ps 51:11 [MT 13]; Isa 63:10f; 1QS 4:21; 8:16; 9:3; 1QH 7:6f; 9:32; also T. Levi 18:7). Likewise, Joseph A. Fitzmyer (*Romans: A New Translation and Commentary*, AB33 [New York: Doubleday, 1993], 236) argues that it is a pre-Pauline, Semitic formula taken over by Paul.

62. Most commentators agree on the future, consummated eschatological context of 1 Thess 3:11–13. See, e.g., Charles A. Wanamaker, *The Epistles to the Thessalonians: A*

which "holiness" is used together with "blameless" (ἄμεμπτος) suggests that "holiness" contains a juridical dimension.[63] Elsewhere in the Pauline corpus, ἄμεμπτος refers either to the state Paul ascribes to himself regarding the law,[64] or to the consummate state of Christians vindicated by God at the eschaton.[65] Lastly, here too, unlike its use in LXX or Rom 1:4, "holiness" does not describe an aspect of God's character, but the holiness of his people as a *consequence of God's work* in their lives.[66] Holiness is one of the primary characteristics of God in the biblical tradition,[67] but both in its present manifestation and an eschatological, juridical context Paul also associates it with the people of God.[68]

This link between the holiness of God and the holiness of his people implies that the divine quality of holiness is shared by God's people by virtue of their moral conformity to the very character of God.[69] Since the church as "God's temple" is to be a community which upholds right belief, keeps moral uprightness, and continues to witness to the power of the gospel, Paul focuses on the moral, spiritual, and faithful quality of the Corinthian community.[70] Thus, "holiness" in 7:1 expresses the essential character of God as separate from all evil and as

Commentary on the Greek Text, NIGTC (Grand Rapids: Eerdmans, 1990), 145; Ben Witherington III, *1 and 2 Thessalonians: A Socio-Rhetorical Commentary* (Grand Rapids: Eerdmans, 2006), 104; G. K. Beale, *1–2 Thessalonians*, The IVPNTC 13 (Downers Grove, IL; Nottingham: InterVarsity Press, 2003), 110; and Gene L. Green, *The Letters to the Thessalonians*, PNTC (Grand Rapids: Leicester: Eerdmans; Apollos, 2002), 179.

63. Wanamaker, *Thessalonians*, 144.

64. E.g., Phil 3:6.

65. E.g., Phil 2:15. See also the adverbial form ἀμέμπτως ("blamelessly") in 1 Thess 2:10; 5:23. Cf. especially the doxological prayer in 1 Thess 5:23: "now may the God of peace himself sanctify you completely, and may *your whole spirit and soul and body* (ὁλόκληρον ὑμῶν τὸ πνεῦμα καὶ ἡ ψυχὴ καὶ τὸ σῶμα) *be kept blameless* (ἀμέμπτως) at the coming of our Lord Jesus Christ" (ESV, emphasis added). Here, "blameless" is used in the same way as "holiness" in 2 Cor 7:1. Thus, Wanamaker, *Thessalonians*, 207: "Paul's intention was not to offer an anthropological definition. Rather he sought to emphasize his desire that God would preserve his readers as *complete* human beings, blameless in the impending judgment of the day of the Lord or parousia" (emphasis added).

66. Therefore, even though "holiness" in 2 Cor 7:1 is anarthrous, it is legitimate to supply the possessive "our" as required by the context. Harris, *Second Corinthians*, 513.

67. Pss 71:22; 89:18; Isa 1:4; Jer 50:9; Ezek 39:7; 1 Pet 1:15–16; John 17:11; Rev 4:8.

68. Thus, Beale (*1–2 Thessalonians*, 110) argues that the holiness of the people of God is the central point of Paul's prayer in 1 Thess 3:11–13.

69. In that "holiness" refers to the holiness of believers, but also indicates the eschatological state that will be vindicated by God, the use of "holiness" in LXX and Rom 1:4 is therefore not totally irrelevant to the interpretation of 2 Cor 7:1 and 1 Thess 3:13. Also, Gerhard Sass, "Noch Einmal: 2 Kor 6,14–7,1: Literarkritische Waffen gegen einen 'unpaulinischen' Paulus?" *ZNW* 84 (1993): 46.

70. Liu, *Temple Purity*, 229–30.

just in his dealings with humanity, the likeness of which believers may possess in greater or lesser degree in proportion to their conformity to the will of God through their pursuit of a life of moral purity.[71] This moral or ethical understanding of ἁγιωσύνη in 7:1 is again confirmed by the parallel in 1 Thess 3:11–13, where the people's holiness is equated with their love for others, a participation in God's moral holiness that is also fundamentally important for Paul in his letter to the Thessalonians (cf. 1 Thess 4:3).[72] Hence, given the Pauline use of "holiness" in 1 Thess 3:13, its use in 2 Cor 7:1 referring to the moral holiness of God's people is not surprising, especially since there is the *same emphasis* on the believers' continuing cleansing in the present in response to the promise of God's presence in their lives.

In this regard, Gerhard Sass rightly argues that the holiness of believers in 2 Cor 7:1 is initiated by the fulfillment of God's promise that the Corinthians, as those called to be separated from the impurities in 6:14–16, are already the temple of the living God (6:16b).[73] At the same time, the Corinthians are exhorted to complete their holiness because of what God has already done, is doing, and promises to do on their behalf. Though the process by which believers attain holiness has been initiated by God in the past, by making them his holy people (6:14–16), it now needs to be carried out by believers in the present until the future eschaton (6:17–18). Therefore, ἐπιτελοῦντες ἁγιωσύνην points to the result of an ongoing process of cleansing, rather than to an already completed condition of believers.[74] And as in 1 Thess 3:11–13, Paul makes it clear to the Corinthians as well that this ongoing process is only possible because of God's continuing grace and the power of the

---

71. James Ayodeji Adewuya, "The People of God in a Pluralistic Society: Holiness in 2 Corinthians," in *Holiness and Ecclesiology in the New Testament*, ed. Kent E. Brower and Andy Johnson (Grand Rapids; Cambridge: Eerdmans, 2007), 214.

72. Wanamaker, *Thessalonians*, 144; Beale, *1–2 Thessalonians*, 110–11. For a more detailed discussion regarding believers' holiness in 1 Thessalonians, see Andy Johnson, "The Sanctification of the Imagination in 1 Thessalonians," in *Holiness and Ecclesiology in the New Testament*, ed. Kent E. Brower and Andy Johnson (Grand Rapids; Cambridge, 2007), 275–92.

73. Gerhard Sass, "Noch Einmal," 46n56.

74. In this regard, see too Martin, *2 Corinthians*, 375: "the idea of advancing in holiness depicts a repeated act of self-consecration, a constant drive to live as God's people." Also, R. Kent Hughes, *2 Corinthians: Power in Weakness* (Wheaton, IL: Crossway, 2006), 258; Harris, *Second Corinthians*, 513. Contra Barnett (*Second Corinthians*, 357), who argues that the holiness in view is covenantal rather than developmental or progressive in character. In other words, for Barnett, the holiness is about their separated *state* from the idol-worshiping cults, and not about an individual's moral and spiritual *development*. Likewise, Green (*Thessalonians*, 180) argues that holiness indicates the *condition* and not the *process* of sanctification. But, although, in 1 Thess 3:13, holiness describes the juridical state of believers in the eschaton, it is inextricably connected to the process of sanctification, which is also expressed as a "cleansing" in 2 Cor 7:1.

Spirit in their lives (cf. 1 Cor 2:12–13; 3:16; 6:19; 15:10; 16:23; 2 Cor 1:12; 3:3, 6, 18; 5:5; 6:1–2; 8:6–7; 9:8; 12:9; 13:14).

Consequently, "completing holiness" contains an eschatological significance, alluding to the final state that both Paul and the Corinthians will reach in the end as they continuously progress in view of God's redemptive acts in the past and promises for the future. Holiness is given to both Paul and the Corinthians as the fulfillment of God's promises, both present and future, but it is also something that they must strive to complete in anticipation of the eschaton.[75] In this regard, Paul's addresses to the Corinthians as "holy ones" (ἁγιάζω, ἅγιοι) in 1 Cor 1:2 and 2 Cor 1:1 are noteworthy because they refer to the Corinthians' present state, as well as implying that they are to live in a way that corresponds to who they are.[76]

This interplay between God's commands and the past and future aspects of his promises on which they depend can be further inferred from the logical relationship in 7:1 between the main verb, καθαρίσωμεν, and the adverbial participle, ἐπιτελοῦντες, concerning which there is some disagreement. Some scholars take the participle as working as an imperative expressing an additional exhortation to supplement the call to cleanse themselves (i.e., Paul's audience in Corinth): "let us cleanse ourselves … and let us complete holiness"[77] or "let us cleanse ourselves … and complete holiness."[78] Others take the participle as expressing the consequence or result of the main verb. In this case, the act of completing holiness becomes an outcome of the cleansing: "let us cleanse ourselves … thus completing holiness."[79] Lastly, it is possible to take the participle instrumentally: "let us cleanse ourselves … by means of completing holiness."[80]

---

75. Throughout the process of sanctification God is intimately related to it. Thus, Charles H. Talbert, *Reading Corinthians: A Literary and Theological Commentary on 1 and 2 Corinthians* (New York: Crossroad, 1987), 172–3: "In Paul sanctification/holiness is not only something God gives (1 Cor 1:30; 2 Thess 2:13) but also something which Christians strive to complete (1 Cor 7:34; 1 Thess 4:1–8; Rom 6:19) as well as something that ultimately God completes (1 Thess 3:13)." The discussion on the role of God's own personal agency in the process of believers' sanctification is beyond the scope of this work.

76. Adewuya, "Holiness," 214: "As used in 2 Cor 7:1, holiness is not 'merely a static condition, a holiness obtained by observance of cultic practices … the context is not one of resting content with an unholy life … but one of acting out one's status in Christ.'"

77. E.g., GNB, REB, NLT, Matera, *II Corinthians*, 157. On this reading, see above, note 56.

78. E.g., TCNT, RSV, NEB, Goodspeed.

79. E.g., NAB, ESV, Martin, *2 Corinthians*, 375–6; Barnett, *Second Corinthians*, 356. Matera (*II Corinthians*, 168) takes the participle as an additional imperative in his translation, but he explains holiness as the goal of the cleansing in his commentary: "By avoiding every defilement, the Corinthians will achieve the goal of the Christian life: 'holiness.'"

80. E.g., the Korean Revised Version: "그런즉 사랑하는 자들아, 이 약속을 가진 우리가 하나님을 두려워하는 가운데서 거룩함을 온전히 이루어 육과 영의 온갖 더러운 것에서 자신을 깨끗케 하자" (Therefore, beloved ones, we, who are having these promises, should cleanse ourselves from every defilement of flesh and spirit, by perfecting holiness in the fear of God). My translation.

Unfortunately, the syntax alone cannot provide a definitive answer to the relationship between "let us cleanse" and "completing." However, as argued above, the most probable reading is to take the participle as a result clause because semantically the use of the notion of "completing" in relation to that of "holiness," in addition to its connection to other words like "blameless" in other Pauline writings (cf. 1 Thess 3:13), suggests that the phrase "completing holiness" denotes a (future) result of a progressive sanctification that comes through "cleansing oneself from every defilement."[81] Conversely, it is difficult to conceptualize a way in which completing holiness would lead to cleansing oneself, as if a progression in holiness were a means to some other human activity, while the move logically and theologically from cleansing oneself to the completion of holiness is a natural one.

4. In the Fear of God

The last phrase of 7:1 concerns the mode or means by which the Corinthians are to fulfill the process of completing holiness, namely, "in/by means of the fear of God" (ἐν φόβῳ θεοῦ).[82] Based on our study of 2 Cor 5:10-11 in Chapter Two, the wider context of the catena of Scripture (6:16c-18) in Chapter Three, and the reception of the biblical tradition in Second Temple Judaism in Chapter Four, Paul's rendering of the fear of God as a motivation for his ministry and for believers' sanctification lends support to an instrumental reading of the preposition ἐν in this context.[83] Moreover, the judgment context of the fear of God which we have seen attested to not only in Paul's own move from 2 Cor 5:10 to 5:11, but also in the wider context of the Scriptural catena in 6:16c-18 and its reception in Jewish tradition, is also the impetus in 7:1 for believers to pursue holiness, which further supports the instrumental reading of the fear of God. Here too, in 7:1, the fear of God, as the motivation for holiness, is to characterize the *present* life of *believers* in anticipation of the day of judgment, at which time they will no longer need to fear God's wrath. For the Corinthians not to fear God now, therefore, would be to risk having accepted God's grace in vain, which would put them in the fearful position

---

81. Thus, Martin, *2 Corinthians*, 375: "[I]dea of advancing in holiness depicts a repeated act of self-consecration, a constant drive to live as God's people."

82. Harris (*Second Corinthians*, 514) suggests three ways of interpreting the preposition ἐν. First, causally: "because we fear God" (NLT) or "out of reverence for God" (NIV). Second, circumstantially: "all the while reverencing God" or "in an atmosphere of reverential fear for God." Third, instrumentally: "by reverence for God" (Goodspeed) or "by living in awe of God" (GNB). Harris argues that a preference may be expressed for the third option because Paul would most naturally indicate the means by which the perfecting of holiness could be achieved since the striving for perfection was a crucial element of his teaching. Also Matera, *II Corinthians*, 168.

83. Contra Stanley E. Porter ("Fear, Reverence," *DPL* 292), who argues that the preposition "refers to the sphere or arena in which sanctification occurs."

of the unbeliever who will be outside of God's salvation on the day of judgment (cf. 6:1–2).

The fear of God therefore functions instrumentally in 7:1 to indicate the means and motive that makes it possible to carry out the process of completing holiness. In other words, the fear of God derived from the realization of the reality of God's eschatological judgment that is reinforced by the dangerous possibility of failing to inherit God's promises (cf. 6:1), motivates believers to continue the process of completing holiness as a result of acting to cleanse themselves. In conclusion, the translation of 2 Cor 7:1 would be as follows:

> Therefore, beloved ones, since we have these promises (which already have been fulfilled among us and are also yet to be fulfilled for us in the eschatological future), let us cleanse ourselves from every defilement regarding flesh and spirit, thus completing holiness, which is brought about by the fear of God.

III. Paul's Eschatology and the Fear of God

Based on our investigations of 2 Cor 5:10–11 and the OT texts in the catena of Scripture in 6:16c–18 we observed the following features of Paul's understanding of the fear of God, which are also traceable in Second Temple Jewish texts: the fear of God derives from the (final) judgment and functions as a motivation for the people to live righteously in anticipation of that judgment. As observed in Chapter Three, in Lev 26:1–2 fearing God thus expresses itself in keeping the law, which in turn determines covenant blessings (vv. 3–13), while failing to show this proper response to God's saving actions results in experiencing the covenant curses (vv. 14–39).

As is well known, this same function of the fear of God, as an essential covenant stipulation for God's people, is further emphasized in the book of Deuteronomy (see, e.g., 6:2, 13, 24; 8:6; 10:12–13, 20; 13:4; 14:23; 17:19; 28:58; 31:12, 13).[84] Even though Paul does not cite Deuteronomy in our passage, this conceptual parallel in Deuteronomy is significant for our study as we seek to put 2 Cor 7:1 into the context of Paul's theology because, as David Lincicum argues, the book of Deuteronomy is essential for understanding the framework of Paul's theology.[85]

---

84. Leland Ryken, "Fear," *DBIM* 277: "Deuteronomy 10:12–13 is an apt summary of what is encompassed in the fear of God." Likewise, Porter, "Fear," *NDBT* 497: "In Deuteronomy, fear of God is linked to love of God, and obedience to his commandments."

85. See David Lincicum, *Paul and the Early Jewish Encounter with Deuteronomy* (Grand Rapids: Baker Academic, 2010). According to Lincicum, 198, "Deuteronomy, mediated through liturgy, has been received by Paul with a threefold construal of the book as ethical authority, theological authority, and a lens for the interpretation of Israel's history." Lincicum, 121, argues that Paul's citations and allusions span all of the major portions of Deuteronomy (except for chs 1–4; 33–4), but there is a sustained interest in Deut 5:1–6:9; 10:12–11:21; 32:1–43.

For, as Lincicum has demonstrated, Paul reads Deuteronomy not only retrospectively to understand Israel's history, but also prospectively in order to apply its message to his and believers' identity and circumstances, which have now begun through Christ and the Spirit:

> Because Paul is convinced that Deuteronomy ultimately speaks to the people of God composed of Jew and Gentile who are welcomed by the one God on the basis of faith in Jesus Christ, he believes that the circumcision of their hearts by the Spirit now enables them to fulfill the law – not as an entrance requirement but as an epistemological guide to what is holy, just and good, though filtered through the apocalyptic disclosure and irruption of the cross and resurrection of Christ. In this sense, the ethical reading of Deuteronomy is grounded in the Christological and pneumatological reading.[86]

Moreover, in relationship to 1 and 2 Corinthians in particular, Brian Rosner argues that the theological or canonical setting of 1 and 2 Corinthians are analogous to that of Deuteronomy, so that, "[i]n one sense, it is not only the Corinthian epistles that look back to Deuteronomy, but Deuteronomy that anticipates 1 and 2 Corinthians ... Paul writes as a minister of the new covenant, a covenant that Deuteronomy does not name but ultimately points forward to."[87]

Within Deuteronomy, it is especially in Deut 10:12–13 that the importance of the fear of God is expressed most clearly:

> So now, O Israel, what does the Lord your God require of you? Only to *fear the Lord your God*, to walk in all his ways, to love him, to serve the Lord your God with all your heart and with all your soul, and to keep the commandments of the Lord your God and his decrees that I am commanding you today, for your own well-being (emphasis added).[88]

In the context of Deut 10:12–13 God commands his people to circumcise their hearts and not to be stubborn any longer (v. 16) in order that they might fear the Lord, as well as walk in his ways by keeping his commandments, loving, and serving him. In order to fulfill this expectation, given that Israel remains in a state

---

86. Ibid., 168.

87. Brian S. Rosner, "Deuteronomy in 1 and 2 Corinthians," in *Deuteronomy in the New Testament: The New Testament and the Scriptures of Israel*, ed. Steve Moyise and Maarten J. J. Menken, LNTS 358 (London; New York: T&T Clark, 2008), 121.

88. According to Lincicum, *Encounter*, 137–42: "The *tefillin* and the *mezuzot*, along with the recitation of the *Shemaʿ* and the excerpted texts from Qumran, all demonstrate a sustained interest in Deut 5:1–6:9; 10:12–11:21, and 32:1–43. This selection of texts corresponds to a significant portion of Paul's quotations from Deuteronomy" (p. 57, repeated in p. 121).

of hardened rebellion against the Lord (31:16–18 cf. 31:27, 29), God promises in ch. 30 a future redemption of his people in which he himself will circumcise their hearts (v. 6) so that they will be able to keep the law (v. 8). The covenant blessings will thus be guaranteed (v. 9) "when you obey the Lord your God by observing his commandments and decrees that are written in this book of the law, because you turn to the Lord your God with all your heart and with all your soul" (v. 10).[89] The motif of the fear of God does not appear in Deut 30, but the similar wording of the covenant obligations in 10:12–13, together with the appearances of the fear of God in the immediate context of Deut 30 itself (cf. 29:58; 31:12, 13), suggest that the fear of God will characterize the new restoration as well.

For our study it is also significant that, again according to Lincicum, Paul fuses the idea of the promised circumcision of the heart in Deuteronomy with God's eschatological enablement of his people to keep the law promised in other prophetic visions, and then interprets this as having come about in his day (Deut 10:16; 30:6; Ezek 36:26–27; Jer 38:33–34 LXX).[90] For as we have seen, here too the prophecy of a coming new covenant in Jer 31:31–34 is linked to the restitution of the fear of God among God's people under the rubric of the Deuteronomic new restoration. Specifically, we observed in Chapter Three that the prophecy of a new, "everlasting covenant" in Jer 32:38–40, as a continuation of the "new covenant" passage from Jer 31:31–4, to which Paul explicitly alludes in 2 Cor 3:6 and as the corollary to Paul's citation of Ezek 37:27 in our passage (cf. the "everlasting covenant" of Ezek 37:26!),[91] declares that under the new, "everlasting covenant" the fear of God as the essential quality of the transformed heart will function as the motivation to pursue righteousness and keep the law.

89. Thus, Rosner, "Deuteronomy," 119: "The new covenant teaching of Jeremiah and Ezekiel, in which the problem of the human heart is resolved, is thus anticipated in Deuteronomy."

90. Lincicum, *Encounter*, 147–53, pointing to Paul's arguments in Rom 2:28–29. Likewise, Roy E. Ciampa, "Deuteronomy in Galatians and Romans," in *Deuteronomy in the New Testament: The New Testament and the Scriptures of Israel*, ed. Steve Moyise and Maarten J. J. Menken, LNTS 358 (London; New York: T&T Clark, 2008), 115: "Leviticus indicates that the way of life is through the Law and Deuteronomy 30 still seems to indicate that a return to faithful keeping of the Law is the key to moving from Israel's experience of the Law's curse to their promised experience of eschatological blessing."

91. Thus, Albert L. A. Hogeterp, "Eschatological Setting of the New Covenant in 2 Cor 3:4–18," in *Theologizing in the Corinthian Conflict: Studies in the Exegesis and Theology of 2 Corinthians*, ed. Reimund Bieringer et al., BTAS 16 (Leuven: Peeters, 2013), 143: "Inaugurated eschatology thus determines the theological perspectives in broader sections of Paul's Second Letter to the Corinthians and in the pericope on the 'new covenant' (2 Cor 3:4–18) in particular." Hogeterp, 141, argues that Jer 31:31–4 LXX is the background of the interpretation of the new covenant in 2 Cor 3. For a more detailed argument regarding the extensive development of this theme and the use of Jer 31:31–4 in 2 Cor 3, see Scott J. Hafemann, *Paul, Moses, and the History of Israel: The Letter/Spirit Contrast and the Argument from Scripture in 2 Corinthians 3*, WUNT 2/81 (Tübingen: J. C. B. Mohr, 1995), 92–186.

Against this backdrop, Paul's reference to the fear of God in 7:1 not only reflects his acknowledgment of his present age as the fulfillment of the promise regarding a new covenant from Jer 31, but also likely alludes to the corresponding passage in Jer 32 as the basis of his understanding of the eschatological gift of "the fear of God" as part of the new covenant restoration of God's people (cf. Jer 33:9). As a servant of this new covenant (2 Cor 3:6), Paul himself experiences the fear of God as a motivation for his ministry (2 Cor 5:11) and consequently exhorts the Corinthians, as members of the new covenant people of God, to cleanse themselves, thereby leading to that holiness which comes about by means of the fear of God (7:1).

This understanding of the fear of God as a reflection of Paul's eschatology sheds light upon the following two issues in the interpretation of 2 Cor 6:14–7:1, to which we will now turn: the temple purity motif and the command to separate. These central theological matters of contention are inextricably linked not only to an understanding of the main verb in 7:1, "let us cleanse," and its consequence for the "holiness" of the Corinthians, but also to the related meaning and role of the fear of God in the life of believers. Paul's exhortation to the Corinthians in 7:1 is part of the temple purity motif, alluding back to their identity as the temple of the living God expressed in 6:16b. This ongoing process of cleansing will bring about the completion of their "holiness," which is linked to the command to separate in 6:17ac. Moreover, none of this will be possible apart from "the fear of God."

1. Temple Purity

In Chapter Three I discussed how the command to fear God's sanctuary in Lev 26:2 is still effective in Ezek 37:26 when God places his sanctuary in the midst of his people. The fear of God's sanctuary as the expression of the fear of God in Lev 26:2 motivates the people's pursuit of a holy life and functions as the covenant stipulation. Moreover, the new covenant context of Ezek 37:27 shows that the people of God are still required to respond properly to God's saving activity, which is here expressed in terms of God's sanctuary having been placed among them. Paul understands that the promises in Lev 26:11–12 are now being fulfilled as a result of the establishment of the new, "everlasting covenant" anticipated in Ezek 37:27 (cf. 2 Cor 6:16b). Under the realities of this new covenant, Paul exhorts the believers to show the proper response to God's salvific acts, i.e., to fear God and pursue holiness as *God's temple*.

In fact, scholars have acknowledged the centrality of the temple motif in relationship to the cleansing and holiness language of 2 Cor 7:1.[92] Paul's use of καθαρίζω, μολυσμός, and ἁγιωσύνη, terms which are typically related to the

---

92. E.g., Hogeterp, *God's Temple*, 295–378; Liu, *Temple Purity*, 106–233; Gordon D. Fee, *The First Epistle to the Corinthians*, NICNT (Grand Rapids: Eerdmans, 1987), 311; G. K. Beale, *The Temple and the Church's Mission: A Biblical Theology of the Dwelling Place of God*, NSBT 17 (Downers Grove, IL: Apollos; InterVarsity Press, 2004), 245–52.

purification of the temple, point back to Paul's announcement in 6:16b of his shared identity with the Corinthians as "the temple of the living God."[93] This is the decisive point at which Paul reminds the community not only of their fundamental identity, but also of their vocation to manifest God's holiness and truthfulness in the world (cf. 6:14–16a), which is further presented in the exhortation of 7:1.[94] Though Paul had already introduced the motif of the church as God's temple in 1 Corinthians and warned them of the eschatological implications of profaning it (cf. 1 Cor 3:9–17; 5:6–8; 6:18–20), it is significant that in our passage Paul explicitly connects his exhortations regarding the "temple" with "the fear of God" (cf. 6:16ab with 7:1). Moreover, although scholars have frequently focused on the temple motif in 2 Cor 6:14–7:1, few have provided an explanation of why and how Paul connects the motif of the fear of God with the motif of temple purity.[95]

Though the temple motif is combined with the fear of God only in 2 Cor 7:1, in 1 Cor 3:9–17; 5:6–8; 6:18–20 Paul associated the temple motif with their holiness in the context of the final judgment. There Paul makes it clear that divine condemnation will be the consequence of believers' failing to fulfill their obligations as "God's temple," which in turn is intended to lead them to pursue holiness. This warning alludes to the eschatological judgment scene, which is also pictured in the previous section when Paul reminds the believers that each of their works will become visible on the "judgment day" through the test of fire (1 Cor 3:13) and that the test will determine their reward or penalty (1 Cor 3:14–15).[96] As such, the judgment theme with regard to the temple in 1 Corinthians has a similar function to the fear of God in 2 Cor 7:1 which is also related to the acknowledgment of the Corinthians as God's temple. It is noteworthy that Paul's concern regarding the eschatological judgment is not for those outside the congregation (cf. 1 Cor 5:12–13), but for the salvation of believers within.[97] Again, the fear of God, for Paul,

---

93. Liu, *Temple Purity*, 229–32.

94. Ibid., 200.

95. For example, Liu (ibid., 199–229) examines the temple purity motif in 1 and 2 Corinthians and explains the fear of God in 2 Cor 7:1 to be the believer's "condition of being conducive to God's mercy and aid," referring to God's providence for the believer. However, he does not provide further explanation for this understanding of the fear of God, nor does he connect this motif with the OT contexts of 2 Cor 6:14–7:1, to which he devotes many pages of thorough analysis. Liu, 230, thus suggests that Paul's use of the phrase "in the fear of God" could echo Isa 66:1–2, and stresses two points: God makes the cosmos his temple and God will look upon people who are "trembling" at his word, though he does not elaborate what the latter means or their interconnection.

96. Hogeterp (*God's Temple*, 320) argues that the "day" in v. 13 indicates the "Day of the Lord" as in 1 Cor 1:8. According to Beale, *Temple*, 250–2, 1 Cor 3:10–17 alludes to Mal 3:1–2 and 4:1, which suggests that "Paul thinks the faithful Corinthians are part of the final end-time temple that will withstand the fiery storm winds of the last judgment" (p. 251).

97. As Fee (*First Corinthians*, 313–14) argues, the judgment in terms of rewards and penalties and the judgment as testing are inseparable in that both concern the salvation of

as in the biblical and Jewish tradition, is a characteristic of the righteous, not the unbeliever. Similarly, in 1 Cor 5:3–4 Paul pronounces "judgment in the name of the Lord Jesus" on the man who commits immorality. As scholars have pointed out, the theme of 5:1–13 is sexual immorality within the Corinthian congregation, which has been described as God's holy temple.[98] Likewise, in 1 Cor 6:12–20 Paul's exhortation, "Shun fornication! (v. 18)," is linked to their identity as God's temple, "your body is a temple of the Holy Spirit within you (v. 19)," and appears in the context of the final judgment: if the admonition is not heeded, "God will destroy both one and the other (v. 13)."[99]

In 1 Corinthians Paul consequently uses the cultic imagery of the temple as part of a coherent moral perspective in his theology,[100] and he exhorts the Corinthians to keep themselves pure and holy, just as God commanded the priests in the OT temple to be holy.[101] In other words, Paul's temple imagery serves a pedagogical purpose, namely, "to teach the Corinthians to live a holy communal way of life, as opposed to their division and quarrels, through his figurative equation of the Corinthians with God's field and God's building."[102] Moreover, Paul's exhortations regarding the church as God's temple appear in the context of a warning that derives from the expectation of divine judgment, which in turn is to motivate believers to pursue a life of moral purity.

The recurring connection in 1 Corinthians between the exhortation to temple purity (based on the church's communal identity as the temple) and the final judgment thus anticipates Paul's exhortation in 2 Cor 7:1, based on the implied admonition in 6:16a for the temple to be free of all associations with idolatry, to purify the temple in the fear of God. And here too Paul's command, motivated by the fear of God, is inextricably linked to the theme of final judgment through the contexts of the catena of Scripture in 6:16c–18. Paul's use of the temple motif and

---

believers. In the same context, George W. E. Nickelsburg argues that the judgment by fire motif (as in 4 Ezra, the Testaments of the Twelve Patriarchs, and the Psalms of Solomon) indicates that "The righteous are rewarded because of their obedience to the Torah, even if they have been rewarded during their lives, and although they may not have suffered or died because of their righteousness. The sinners are condemned for their wickedness in general and not specifically because they have maltreated the righteous." George W. E. Nickelsburg, *Resurrection, Immortality, and Eternal Life in Intertestamental Judaism and Early Christianity*, expanded ed., HTS 56 (Cambridge, MA; London: Harvard University Press, 2006), 177. For a more detailed argument concerning the motif of the eschatological judgment by fire, see Hogeterp, *God's Temple*, 320–22; Fee, *First Corinthians*, 312–13.

98. Hogeterp, *God's Temple*, 331–36; Liu, *Temple Purity*, 127–45.

99. Both Hogeterp (*God's Temple*, 336–47) and Liu (*Temple Purity*, 147–73) focus on Paul's use of the temple motif for the body, but do not discuss the connection between the judgment theme and the temple motif.

100. Hogeterp, *God's Temple*, 298.

101. Beale, *Temple*, 256.

102. Hogeterp, *God's Temple*, 317. So too Liu, Temple Purity, 115.

its related motif of the fear of God is therefore based on his underlying conviction that the Corinthians, through the atonement of Jesus, are now the new covenant community, which is the spiritually transformed dwelling of the living God (6:16b), whose holiness they are to manifest through the life they lead.[103]

Moreover, the fear of God and the context of eschatological judgment that lie in the background of Paul's identification of believers as God's temple and his corresponding exhortations to them indicate that the process of sanctification has not yet reached the terminal point and will not be fully achieved until a consummative point in the future. Paul therefore combines the temple motif with the themes of eschatological judgment and its consequent "fear of God" in order to stress that believers must continue to pursue holiness as God's people until the eschatological day of judgment.

2. The Command to Separate

As David I. Starling argues, one of the greatest difficulties in understanding 6:14–7:1 is being able to explain the connection between the negative call to separation in 6:14–16a, 17 and the appeal for reconciliation in the previous section (cf. 5:19–20; 6:11–12).[104] To solve this problem, we have to consider two things: Paul's intention behind his exhortation to the Corinthians to reconcile with God and himself and the function of the fear of God in relationship to Paul's exhortations. Paul exhorts the Corinthians to be reconciled because they have become God's people in the new covenant (5:20; 6:16b) and therefore possess God's promises (7:1 cf. 6:16d–18a). However, their questioning the divine authority of Paul's apostleship reflects the fact that their actions do not match their identity. Paul consequently warns them that, "If this alienation between Paul and his readers continues, it will also be an alienation from God since Paul represents God's authority and it is actually God who is 'entreating' through him (5:20; cf. 2:14–17; 3:6; 6:7; 10:8; 13:3)."[105] In other words, rejecting Paul's authority and siding with his opponents are not matters of individual preference, but are directly connected to their salvation.

As we have observed above, Paul's warning in 6:1 that "they might accept God's grace in vain" thus expresses what is at stake for the Corinthians in their rejection of Paul's authority and message.[106] With this same urgency, Paul exhorts the Corinthians to separate from unbelievers and to cleanse themselves from every defilement, and he asks them to do these tasks in the fear of God (6:14a, 17a; 7:1b). Like the warning in 6:1, the judgment implied in the fear of God highlights the situation into which the Corinthians might fall if they do not follow the admonitions

---

103. Hogeterp, *God's Temple*, 376. Also Thrall, *Second Corinthians*, 1:480; Liu, *Temple Purity*, 205–8, 229–30; Martin, *2 Corinthians*, 375–6.
104. Starling, *Not My People*, 87.
105. Beale, "Reconciliation," 224.
106. Hafemann, "Old Testament in 2 Corinthians," 252.

of Paul and the Scriptures (cf. Paul's use of Isa 49:8 in 2 Cor 6:2 with the catena of Scripture in 6:16c–18).

In the eschaton that has now dawned (6:2), Paul claims that reconciliation with God through Christ in response to Paul's ministry of reconciliation (5:18–21) is the beginning of the eschatological redemption of the world, which is also called the new creation (5:17).[107] As a result of this new reality, the Corinthians should act like reconciled people by opening their heart to Paul positively (6:13) and by not bearing a yoke with unbelievers negatively (6:14).[108] Hence, the positive and negative exhortations do not contradict each other because in their identity as part of the "new creation" (5:17) the Corinthians' separation from unbelievers is merely a natural expression of their reconciliation with God and Paul. In other words, Paul exhorts the Corinthians, as the people of God, to maintain their "new creation" identity through reconciliation (with Paul and thus with God) and separation

---

107. Ibid.

108. Scholarly positions on the issue of the identity of "unbelievers" (ἄπιστοι) in 6:14a are divided. The traditional theory understands the unbelievers to be the pagan idolaters outside the Corinthian community, e.g., Fee, "Idols," 156–9; Webb, *Returning Home*, 184–99; Witherington, *Conflict*, 402–6; Barnett, *Second Corinthians*, 341–3; Harris, *Second Corinthians*, 499–501; Martin, *2 Corinthians*, 361–2. On the other hand, the alternative theory claims that the unbelievers are Paul's opponents within the community, whom Paul depicts in 2 Cor 10–13 as "false apostles" (ψευδαπόστολοι), e.g., Nils Alstrup Dahl, "A Fragment and Its Context: 2 Corinthians 6:14–7:1," in *Studies in Paul: Theology for the Early Christian Mission* (Minneapolis: Augsburg Fortress, 1977), 62–9; Jerome Murphy-O'Connor, "Relating 2 Corinthians 6:14–7:1 to Its Context," *NTS* 33 (1987): 272–3; James M. Scott, *2 Corinthians*, NIBCNT 8 (Peabody, MA: Carlisle: Hendrickson; Paternoster, 1998), 152–3; Scott J. Hafemann, *2 Corinthians*, NIVAC (Grand Rapids: Zondervan, 2000); Craig S. Keener, *1–2 Corinthians*, NCBC (Cambridge: Cambridge University Press, 2005), 192–93. Also see Webb (*Returning Home*, 184–99), who examines five possible referents for "unbelievers": (1) untrustworthy persons; (2) Gentile Christians who do not keep the Torah; (3) the immoral within the church community; (4) the false apostles, and (5) non-Christians, pagans outside the church community. Two scholars have recently attempted to provide a fresh perspective on this issue. David I. Starling, "The ἄπιστοι of 2 Cor 6:14: Beyond the Impasse," *NT* 55 (2013): 45–60, argues that the holiness in 2 Cor 7:1 is a broad, comprehensive concept that includes a separation from the pagan fleshly wisdom (influenced by sophistic tradition) that has made them side with the false apostles who oppose Paul. The false apostles are not themselves the unbelievers in 6:14, but the principle issue from which Paul is urging the Corinthians to separate is not the cultic or sexual entanglements he addressed elsewhere, but the fleshly wisdom that stands behind the false apostles. On the other hand, Volker Rabens, "Paul's Rhetoric of Demarcation: Separation from 'Unbelievers' (2 Cor 6:14–7:1) in the Corinthian Conflict," in *Theologizing in the Corinthian Conflict: Studies in the Exegesis and Theology of 2 Corinthians*, ed. Reimund Bieringer et al., BTAS 16 (Leuven: Peeters, 2013), 229–54, argues that 2 Cor 6:14–7:1 can be read as a double entendre referring to a demarcation both from idolatrous people outside the church (= unbelievers) and idolatrous people inside the church (= unbelievers).

(from unbelievers), both of which can be understood as acts of cleansing (expressed in an ethical sense).[109] For as Beale rightly observes, "Paul can only issue *negative* imperatives not to identify with the unbelieving world on the *positive* basis that the readers are already possessors of these Old Testament restoration promises."[110]

Furthermore, the Corinthians are facing a serious situation in that their very salvation is at stake in these positive and negative admonitions. However, in order to understand the gravity of Paul's admonitions and warnings, the positive and negative exhortations in 5:19–6:1 and 6:14–7:1, including the role of the fear of God in 5:11 and 7:1, need to be put in their salvation-historical context. Only when we take into account that the OT quotations in 6:16c–18 contain not only the promises of Israel's restoration, but also a warning of judgment in the case of failure,[111] can we explain why Paul begins his argument in the larger context with reference to his own fear of the Lord (5:11) and concludes it with an exhortation to pursue holiness in the fear of God (7:1). In this context, Paul's negative exhortation to separate from unbelievers will lead believers to become more confirmed in their positive identity as those reconciled with God and his apostle, and in so doing eventually lead them to be able to keep the further positive exhortations of Chapters Eight and Nine. As Hafemann rightly argues:

> if 6:14–7:1 expresses in a negative vein the new covenant status and obligations of God's restored people, then their renewed willingness to participate in the collection for Jerusalem will be an undeniable positive expression of this same status.[112]

---

109. Adewuya, "Holiness," 207–15.
110. Beale, "Reconciliation," 236, emphasis added.
111. Thus, ibid., 241.
112. Hafemann, "Old Testament in 2 Corinthians," 253.

Chapter 6

CONCLUSION

I. Overview

This study has sought to demonstrate Paul's coherent understanding of the fear of God in 2 Cor 7:1 within the contexts of the canonical letter, the OT, and Paul's Jewish contemporaries. Scholars have repeatedly pointed to 2 Cor 6:14–7:1 as an interpolation from an extra-biblical source, arguing that Paul's appeal in this section does not fit with the larger context, nor match Paul's use of language and themes in other writings. This study, however, has contended that the fear of God in 7:1 is not only the *crux interpretum* to Paul's argument of 6:14–7:1, especially in terms of the Scriptures to which Paul appeals in 6:16c–18, but also that it coheres both with the developing argument of 2 Corinthians and with his eschatology.

In support of this thesis, Chapter Two examined 2 Cor 5:10–11 and showed that the fear of the Lord referenced in 5:11 derives from Paul's acknowledgment of the judgment seat of Christ in 5:10. It was this fear that motivated Paul in his ministry. We also argued that "the fear of the Lord" in 5:11 refers not to Christ, but to the fear of God by examining the content of Paul's fear (cf. 6:1) and the Isaianic background of 2 Cor 4–6.

In Chapter Three we turned to the broader context of the OT citations that Paul quotes in 2 Cor 6:16c–18, which we saw in each case provided the implied Scriptural background for the motif of the fear of God in 2 Cor 7:1. An examination of the commands in Isa 52:11 within the context of Isa 50:4–52:11 discovered that these commands were intended to express the proper reaction of the people of God to God's salvation, which contextually is also described in Isa 50:10 as "fearing God." This fear of God among God's people thus forms an essential contrast to those who will be condemned under God's judgment (50:11). In regard to the two promises of God that appear in the composite citation of Lev 26:11–12 and Ezek 37:27, the fear of God in Lev 26:2, expressed in the fear of God's sanctuary, was seen to function as the covenant stipulation that determines the covenant blessings (vv. 4–13), and curses (vv. 14–39). The covenant formula, which is expressed in the promise cited from Ezek 37:27, then, places the promise from Lev 26:11–12 within the context of the new covenant. This recalls Paul's comparison of the new covenant passages from Ezekiel and Jeremiah in 2 Cor 3:3 and 6, by which Paul describes his new covenant ministry. As was clear in the context of Lev 26:1–2 and 11–12, the sanctuary that God will set in the midst of his people demands that the people fear his sanctuary as that which will motivate them to keep his commandments. So too in Ezek 37:26, placing God's sanctuary in the midst of his people will lead to the overcoming their idolatry and cause them to keep God's statues (vv. 23–5). The composite citation of Lev 26:11–12 and Ezek 37:27 in 2 Cor 6:16de therefore reveals that, for Paul, the fear of God continues to play a significant role in the life of God's people under the rubric of the new, "everlasting covenant" (cf. Jer 32:38–41). Moreover, the brief examination of the context of Ezek 20:34 (cf. 2 Sam 7:14), to which Paul also refers in the catena of Scripture, showed the context of God's judgment upon his people, and thus further provides the biblical context for the fear of God already established by the link between 2 Cor 5:11 and 7:1.

In order to provide a point of comparison and contrast for better understanding Paul's own adaptation of this biblical material, Chapter Four then examined four exemplary texts from the history of Paul's tradition as paradigmatic indicators of the spectrum of the Jewish understanding of the fear of God in the Second Temple period. In the Psalms of Solomon, as in the biblical material, the fear of God functions as a characteristic of the righteous and derives from the motif of God's judgment. Moreover, the examination of Ps. Sol. 17 showed that the fear of God also characterizes the eschatological reign of the Messiah during which it continues to motivate all people (including the nations) to live righteously. Jubilees shares many similarities with 2 Cor 6:14–7:1, but the motif of the fear of God appears only a few times without explicit function. Nevertheless, the assumed link between the fear of God and his judgment indicates that where judgment is given as the motivation, fearing God is also implied. In 4 Ezra, here too the fear of God derives from God's judgment and thereby functions as a motivation for the people. Moreover, 4 Ezra shows that those who fear God in the present, as manifest in their keeping of the law, will not fear God on the day of judgment. In contrast, the stance of the unrighteous ones, who did not fear God in the present and despised his law will fear God on the day of judgment. Again, there are not two kinds of "fear," but only one fear that derives from the final judgment of God and functions differently in relationship to two types of persons and times in which this fear is experienced. The motivational function of the fear of God becomes more apparent in 6 Ezra, which is a later Christian redaction. The comparison of 4 and 6 Ezra helped us to see how the Christian redactor used the theme of the fear of God in congruence with the Jewish tradition. This observation was further supported by our examination of the Testaments of the Twelve Patriarchs against its Jewish and Christian backgrounds, where the fear of God expresses itself in the keeping of God's law and is connected to the judgment of God, thereby once again functioning as a motivation for the righteous life.

With this survey in view, the study returned in Chapter Five to 2 Cor 6:14–7:1 for a close reading of Paul's argument. Against the backdrop of its use in both the OT and Second Temple Judaism, we argued that Paul's use of the fear of God in 7:1, concluding his former argument of 6:14–18, is striking in that Paul understood his present age as the beginning of a new age of the new covenant (6:16) in which the fear of God nevertheless continues to function as a motivation for believers in view of the judgment of God still to come. Thus, just as the fear of the Lord motivated Paul in his own ministry toward others, knowing that they would one day face the judgment seat of Christ (5:10–11), so too the fear of God is to motivate believers to cleanse themselves so that they complete holiness in their lives (7:1). The study then showed how this new understanding of the fear of God sheds light on the literary and theological issues that have been raised regarding 2 Cor 6:14–7:1.

II. Implications for Reading Second Corinthians

If our observations are correct, they can help us to understand Paul's coherent use of the fear of God as his argument continues in 2 Corinthians, in which the motif of fear appears five more times, subsequent to its use in 5:11 and 7:1 (7:5, 11, 15; 11:3; 12:20). Among these texts fear appears without a specific reference to its object and thus its connection to the fear of the Lord/God in 5:11 and 7:1 is not immediately clear. In this regard, George H. Guthrie, representative of many, argues that the other occurrences of fear in 2 Corinthians "seem to refer to an emotional state of being afraid or anxious, or at least deeply sobered by a situation."[1] However, given our understanding of the meaning and motivational function of the fear of God in the life of the believer as reflected in 5:11 and 7:1, Paul may be seen to be presenting the same or similar perspectives regarding the fear of God as his argument continues throughout the rest of 2 Corinthians.

1. 2 Cor 7:5, 11, 15

Second Corinthians 7:5–16 focuses on the joy Paul experienced as a result of the encouraging report about the Corinthians' response to his earlier "tearful letter" (cf. 2:1–4 with 7:8) that Paul received from Titus upon meeting him in Macedonia (7:7). In this section "fear" appears three times and plays a significant role in Paul's argument. Even though fear appears without a specific referent to its object, a closer examination will show that each case shares similarities with the perspectives on the fear of God established in 5:11 and 7:1.

In 7:5 Paul confesses that "when we came into Macedonia, our bodies had no rest, but we were afflicted at every turn—fightings without and *fears within* (ἔξωθεν μάχαι, ἔσωθεν φόβοι)" (emphasis added). The "fightings without" seem to refer either to the persecution of the church in Macedonia or to quarrels among believers in Macedonia, both of which would have impacted Paul.[2] On the other hand, the "fears within" appear to reflect Paul's worry about the Corinthians—they

---

1. George H. Guthrie, *2 Corinthians*, BECNT (Grand Rapids: Baker Academic, 2015), 381.
2. Paul Barnett, *The Second Epistle to the Corinthians*, NICNT (Grand Rapids: Eerdmans, 1997), 368.

might be a reference to Paul's fear about his own safety, but the plural form of fear is better taken to denote Paul's concern about the Corinthians' response to the harsh letter that he had sent via Titus (2:4).[3] Thus, Paul's fear in 7:5 is linked to the fear of God in that it concerned the danger of God's judgment faced by the Corinthians if they had not repented of their rebellion against Paul and his gospel in response to his letter, which was an extension of his apostolic ministry to them (5:11). In other words, Paul had many fears that the Corinthians may have received God's grace in vain (6:1).[4]

Nevertheless, despite those previous fears, Paul was now excited about Titus' report (7:9) because the majority of the Corinthians had received Paul's harsh letter with the "godly sorrow" (7:10) that led them to "repentance" (vv. 9, 10), producing "eagerness (to clear oneself), indignation, *fear* (φόβον), longing, zeal, and punishment" (v. 11).[5] It is noteworthy that fear appears among the seven responses listed here that Paul regards as proper responses to God's grace in their lives.[6] That the Corinthians' fear is closely connected to the judgment context is supported by Paul's conclusion in v. 11 that, by their repentance, the Corinthians have now proved themselves "guiltless (ἁγνός) in the matter" of their previous rebellion. The reference to their being "guiltless" clearly shows a juridical context for their fear.[7] Moreover, the judgment context of the Corinthians' fear is further

---

3. Barnett (ibid.); Murray J. Harris, *The Second Epistle to the Corinthians: A Commentary on the Greek Text*, NIGTC (Grand Rapids; Milton Keynes: Eerdmans; Paternoster, 2005), 527; Guthrie, *2 Corinthians*, 372–3. Moreover, Paul mentions several times in his letters about the life of believers without fear (for other object), e.g., Rom 8:15; Phil 1:14; also Gal 2:12, where Paul rebukes Peter's improper "fear of the circumcision faction" (φοβούμενος τοὺς ἐκ περιτομῆς). Thus, it is more probable that Paul's fear(s) in 2 Cor 7:5 refers to his concern about the Corinthians, and not to his fear of people or circumstances regarding his safety.

4. Paul's fear in 2 Cor 7:5 is similar to Gal 4:11, where Paul fears that his work for the Galatians might become in vain (εἰκῇ) (cf. 1 Cor 15:2).

5. Barnett (*Second Corinthians*, 372) and Harris (*Second Corinthians*, 541–2) take the "fear" as "alarm"; Guthrie (*2 Corinthians*, 380) takes it as "a deep, awe-inspired reverence."

6. Scholarly opinion has been divided regarding the fear in v. 11. For example, Harris (*Second Corinthians*, 542) argues that fear indicates the uncertainty of the Corinthians about the consequences that their disloyalty on Paul will bring on his visit 'with a rod' (1 Cor 4:21). Ralph P. Martin (*2 Corinthians*, 2nd rev., WBC 40 [Grand Rapids: Zondervan, 2014], 402) argues that this fear can mean both the Corinthians' (negative) fear regarding Paul (cf. 1 Cor 4:21) or God (cf. 2 Cor 5:11). Martin comments that this use of fear suggests reverential awe, but does not further explain how the negative fear acts in a positive aspect. Mark A. Seifrid (*The Second Letter to the Corinthians*, PNTC [Grand Rapids; Nottingham, England: Eerdmans; Apollos, 2014], 310) argues that this fear refers not to a fear of Paul, but of God, who has given him apostolic authority.

7. According to Barnett (*Second Corinthians*, 379) and Harris (*Second Corinthians*, 542–3), this phrase means the Corinthians are now declared to be "blameless."

emphasized by Paul's statement in v. 12 that he had written his painful letter so that the Corinthians' earnestness for him "might be revealed (φανερωθῆναι) before God (ἐνώπιον τοῦ θεοῦ)."[8] From the context it is thus clear that the Corinthians' fear produced by their repentance, as the evidence and characteristic of their salvation (cf. 7:10), derives from their acknowledgment of God's judgment.[9] This again fits with the fact that, as we observed both in the OT (e.g., Isa 50:10; Jer 32:40; etc.) and in Second Temple Judaism (e.g., Ps. Sol. 18:7-9; 4 Ezra 7:[79]; 8:28; etc.), the fear of God characterizes the righteous in the present, whose fear of the future judgment motivates them to pursue holiness. In contrast, the wicked do not fear in the present, but will fear when they fall under God's condemnation in the future (cf. 4 Ezra 7:[87]). Thus, it is not two "kinds" of fear that distinguish the righteous from the wicked, but rather whether one experiences the fear of God in view of his future judgment, which leads those who fear God's judgment to pursue a holy life in the present.

Hence, 2 Cor 7:15 shows that the repentant Corinthians' fear (of God's judgment; cf. 7:11-12) motivated them to show a proper response (to God and also to Paul's letter) in that they expressed their "obedience" (ὑπακοή) by welcoming Titus "with fear and trembling" (μετὰ φόβου καὶ τρόμου).[10] Thus, 7:5-16 begins with Paul's *fear(s)* as in 5:11, yet it ends with his joy because of the Corinthians' *fear* as called for in 7:1. Paul himself rejoices because he now has perfect confidence in the Corinthians (v. 16) that they too will follow Paul's example, since, as with Paul (5:10-11), the fear (of God) in response to God's coming judgment is once again motivating the Corinthians to obey.[11]

The fear and trembling alludes back to 1 Cor 2:3, where Paul came to the Corinthians not with self-aggrandizing sophisticated rhetoric, but in weakness

---

8. Cf. Rom 3:20; 14:22; 1 Cor 1:29; 2 Cor 4:2; 8:21; Gal 1:20. Most of the scholars argue that v. 12 refers to the judgment of God. E.g., Barnett, *Second Corinthians*, 381-82; Harris, *Second Corinthians*, 546; Martin, *2 Corinthians*, 406. Also note the same verb, φανερόω, in v. 12 alludes back to Paul's earlier argument regarding the judgment seat in 5:10.

9. Thus, B. J. Oropeza (*Exploring Second Corinthians: Death and Life, Hardship and Rivalry*, RRA 3 [Atlanta: SBL Press, 2016], 474-5) argues that the fear in v. 11 seems to anticipate divine retribution. In contrast to the fear of the Corinthians in 7:11, Rom 3:18 describes unbelievers as those for whom, "there is no fear of God before their eyes."

10. Thus, Guthrie, *2 Corinthians*, 384-5; Barnett, *2 Corinthians*, 382; Harris, *2 Corinthians*, 522; Seifrid, *Second Corinthians*, 312. Barnett, *2 Corinthians*, 385 and Harris, *2 Corinthians*, 552 acknowledge the OT allusion in the phrase "fear and trembling" to Exod 15:16; Deut 2:25; 11:25; Isa 19:16. For a more detailed argument about the use of this phrase, see Oropeza, *Second Corinthians*, 477n335.

11. For a more detailed argument about Phil 2:12, see J. Ross Wagner, "Working out Salvation: Holiness and Community in Philippians," in *Holiness and Ecclesiology in the New Testament*, ed. Kent E. Brower and Andy Johnson (Grand Rapids; Cambridge: Eerdmans, 2007), 257-74. Wagner, 263, acknowledges "fear and trembling" to be the Philippians' response to God's presence, but does not discuss its judgment context.

and "in fear and in much trembling" (ἐν φόβῳ καὶ ἐν τρόμῳ πολλῷ) as befits a servant of Christ who is aware of God's judgment (cf. 1 Cor 4:1-5), which demonstrated God's Spirit and power (2:4). Against this backdrop, in 2 Cor 7:15 Paul is rejoicing that the Corinthians also follow Paul's example. Moreover, 2 Cor 7:15 is also closely linked to Paul's exhortation to believers in Philippians:

> Therefore, my beloved, just as you have always obeyed me, not only in my presence, but much more now in my absence, *work out your own salvation with fear and trembling* (μετὰ φόβου καὶ τρόμου τὴν ἑαυτῶν σωτηρίαν κατεργάζεσθε)
> Phil 2:12, emphasis added.

The context reveals that here too Paul is referring to the fear of God. First, the outcome of the exhortation is the Philippians' becoming "blameless and without blemish" (ἄμεμπτοι καὶ ἀκέραιοι) at the day of judgment (2:15; cf. my discussion of 1 Thess 3:11-13 in Chapter Five). Second, the content of the fear is that if they fail in keeping Paul's exhortation, then Paul's "running and labor" as an apostle will be "in vain" (εἰς κενόν) (2:16). Third, just as the Corinthians' fear and trembling was expressed in their obedience (2 Cor 7:15), so too Paul calls attention to the obedience of the Philippians in Phil 2:12. Lastly, the OT quotation from Isa 45:23 in Phil 2:9-11 implies judgment context (cf. Rom 14:10-11).[12]

2. 2 Cor 11:3; 12:20-1

In 2 Cor 11:3 and 12:20-1 Paul warns the Corinthians of the danger into which they might fall, which he expressed in both cases with "fear." In 11:3 Paul expresses his fear of the danger caused by the false apostles:

> But I *fear* (φοβοῦμαι) that as the serpent deceived Eve by its cunning, your thoughts will be led astray from a sincere and pure devotion to Christ (emphasis added).

Later, in 12:20-1 Paul expresses his fear that despite his attempts to win them back, he will still find some of the Corinthians not repenting:[13]

> For I *fear* (φοβοῦμαι) that when I come, I may find you not as I wish, and that you may find me not as you wish; [for I fear] that there may perhaps be quarreling, jealousy, anger, selfishness, slander, gossip, conceit, and disorder; [for I fear] that when I come again, my God may humble me before you, and that I may have to mourn over many who previously sinned and *have not repented* of the impurity, sexual immorality, and licentiousness that they have practiced (emphasis added).

---

12. See my argument in Chapter Two.
13. Paul describes the situation in three long clauses starting with μή that are all referring back to Paul's fear. Barnett, *Second Corinthians*, 594.

Two things can be observed from the context surrounding Paul's "fear" in 11:3 and 12:20-1. First, as in the other occurrences of fear in 2 Corinthians, divine judgment appears as the context. Paul continuously warns the Corinthians against the false apostles in 11:13-14 by explaining the eschatological, juridical consequences facing those "apostles" (and their followers): "their end will match their deeds."[14] Likewise, Paul claims in 12:19 that he is speaking "before God and in Christ," which, as we mentioned in Chapter Two, carries the idea of judgment (cf. 2 Cor 2:17).[15] Second, along with the reference to fear, Paul describes the proper responses of the Corinthians in contrast to their failed responses. The Corinthians were supposed to show "a sincere and pure devotion to Christ" (11:3) and "repentance" (12:21); however, if they are "being led astray" (11:3), there may be "quarreling, jealousy, anger, selfishness, slander, gossip, conceit, and disorder" (12:20), in that they have "sinned and have not repented of the impurity, sexual immorality, and licentiousness that they have practiced" (12:21).[16] In other words, Paul's fear derives from the recognition that the Corinthians did not show a proper response to Paul's gospel according to their new identity, but instead acted in a way that led them to receive God's grace in vain. In this regard, Paul's fear in 11:3 and 12:20-1 reveals similarities with the features of the fear of God we have seen in 5:11 and 7:1.[17] Therefore, Paul ends his letter by exhorting those Corinthians still in rebellion against him and his gospel to examine their deeds, motives, and relationship with God in the light of the reality of God's eschatological judgment, because these will reveal the truth about their standing before God: "Examine yourselves to see whether you are living in the faith. Test yourselves" (13:5).[18] In

---

14. Thus, Barnett, *Second Corinthians*, 527; Harris, *Second Corinthians*, 776; Martin, *2 Corinthians*, 539-40; Guthrie, *2 Corinthians*, 529; Oropeza, *Second Corinthians*, 607, 615: "As such Paul implies that their end will be final judgment. The Corinthians might infer from this that they, too, stand in jeopardy of divine judgment if they continue following the ministers of Satan" (p. 615).

15. Barnett, *Second Corinthians*, 591-2; Martin, *2 Corinthians*, 656; Oropeza, *Second Corinthians*, 704.

16. Different from Barnett (*Second Corinthians*, 595), who argues that 12:20 and 21 each describe two groups existing in the Corinthian community, Martin (*2 Corinthians*, 650) argues that the lists in both verses describe the present situation at Corinth.

17. Likewise, G. K. Beale ("The Old Testament Background of Reconciliation in 2 Corinthians 5-7 and Its Bearing on the Literary Problem of 2 Corinthians 6:14-7:1," in *The Right Doctrine from the Wrong Texts? Essays on the Use of the Old Testament in the New* [Grand Rapids: Baker Books, 1994], 239) argues that there is a close connection between 2 Cor 6:14-7:1 and 12:20-1 in that the former anticipates the continuing problem of the Corinthians' behavior, as described in the latter, which is probably related in part to the false apostles' influence but not necessarily exhaustively so.

18. Likewise, Oropeza, *Second Corinthians*, 712. In this regard, Paul exhorts his listeners and readers in Romans to "not to become proud, but fear (μὴ ὑψηλὰ φρόνει, ἀλλὰ φοβοῦ)" in Rom 11:20. Their attitude of fear is further elaborated as to be constantly cognizant of

other words, they should "cleanse themselves, thus completing holiness, which is brought about by the fear of God" (7:1).

This work has argued that Paul understands the fear of God in 2 Cor 7:1 as deriving from the recognition that an eschatological judgment will come to all people and that it is thus this fear that motivates believers to live a holy life, just as it motivates him for his ministry toward others (2 Cor 5:10–11). In contrast, unbelievers have no such fear of God or his judgment and hence remain in their sinful ways (cf. Rom 3:18 with 2 Cor 4:3–4; 11:3). This understanding of Paul's singular perspective on the fear of God, based on his reception of the OT tradition concerning this motif, differs from the traditional "dual understanding" of the fear of God that posits two kinds of fear—a negative "terror" that derives from God's experienced by unbelievers and a positive "reverence" that motivates believers' obedience. Rather, for Paul, the single fear of God, which can be expressed as "one's feeling of alarm or trepidation in regard to God that is brought about by the realization of the reality of God's eschatological judgment," functions differently in relationship to two types of persons and times. Thus, believers who are living in the eschaton are to be characterized by the fear of God that motivates them to pursue a holy life in anticipation of the judgment to come in the future. This understanding of Paul's fear of God was supported by his use of "the fear of the Lord" in 2 Cor 5:10–11, and, furthermore, by the OT contexts of the catena of Scripture that he quotes in 6:16c–18. We observed that the OT contexts denote references to the fear of God as a covenant stipulation (Lev 26:2) and/or as an expression of obedience (Isa 50:10), and that in both cases the fear of God appears in the context of God's judgment on his people (Lev 26:14–39; Isa 50:11). This judgment context was also apparent in the rest of the OT texts in the catena of Scripture, even though they do not refer explicitly to fearing God (2 Sam 7: 14; Ezek 20:34). We also observed that this motivational function of the fear of God is apparent in Second Temple Judaism either through direct references to the fear of God (the Psalms of Solomon, 4 Ezra, the Testaments of the Twelve Patriarchs) or through depictions of God's judgment (Jubilees). Therefore, our examination of Paul's understanding of the fear of God is justified both by Paul's own theology, which derives from his understanding of the OT Scriptures when read in their original contexts, and by its correspondence to the Jewish traditions regarding the fear of God that formed the larger context of his thoughts, which likewise received the same Scriptures.

---

both God's "kindness" and his "sternness" in the context of God's salvation (v. 22) and his judgment (vv. 21–2). Thomas R. Schreiner, *Romans*, BECNT (Grand Rapids: Baker Academic, 1998), 607–8; Richard N. Longenecker, *The Epistle to the Romans: A Commentary on the Greek Text*, NIGTC (Grand Rapids: Eerdmans, 2016), 894.

BIBLIOGRAPHY OF WORKS CITED

Achtemeier, Paul J. *1 Peter: A Commentary on First Peter*. Edited by Eldon Jay Epp. Hermeneia. Minneapolis: Augsburg Fortress, 1996.

Adams, Sean A. and Ehorn, Seth M. "What Is a Composite Citation? An Introduction." Pages 1–16 in *Composite Citations in Antiquity. Vol. 1*. Edited by Sean A. Adams and Seth M. Ehorn. LNTS 525. London: T&T Clark, 2016.

———. "Introduction." Pages 1–15 in *Composite Citations in Antiquity. Vol. 2*. Edited by Sean A. Adams and Seth M. Ehorn. LNTS 593. London: T&T Clark, 2018.

———. "Conclusion." Pages 209–49 in *Composite Citations in Antiquity. Vol. 2*. Edited by Sean A. Adams and Seth M. Ehorn. LNTS 593. London: T&T Clark, 2018.

Adewuya, James Ayodeji. "The People of God in a Pluralistic Society: Holiness in 2 Corinthians." Pages 201–18 in *Holiness and Ecclesiology in the New Testament*. Edited by Kent E. Brower and Andy Johnson. Grand Rapids; Cambridge: Eerdmans, 2007.

Aernie, Jeffrey W. *Is Paul also among the Prophets? An Examination of the Relationship between Paul and the Old Testament Prophetic Tradition in 2 Corinthians*. LNTS 467. London: T&T Clark, 2012.

Amador, James D. H. "Revisiting 2 Corinthians: Rhetoric and the Case for Unity." *NTS* 46 (2000): 92–111.

Andersen, Francis I. "2 Enoch." Pages 90–221 in *The Old Testament Pseudepigrapha Vol. 1*. Edited by James H. Charlesworth. 3rd ed. Peabody, MA: Hendrickson, 2013.

Aune, David Edward. "The Judgment Seat of Christ (2 Cor. 5.10)." Pages 68–86 in *Pauline Conversations in Context: Essays in Honor of Calvin J. Roetzel*. JSNTSup 221. London; New York: Sheffield Academic Press, 2002.

Baltzer, Klaus. *Deutero-Isaiah: A Commentary on Isaiah 40–55*. Hermeneia. Minneapolis: Fortress, 2001.

Barclay, John M. G. *Paul and the Gift*. Grand Rapids: Eerdmans, 2015.

Barnett, Paul. *The Second Epistle to the Corinthians*. NICNT. Grand Rapids: Eerdmans, 1997.

Barrett, C. K. *A Commentary on the Second Epistle to the Corinthians*. BNTC. London: Black, 1973.

Beale, G. K. *1–2 Thessalonians*. The IVPNTC 13. Downers Grove, IL; Nottingham, England: InterVarsity Press, 2003.

———. *A New Testament Biblical Theology: The Unfolding of the Old Testament in the New*. Grand Rapids: Baker Academic, 2011.

———. *The Book of Revelation: A Commentary on the Greek Text*. NIGTC. Grand Rapids: Carlisle: Eerdmans; Paternoster, 1999.

———. "The Old Testament Background of Reconciliation in 2 Corinthians 5–7 and Its Bearing on the Literary Problem of 2 Corinthians 6:14–7:1." Pages 217–47 in *The Right Doctrine from the Wrong Texts? Essays on the Use of the Old Testament in the New*. Grand Rapids: Baker Books, 1994.

———. *The Temple and the Church's Mission: A Biblical Theology of the Dwelling Place of God*. NSBT 17. Downers Grove, IL: Apollos; InterVarsity Press, 2004.

Becker, Joachim. *Gottesfurcht im Altem Testament*. Anbib 25. Rome: Pontificio Instituto Biblico, 1965.

Becker, Jürgen. *Die Testamente der Zwölf Patriarchen.* JSHRZ 1. Gütersloh: Mohn, 1974.
Bergren, Theodore A. "Christian Influence on the Transmission History of 4, 5, and 6 Ezra." Pages 102–28 in *The Jewish Apocalyptic Heritage in Early Christianity.* Edited by James C. VanderKam and William Adler. CRINT 4. Minneapolis; Assen: Fortress; Van Gorcum, 1996.
———. "Fifth Ezra: A New Translation and Introduction." Pages 467–82 in *Old Testament Pseudepigrapha: More Noncanonical Scriptures.* Edited by Richard Bauckham, James R. Davila, and Alexander Panayotov. Vol. 1. Grand Rapids; Cambridge: Eerdmans, 2013.
———. "Prophetic Rhetoric in 6 Ezra." Pages 25–32 in *For a Later Generation: The Transformation of Tradition in Israel, Early Judaism, and Early Christianity.* Edited by Randal A. Argall, Beverly A. Bow, and Rodney Alan Werline. Harrisburg: Trinity Press International, 2000.
———. "Sixth Ezra: A New Translation and Introduction." Pages 483–97 in *Old Testament Pseudepigrapha: More Noncanonical Scriptures.* Edited by Richard Bauckham, James R. Davila, and Alexander Panayotov. Vol. 1. Grand Rapids; Cambridge: Eerdmans, 2013.
———. *Sixth Ezra: The Text and Origin.* New York; Oxford: Oxford University Press, 1998.
Betz, Hans Dieter. "2 Cor 6:14–7:1: An Anti-Pauline Fragment?" *JBL* 92 (1973): 88–108.
Beuken, W. A. M. "Jes 50:10–11, Eine Kultische Paränese zur Dritten Ebed-Prophetie." *ZAW* 85 (1973): 168–82.
Bieringer, Reimund. "2 Korinther 6,14–7:1 im Kontext des 2. Korintherbriefes. Forschungsüberblick und Versuch eines eigenes Zugangs." Pages 551–70 in *Studies on 2 Corinthians.* Edited by Reimund Bieringer and Jan Lambrecht. BETL 122. Leuven: Leuven University Press; Peeters, 1994.
Blenkinsopp, Joseph. *Isaiah 40–55: A New Translation with Introduction and Commentary.* AB 19A. New York: Doubleday, 2000.
Blum, Erhard. *Studien zur Komposition des Pentateuch.* BZAW 189. Berlin; New York: de Gruyter, 1990.
Bonnard, Pierre. *Le Second Isaïe, Son Disciple et Leurs Éditeurs: Isaïe 40–66. Ebib.* Paris: Gabalda, 1972.
Brooke, George J. "2 Corinthians 6:14–7:1 Again: A Change in Perspective." Pages 1–16 in *The Dead Sea Scrolls and Pauline Literature.* STDJ 102. Leiden: Brill, 2014.
———. *Exegesis at Qumran: 4QFlorilegium in Its Jewish Context. JSOT* 29. Sheffield: JSOT Press, 1985.
Brown, Derek R. *The God of This Age: Satan in the Churches and Letters of the Apostle Paul.* WUNT 2/409. Tübingen: Mohr Siebeck, 2015.
Bultmann, Rudolf Karl. *The Second Letter to the Corinthians.* Translated by Erich Dinkler. Minneapolis: Augsburg, 1985.
Byrne, Brendan. *Romans.* SP 6. Collegeville, MN: Liturgical Press, 2007.
Caird, G. B. *The Revelation of Saint John.* BNTC. Peabody, MA: Hendrickson, 1966.
Charles, R. H., ed. *The Greek Versions of the Testaments of the Twelve Patriarchs: Edited from Nine Mss.: Together with the Variants of the Armenian and Slavonic Versions and some Hebrew Fragments.* Oxford: Clarendon, 1908.
Childs, Brevard S. *Isaiah.* OTL. Louisville: Westminster John Knox, 2001.
Ciampa, Roy E. "Deuteronomy in Galatians and Romans." Pages 99–117 in *Deuteronomy in the New Testament: The New Testament and the Scriptures of Israel.* Edited by Steve Moyise and Maarten J. J. Menken. LNTS 358. London; New York: T&T Clark, 2008.
———. "Composite Citations in 1–2 Corinthians and Galatians." Pages 159–89 in *Composite Citations in Antiquity.* Vol. 2. Edited by Sean A. Adams and Seth M. Ehorn. LNTS 593. London: T&T Clark, 2018.

Ciampa, Roy E., and Brian S. Rosner. *The First Letter to the Corinthians*. PNTC. Grand Rapids; Nottingham, England: Eerdmans; Apollos, 2010.

Conway, Kevin P. *The Promises of God: The Background of Paul's Exclusive Use of "Epangelia" for the Divine Pledge*. BZNW 211. Berlin; Munich; Boston: de Gruyter, 2014.

Crane, Ashley S. *Israel's Restoration: A Textual-Comparative Exploration of Ezekiel 36–39*. VTSup 122. Leiden; Boston: Brill, 2008.

Cranfield, C. E. B. *A Critical and Exegetical Commentary on the Epistle to the Romans*. 6th ed. ICC. Edinburgh: T&T Clark, 1975.

Dahl, Nils Alstrup. "A Fragment and Its Context: 2 Corinthians 6:14–7:1." Pages 62–9 in *Studies in Paul: Theology for the Early Christian Mission*. Minneapolis: Augsburg Fortress, 1977.

Davila, James R. "Testaments of the Twelve Patriarchs." *Old Testament Pseudepigrapha— School of Divinity, University of St Andrews*, February 1997. https://www.st-andrews.ac.uk/divinity/rt/otp/abstracts/testoftwelve/.

———. *The Provenance of the Pseudepigrapha: Jewish, Christian, or Other?* JSJSup 105. Leiden; Boston: Brill, 2005.

De Jonge, Marinus. *Pseudepigrapha of the Old Testament as Part of Christian Literature: The Case of the Testaments of the Twelve Patriarchs and the Greek Life of Adam and Eve*. SVTP 18. Leiden: Brill, 2003.

———. "The Main Issues in the Study of the Testaments of the Twelve Patriarchs." Pages 148–63 in *Jewish Eschatology, Early Christian Christology, and the Testaments of the Twelve Patriarchs: Collected Essays of Marinus de Jonge*. NovTSup 63. Leiden: Brill, 1991.

———. "The Testaments of the Twelve Patriarchs: Christian and Jewish. A Hundred Years after Friedrich Schnapp." Pages 233–43 in *Jewish Eschatology, Early Christian Christology, and the Testaments of the Twelve Patriarchs: Collected Essays of Marinus de Jonge*. NovTSup 63. Leiden: Brill, 1991.

———. "The Two Great Commandments in the Testaments of the Twelve Patriarchs." *NovT* 44, (2002): 371–92.

Dimant, Devorah. "Between Qumran Sectarian and Non-Sectarian Texts: The Case of Belial and Mastema." Pages 235–56 in *Dead Sea Scrolls and Contemporary Culture: Proceedings of the International Conference Held at the Israel Museum, Jerusalem (July 6–8, 2008)*. Leiden: Brill, 2011.

Dodd, C. H. *According to the Scripture: The Sub-Structure of New Testament Theology*. London: Nisbet, 1953.

Dunn, James D. G. "Jesus the Judge: Further Thoughts of Paul's Christology and Soteriology." Pages 34–54 in *The Convergence of Theology: A Festschrift Honoring Gerald O'Collins, S. J.* Edited by Daniel Kendall and Stephen T. Davis. New York: Paulist, 2001.

Eichrodt, Walther. *Ezekiel: A Commentary*. OTL. London: SCM, 1970.

Ekblad Jr., Eugene Robert. *Isaiah's Servant Poems According to the Septuagint: An Exegetical and Theological Study*. CBET 23. Leuven: Peeters, 1999.

Ellis, E. Earle. *The Old Testament in Early Christianity: Canon and Interpretation in the Light of Modern Research*. WUNT 54. Tübingen: J. C. B. Mohr, 1991.

Evans, Craig A. "From Gospel to Gospel: The Function of Isaiah in the New Testament." Pages 682–91 in *Writing and Reading the Scroll of Isaiah: Studies of an Interpretive Tradition*. Edited by Craig C. Broyles and Craig A. Evans. Vol. 2. VTSup 70. Leiden; New York: Brill, 1997.

Fee, Gordon D. "II Corinthians vi. 14–vii. 1 and Food Offered to Idols." *NTS* 23 (1977): 140–61.

———. *Pauline Christology: An Exegetical-Theological Study*. Peabody, MA: Hendrickson, 2007.

———. *The First Epistle to the Corinthians*. NICNT. Grand Rapids: Eerdmans, 1987.

Fitzmyer, Joseph A. "Qumrân and the Interpolated Paragraph in 2 Cor 6,14–7,1." *CBQ* 23 (1961): 271–80.

———. *Romans: A New Translation and Commentary*. AB 33. New York: Doubleday, 1993.

———. "Use of Explicit Old Testament Quotations in Qumran Literature and in the New Testament." *NTS* 7 (1961): 297–333.

Furnish, Victor Paul. *II Corinthians*. AB 32A. Garden City, NY: Doubleday, 1984.

Gane, Roy. *Leviticus, Numbers*. NIVAC. Grand Rapids: Zondervan, 2004.

Garland, David E. *1 Corinthians*. BECNT. Grand Rapids: Baker Academic, 2003.

———. *2 Corinthians*. NAC 29. Nashville: Broadman & Holman, 1999.

Gärtner, Bertil. *The Temple and the Community in Qumran and the New Testament*. SNTSMS 1. Cambridge: Cambridge University Press, 1965.

Gerstenberger, Erhard S. *Leviticus: A Commentary*. OTL. Louisville: Westminster John Knox, 1996.

Gignilliat, Mark. "2 Corinthians 6:2: Paul's Eschatological 'Now' and Hermeneutical Invitation." *WTJ* 67 (2005): 147–61.

———. *Paul and Isaiah's Servants: Paul's Theological Reading of Isaiah 40–66 in 2 Corinthians 5:14–6:10*. LNTS 330. London: T&T Clark, 2007.

Gnilka, Joachim. "2 Cor 6:14–7:1 in the Light of the Qumran Texts and the Testaments of the Twelve Patriarchs." Pages 48–68 in *Paul and Qumran: Studies in New Testament Exegesis*. Edited by Jerome Murphy-O'Connor. London: G. Chapman, 1968.

Goldingay, John. *Isaiah*. NIBCOT 13. Peabody, MA: Carlisle: Hendrickson; Paternoster, 2001.

———. *The Message of Isaiah 40–55: A Literary-Theological Commentary*. London: T&T Clark, 2005.

Goldingay, John, and David Payne. *A Critical and Exegetical Commentary on Isaiah 40–55*. Vol. 2. ICC. London: T&T Clark, 2005.

Green, Gene L. *The Letters to the Thessalonians*. PNTC. Grand Rapids: Leicester: Eerdmans; Apollos, 2002.

Greenberg, Moshe. *Ezekiel 1–20: A New Translation with Introduction and Commentary*. AB 22. New York: Doubleday, 1983.

———. *Ezekiel 21–37: A New Translation with Introduction and Commentary*. AB 22A. New York: Doubleday, 1997.

Gundry Volf, Judith M. *Paul and Perseverance: Staying In and Falling Away*. Louisville: Westminster John Knox, 1990.

Guntermann, Friedrich. *Die Eschatologie des Hl. Paulus*. NTAbh 13. Münster: Aschendorff, 1932.

Guthrie, George H. *2 Corinthians*. BECNT. Grand Rapids: Baker Academic, 2015.

Hafemann, Scott J. *2 Corinthians*. NIVAC. Grand Rapids: Zondervan, 2000.

———. *Paul, Moses, and the History of Israel: The Letter/Spirit Contrast and the Argument from Scripture in 2 Corinthians 3*. WUNT 2/81. Tübingen: J. C. B. Mohr, 1995.

———. "Paul's Argument from the Old Testament and Christology in 2 Cor 1–9." Pages 277–303 in *The Corinthian Correspondence*. Edited by Reimund Bieringer. BETL 125. Leuven: Leuven University Press; Peeters, 1994.

———. "Paul's Use of the Old Testament in 2 Corinthians." *Int* 52 (1998): 246–57.

———. *Suffering and the Spirit: An Exegetical Study of II Cor. 2:14–3:3 within the Context of the Corinthian Correspondence*. WUNT 2/19. Tübingen: J. C. B. Mohr, 1986.

———. "The Covenant Relationship." Pages 20–65 in *Central Themes in Biblical Theology: Mapping Unity in Diversity*. Edited by Scott J. Hafemann and Paul R. House. Nottingham, England: Apollos, 2007.

Han, Paul. *Swimming in the Sea of Scripture: Paul's Use of the Old Testament in 2 Corinthians 4.7–13.13*. LNTS 519. London: Bloomsbury, 2014.

Harmon, Matthew S. *She Must and Shall Go Free: Paul's Isaianic Gospel in Galatians*. BZNW 168. Berlin; New York: de Gruyter, 2010.

Harris, Murray J. *The Second Epistle to the Corinthians: A Commentary on the Greek Text*. NIGTC. Grand Rapids; Milton Keynes: Eerdmans; Paternoster, 2005.

Hartley, John E. *Leviticus*. WBC 4. Nashville: Thomas Nelson, 1992.

Hayes, Elizabeth R. "The Influence of Ezekiel 37 on 2 Corinthians 6:14–7:1." Pages 123–36 in *The Book of Ezekiel and Its Influence*. Edited by Henk Jan de Jonge and Johannes Tromp. Aldershot; Burlington, VT: Ashgate, 2007.

Hays, Richard B. *Echoes of Scripture in the Letters of Paul*. New Haven: Yale University Press, 1989.

Heil, Christoph. "Die Sprache der Absonderung in 2 Kor 6,17 und bei Paulus." Pages 717–29 in *The Corinthian Correspondence*. Leuven: Leuven University Press, 1996.

Herford, R. Travers. *Talmud and Apocrypha: A Comparative Study of the Jewish Ethical Teaching in the Rabbinical and Non-Rabbinical Sources in the Early Centuries*. London: Soncino, 1933.

Hogeterp, Albert L. A. "Community as a Temple in Paul's Letters: The Case of Cultic Terms in 2 Corinthians 6:14–7:1." Pages 281–95 in *Anthropology and Biblical Studies: Avenues of Approach*. Leiderdorp: Deo, 2004.

———. *Paul and God's Temple: A Historical Interpretation of Cultic Imagery in the Corinthian Correspondence*. BTAS 2. Leuven; Dudley, MA: Peeters, 2006.

———. "The Eschatological Setting of the New Covenant in 2 Cor 3:4–18." Pages 131–44 in *Theologizing in the Corinthian Conflict: Studies in the Exegesis and Theology of 2 Corinthians*. Edited by Reimund Bieringer, Ma. Marilou S. Ibita, Dominika A. Kurek-Chomycz, and Thomas A. Vollmer. BTAS 16. Leuven: Peeters, 2013.

Hollander, Harm W. *Joseph as an Ethical Model in the Testaments of the Twelve Patriarchs*. SVTP 6. Leiden: Brill, 1981.

Hollander, Harm W. and Marinus De Jonge. *The Testaments of the Twelve Patriarchs: A Commentary*. SVTP 8. Leiden: Brill, 1985.

Hubbard, Moyer V. *New Creation in Paul's Letters and Thoughts*. SNTSMS 119. Cambridge; New York: Cambridge University Press, 2002.

Hughes, R. Kent. *2 Corinthians: Power in Weakness*. Wheaton, IL: Crossway, 2006.

Hurtado, Larry *Lord Jesus Christ: Devotion to Jesus in Earliest Christianity*. Grand Rapids: Eerdmans, 2003.

Jackson, T. Ryan. *New Creation in Paul's Letters: A Study of the Historical and Social Setting of a Pauline Concept*. WUNT 2/272. Tübingen: Mohr Siebeck, 2010.

Janzen, J. Gerald. "Rivers in the Desert of Abraham and Sarah and Zion (Isaiah 51:1–3)." *HAR* 10 (1986): 139–55.

Jenson, Robert W. *Ezekiel*. BTCB. Grand Rapids: Brazos, 2009.

Jewett, Robert. *The Redaction of I Corinthians and the Trajectory of the Pauline School*. JAARSup 44. Missoula, MT: American Academy of Religion, 1978.

Johnson, Andy. "The Sanctification of the Imagination in 1 Thessalonians." Pages 275–92 in *Holiness and Ecclesiology in the New Testament*. Edited by Kent E. Brower and Andy Johnson. Grand Rapids; Cambridge, 2007.

Joyce, Paul. *Divine Initiative and Human Response*. JSOTSup 51. Sheffield: JSOT Press, 1989.
Kee, H. C. "Testaments of the Twelve Patriarchs: A New Translation and Introduction." Pages 775–828 in *The Old Testament Pseudepigrapha Vol. 1*. Edited by James H. Charlesworth. 3rd ed. Peabody, MA: Hendrickson, 2013.
Keener, Craig S. *1–2 Corinthians*. NCBC. Cambridge: Cambridge University Press, 2005.
Klinzing, Georg. *Die Umdeutung des Kultus in der Qumrangemeinde und im Neuen Testament*. SUNT 7. Göttingen: Vandenhoeck & Ruprecht, 1971.
Knight, George Angus Fulton. *Servant Theology: A Commentary on the Book of Isaiah 40–55*. ITC. Edinburgh: Handsel, 1984.
Koch, Dietrich-Alex. *Die Schrift als Zeuge des Evangeliums: Untersuchungen zur Verwendung und zum Verständnis der Schrift bei Paulus*. BHT 69. Tübingen: Mohr Siebeck, 1986.
Koch, Klaus. *The Prophets. Vol. 2: The Babylonian and Persian Periods*. London: SCM, 1983.
Koole, Jan Leunis. *Isaiah III*. Vol. 2. HCOT. Leuven: Peeters, 1998.
———. *Isaiah III*. Vol. 3. HCOT. Leuven: Peeters, 2001.
Kreitzer, L. Joseph. *Jesus and God in Paul's Eschatology*. JSNT 19. Sheffield: JSOT Press, 1987.
Krüger, Thomas. "Transformation of History in Ezekiel 20." Pages 159–86 in *Transforming Visions: Transformations of Text, Tradition, and Theology in Ezekiel*. Edited by William A. Tooman and Michael A. Lyons. Cambridge: James Clarke, 2010.
Kugel, James L. *A Walk through Jubilees: Studies in the Book of Jubilees and the World of Its Creation*. JSJSup 156. Leiden; Boston: Brill, 2012.
Kugler, Robert A. *The Testaments of the Twelve Patriarchs*. GAP 10. Sheffield: Sheffield Academic Press, 2001.
Lambrecht, Jan. *Second Corinthians*. SP 8. Collegeville, MN: Liturgical Press, 1999.
———. "The Fragment 2 Cor 6:14–7:1: A Plea for Its Authenticity." Pages 143–61 in *Miscellanea Neotestamentica*. Vol. 2. Leiden: Brill, 1978.
Leene, Henk. "Ezekiel and Jeremiah: Promises of Inner Renewal in Diachronic Perspective." Pages 150–75 in *Past, Present, Future: The Deuteronomistic History and the Prophets*. Edited by Harry F. van Rooy and Johannes Cornelis De Moor. OtSt 44. Leiden; Boston; Kolun: Brill, 2000.
———. "History and Eschatology in Deutero-Isaiah." Pages 223–50 in *Studies in the Book of Isaiah: Festschrift Willem A.M. Beuken*. Edited by Jacque Van Ruiten and Marc Vervenne. BETL 132. Leuven: Leuven University Press; Peeters, 1997.
———. *Newness in Old Testament Prophecy: An Intertextual Study*. OTS 64. Leiden; Boston: Brill, 2014.
Lim, Timothy H. *Holy Scripture in the Qumran Commentaries and Pauline Letters*. Oxford; New York: Clarendon; Oxford University Press, 1977.
Lincicum, David. *Paul and the Early Jewish Encounter with Deuteronomy*. Grand Rapids: Baker Academic, 2010.
Liu, Yulin. *Temple Purity in 1–2 Corinthians*. WUNT 2/343. Tübingen: Mohr Siebeck, 2013.
Longenecker, Bruce W. *2 Esdras*. GAP. Sheffield: Sheffield Academic Press, 1995.
Longenecker, Richard N. *The Epistle to the Romans: A Commentary on the Greek Text*, NIGTC. Grand Rapids: Eerdmans, 2016.
Longman III, Tremper. *The Fear of the Lord Is Wisdom: A Theological Introduction to Wisdom in Israel*. Grand Rapids: Baker Academic, 2017.
Lust, Johan. "Ezekiel 36–40 in the Oldest Greek Manuscript." *CBQ* 43 (1981): 517–33.

Lyons, Michael A. "Transformation of Law: Ezekiel's Use of the Holiness Code (Leviticus 17–26)." Pages 1–32 in *Transforming Visions: Transformations of Text, Tradition, and Theology in Ezekiel*. Edited by William A. Tooman and Michael A. Lyons. Cambridge: James Clarke, 2010.

Mack, Burton L. "Sirach." Page 1378–80 in *The HarperCollins Study Bible*. Edited by Harold W. Attridge and Wayne A. Meeks. Revised ed. San Francisco: Harper One, 2006.

Martin, Ralph P. *2 Corinthians*. 2nd rev. WBC 40. Grand Rapids: Zondervan, 2014.

Matera, Frank J. *II Corinthians: A Commentary*. NTL. Louisville; London: Westminster John Knox, 2003.

McKelvey, R. J. *The New Temple: The Church in the New Testament*. Oxford Theological Monographs. London: Oxford University Press, 1969.

Melugin, Roy F. *The Formation of Isaiah 40–55*. BZAW 141. Berlin; New York: de Gruyter, 1976.

Mettinger, Tryggve N. D. "In Search of the Hidden Structure: YHWH as King in Isaiah 40–55." Pages 143–54 in *Writing and Reading the Scroll of Isaiah*. Vol. 1. Leiden: Brill, 1997.

Metzger, Bruce Manning. "4 Ezra." Pages 517–59 in *The Old Testament Pseudepigrapha Vol. 1*. Edited by James H. Charlesworth. 3rd ed. Peabody, MA: Hendrickson, 2013.

———. *A Textual Commentary on the Greek New Testament: A Comparison Volume to the United Bible Societies' Greek New Testament*. 3rd ed. London: United Bible Societies, 1975.

Michaels, J. Ramsey. *Revelation*. The IVPNTC 20. Downers Grove, IL: InterVarsity Press, 1997.

Milgrom, Jacob. *Leviticus 17–22: A New Translation with Introduction and Commentary*. AB 3A. New York: Doubleday, 2000.

———. *Leviticus 23–27: A New Translation with Introduction and Commentary*. AB 3B. New York: Doubleday, 2001.

Moo, Douglas J. *The Epistle to the Romans*. NICNT. Grand Rapids: Eerdmans, 1996.

Morales, Rodrigo Jose. *The Spirit and the Restoration of Israel: New Exodus and New Creation Motifs in Galatians*. WUNT 2/282. Tübingen: Mohr Siebeck, 2010.

Morris, Leon. *Revelation*. TNTC 20. Downers Grove, IL: InterVarsity Press, 2009.

Motyer, J. Alec. *The Prophecy of Isaiah*. Downers Grove, IL: InterVarsity Press, 1993.

Mounce, Robert H. *The Book of Revelation*. NICNT. Grand Rapids: Eerdmans, 1977.

Moyise, Steve. "Does Paul Respect the Context of His Quotations?" Pages 97–114 in *Paul and Scripture: Extending the Conversation*. Edited by Christopher D. Stanley. Atlanta: SBL Press, 2012.

———. *Paul and Scripture: Studying the New Testament Use of the Old Testament*. Grand Rapids: Baker Academic, 2010.

———. "Quotations" Pages 18–29 in *As It Is Written: Studying Paul's Use of Scripture*. Edited by Stanley E. Porter and Christopher D. Stanley. SBLSymS 50. Atlanta: SBL Press, 2008.

Murphy-O'Connor, Jerome. "Philo and 2 Cor 6:14–7:1." *RB* 95 (1988): 55–69.

———. "Philo and 2 Cor 6:14–7:1." Pages 121–39 in *Keys to Second Corinthians: Revisiting the Major Issues*. Oxford; New York: Oxford University Press, 2010.

———. "Relating 2 Corinthians 6:14–7:1 to Its Context." *NTS* 33 (1987): 272–5.

Nathan, Emmanuel. "Fragmented Theology in 2 Corinthians: The Unsolved Puzzle of 6:14–7:1." Pages 211–28 in *Theologizing in the Corinthian Conflict: Studies in the Exegesis and Theology of 2 Corinthians*. Edited by Bieringer, Reimund, Ma. Marilou S. Ibita, Dominika A. Kurek-Chomycz, and Thomas A. Vollmer. BTAS 16. Leuven: Peeters, 2013.

Newton, Michael. *The Concept of Purity at Qumran and in the Letters of Paul.* SNTSMS 53. Cambridge: Cambridge University Press, 1985.

Nickelsburg, George W. E. *Resurrection, Immortality, and Eternal Life in Intertestamental Judaism and Early Christianity.* Expanded ed. HTS 56. Cambridge, MA; London: Harvard University Press, 2006.

Novenson, Matthew V. *Christ among the Messiahs: Christ Language in Paul and Messiah Language in Ancient Judaism.* New York; Oxford: Oxford University Press, 2012.

Oropeza, B. J. *Exploring Second Corinthians: Death and Life, Hardship and Rivalry.* RRA 3. Atlanta: SBL Press, 2016.

———. *Paul and Apostasy: Eschatology, Perseverance, and Falling Away in the Corinthian Congregation.* WUNT 2/115. Tübingen: Mohr Siebeck, 2000.

Osborne, Grant R. *Revelation.* BECNT. Grand Rapids: Baker Academic, 2002.

Oswalt, John. *The Book of Isaiah.* NICOT. Grand Rapids: Eerdmans, 1998.

Pálfy, Miklós. "Allgemein-Menschliche Beziehungen der Furcht im Alten Testament." Pages 23-7 in *Schalom: Studien zu Glaube und Geschichte Israels: Alfred Jepsen zum 70sten Geburtstag.* Edited by Karl-Heinz Bernhardt. AVTRW. Stuttgart: Calwer Verlag, 1971.

Paul, Shalom M. *Isaiah 40-66: Translation and Commentary.* ECC. Grand Rapids; Cambridge: Eerdmans, 2012.

Philo. *Philo.* Translated by F. H. Colson and G. H. Whitaker. LCL 226-7, 247, 261, 275, 289, 320, 341, 363, 379. Cambridge, MA: Harvard University Press, 2014.

Plath, Siegfried. *Furcht Gottes: Der Begriff Yārā im Alten Testament.* Stuttgart: Calwer Verlag, 1963.

Porter, Stanley E. "Allusions and Echoes." Pages 29-40 in *As It Is Written: Studying Paul's Use of Scripture.* Edited by Stanley E. Porter and Christopher D. Stanley. SBLSymS 50. Atlanta: SBL, 2008.

Porter, Stanley E., and Christopher D. Stanley, eds. *As It Is Written: Studying Paul's Use of Scripture.* SBLSymS 50. Atlanta SBL, 2008.

Rabens, Volker. "Paul's Rhetoric of Demarcation: Separation from 'Unbelievers' (2 Cor 6:14-7:1) in the Corinthian Conflict." Pages 229-54 in *Theologizing in the Corinthian Conflict: Studies in the Exegesis and Theology of 2 Corinthians.* Edited by Reimund Bieringer, Ma. Marilou S. Ibita, Dominika A. Kurek-Chomycz, and Thomas A. Vollmer. BTAS 16. Leuven: Peeters, 2013.

von Rad, Gerhard. *Old Testament Theology: The Theology of Israel's Prophetic Traditions.* Vol. 2. London: SCM, 1975.

Rendtorff, Rolf. *The Covenant Formula: An Exegetical and Theological Investigation.* Edinburgh: T&T Clark, 1998.

Roetzel, Calvin J. *Judgement in the Community: A Study of the Relationship between Eschatology and Ecclesiology in Paul.* Leiden: Brill, 1972.

Rosner, Brian S. "Deuteronomy in 1 and 2 Corinthians." Pages 118-35 in *Deuteronomy in the New Testament: The New Testament and the Scriptures of Israel.* Edited by Steve Moyise and Maarten J. J. Menken. LNTS 358. London; New York: T&T Clark, 2008.

Runge, Steven E. *Discourse Grammar of the Greek New Testament: A Practical Introduction for Teaching and Exegesis.* Peabody, MA: Hendrickson, 2010.

Ruwe, Andreas. *"Heiligkeitsgesetz" und "Priesterschrift": Literaturgeschichtliche und Rechtssystematische Untersuchungen zu Leviticus 17,1-26,2.* FAT 26. Tübingen: Mohr Siebeck, 1999.

Sass, Gerhard. "Noch Einmal: 2 Kor 6,14-7,1: Literarkritische Waffen gegen einen 'Unpaulinischen' Paulus?" *ZNW* 84 (1993): 36-64.

Scheuer, Blaženka. *The Return of YHWH: The Tension between Deliverance and Repentance in Isaiah 40–55*. BZAW 377. Berlin; New York: de Gruyter, 2008.

Schmeller, Thomas. *Der Zweite Brief an die Korinther*. EKK 8. Neukirchen-Vluyn: Ostfildern: Neukirchener Theologie; Patmos-Verlag, 2010.

Schreiner, Thomas R. *Romans*. BECNT. Grand Rapids: Baker Academic, 1998.

Scott, James M. *2 Corinthians*. NIBCNT 8. Peabody, MA: Carlisle: Hendrickson; Paternoster, 1998.

———. *Adoption as Sons of God: An Exegetical Investigation into the Background of ΥΙΟΘΕΣΙΑ in the Pauline Corpus*. WUNT 2/48. Tübingen: J. C. B. Mohr, 1992.

———. "The Use of Scripture in 2 Corinthians 6.16c–18 and Paul's Restoration Theology." *JSNT* 56 (1994): 73–99.

Segal, Michael. *The Book of Jubilees: Rewritten Bible, Redaction, Ideology and Theology*. JSJSup 117. Leiden; Boston: Brill, 2007.

Seifrid, Mark A. *The Second Letter to the Corinthians*. PNTC. Grand Rapids; Nottingham, England: Eerdmans; Apollos, 2014.

Silva, Moisés. "Philippians." Pages 835–9 in *Commentary on the New Testament Use of the Old Testament*. Edited by G. K. Beale and D. A. Carson. Grand Rapids: Baker Academic, 2007.

Smith, D. Moody. "The Pauline Literature." Pages 265–91 in *It Is Written: Scripture Citing Scripture: Essays in Honour of Barnabas Lindars*. Edited by D. A. Carson and H. G. M. Williamson. Cambridge: Cambridge University Press, 1988.

Stanley, Christopher D. *Arguing with Scripture: The Rhetoric of Quotations in the Letters of Paul*. New York: T&T Clark, 2004.

———. "Composite Citations: Retrospect and Prospect." Pages 203–9 in *Composite Citations in Antiquity. Vol. 1*. Edited by Sean A. Adams and Seth M. Ehorn. LNTS 525. London: T&T Clark, 2016.

———. *Paul and the Language of Scripture*. SNTSMS 74. Cambridge: Cambridge University Press, 1992.

———. "Paul's 'Use' of Scripture: Why the Audience Matters." Pages 125–55 in *As It Is Written*. Edited by Stanley E. Porter and Christopher D. Stanley. SBLSymS 50. Atlanta: SBL Press, 2008.

———. "What We Learned—and What We Didn't." Pages 321–30 in *Paul and Scripture: Extending the Conversation*. Edited by Christopher D. Stanley. Atlanta: SBL Press, 2012.

Starling, David I. *Not My People: Gentiles as Exiles in Pauline Hermeneutics*. BZNW 184. Berlin; New York: de Gruyter, 2011.

———. "The Ἄπιστοι of 2 Cor 6:14: Beyond the Impasse." *NovT* 55 (2013): 45–60.

———. "The Yes to All God's Promises: Jesus, Israel and the Promises of God in Paul's Letters." *RTR* 71 (2012): 185–204.

Steck, Odil Hannes. "Jahwes Feinde in Jesaja 59." Pages 187–91 in *Studien zu Tritojesaja*. BZAW 203. Berlin; New York: de Gruyter, 1991.

Steudel, Annette. "God and Belial." Pages 334–40 in *The Dead Sea Scrolls Fifty Years After Their Discovery: Proceedings of the Jerusalem Congress, July 20–25, 1997*. Edited by Lawrence H. Schiffman, Emanuel Tov, James C. VanderKam, and Galen Marquis. Jerusalem: Israel Exploration Society in cooperation with the Shrine of the Book, Israel Museum, 2000.

Stone, Michael Edward. "2 Esdras." Page 1588–89 in *The HarperCollins Study Bible*. Edited by Harold W. Attridge and Wayne A. Meeks. Revised ed. San Francisco: Harper One, 2006.

———. *Fourth Ezra: A Commentary on the Book of Fourth Ezra.* Hermeneia. Minneapolis: Fortress, 1990.

Stuckenbruck, Loren T. "The Demonic World of the Dead Sea Scrolls." Pages 51-70 in *Evil and the Devil*. Edited by Ida Fröhlich and Erkki Koskenniemi. ISCO 481. London: Bloomsbury T&T Clark, 2013.

Swete, Henry Barclay. *An Introduction to the Old Testament in Greek*. Edited by Richard Rusden Ottley. 2nd ed. Cambridge: Cambridge University Press, 1991.

Talbert, Charles H. *Reading Corinthians: A Literary and Theological Commentary on 1 and 2 Corinthians*. New York: Crossroad, 1987.

Thompson, Michael E. W. *Isaiah: Chapters 40-66*. EC. London: Epworth, 2001.

Thrall, Margaret E. *A Critical and Exegetical Commentary on the Second Epistle to the Corinthians: Introduction and Commentary on II Corinthians I-VII.* Vol. 1. ICC. Edinburgh: T&T Clark, 1994.

Thüsing, Wilhelm. *Per Christum in Deum: Studien zum Verhältnis von Christozentrik und Theozentrik in den Paulinischen Hauptbriefen*. 2nd ed. NTAbh 1. Münster: Aschendorff, 1969.

Tigchelaar, Eibert J. C., and Florentino García Martínez, eds. *The Dead Sea Scrolls Study Edition*. Leiden; New York; Grand Rapids: Brill; Eerdmans, 2000.

Tomson, Peter J. "Christ, Belial, and Women: 2 Cor 6:14-7:1 Compared with Ancient Judaism and with the Pauline Corpus." Pages 79-131 in *Second Corinthians in the Perspective of Late Second Temple Judaism*. Edited by Reimund Bieringer. CRINT 14. Leiden; Boston: Brill, 2014.

Tooman, William A. *Gog of Magog: Reuse of Scripture and Compositional Technique in Ezekiel 38-39*. FAT 2/52. Tübingen: Mohr Siebeck, 2011.

Tov, Emmanuel. "The Status of the Masoretic Text in Modern Text Editions of the Hebrew Bible: The Relevance of Canon." Pages 234-51 in *The Canon Debate: On the Origins and Formation of the Bible*. Edited by Lee Martin McDonald and James A. Sanders. Peabody, MA: Hendrickson, 2002.

Trafton, Joseph L. "What Would David Do? Messianic Expectation and Surprise in Ps. Sol. 17." Pages 155-74 in *The Psalms of Solomon: Language, History, Theology*. Edited by Eberhard Bons and Patrick Pouchelle. SBLEJL 40. Atlanta: SBL Press, 2015.

VanderKam, James C. "Recent Scholarship on the Book of Jubilees." *CurBR* 6 (2008): 405-31.

———. *The Book of Jubilees*. GAP. Sheffield: Sheffield Academic Press, 2001.

———. *The Book of Jubilees: A Critical Text*. CSCO 87, 88. Leuven: Peeters, 1989.

Wagner, J. Ross. *Heralds of the Good News: Isaiah and Paul "in Concert" in the Letter to the Romans*. NovTSup 101. Leiden: Brill, 2002.

———. "Working out Salvation: Holiness and Community in Philippians." Pages 257-74 in *Holiness and Ecclesiology in the New Testament*. Edited by Kent E. Brower and Andy Johnson. Grand Rapids; Cambridge: Eerdmans, 2007.

Walker, William O., Jr. "2 Cor 6.14-7.1 and the Chiastic Structure of 6.11-13; 7.2-3." *NTS* 48 (2002): 142-4.

———. *Interpolations in the Pauline Letters*. JSNTSup 213. London: Sheffield Academic Press, 2001.

Wallace, Daniel B. *Greek Grammar beyond the Basics: An Exegetical Syntax of the New Testament*. Grand Rapids: Zondervan, 1996.

Walsh, Jerome T. "Summons to Judgement: A Close Reading of Isaiah XLI 1-20." *VT* 43 (1993): 351-71.

Wanamaker, Charles A. *The Epistles to the Thessalonians: A Commentary on the Greek Text*. NIGTC. Grand Rapids: Eerdmans, 1990.

Ward, Richard F. "Pauline Voice and Presence as Strategic Communication." Pages 95–107 in *Orality and Textuality in Early Christian Literature. Semeia* 65. Atlanta: Scholars, 1995.
Watson, Francis. *Paul and the Hermeneutics of Faith*. London; New York: T&T Clark, 2004.
Webb, William J. *Returning Home: New Covenant and Second Exodus as the Context for 2 Corinthians 6.14–7.1.* JSNTSup 85. Sheffield: JSOT Press, 1993.
Wenham, Gordon J. *The Book of Leviticus*. NICOT. Grand Rapids: Eerdmans, 1979.
Wevers, John William, and U. Quast, eds. *Leviticus*. SVTG v. II, 2. Göttingen: Vandenhoeck & Ruprecht, 1986.
Whybray, Roger Norman. *Isaiah 40–66*. CB. London: Oliphants, 1975.
———. *The Second Isaiah*. OTG 1. Sheffield: JSOT Press, 1983.
Wilk, Florian. *Die Bedeutung des Jesajabuches für Paulus*. FRLANT 179. Göttingen: Vandenhoeck & Ruprecht, 1998.
———. "Gottes Wort und Gottes Verheißungen. Zur Eigenart der Schriftverwendung in 2 Kor 6,14–7,1." Pages 673–96 in *Die Septuaginta – Texte, Kontexte, Lebenswelten: Internationale Fachtagung Veranstaltet von Septuaginta Deutsch (LXX.D), Wuppertal 20.–23. Juli 2006*. Edited by Martin Karrer and Wolfgang Kraus. WUNT 213. Tübingen: Mohr Siebeck, 2008.
———. "Isaiah in 1 and 2 Corinthians." Pages 133–58 in *Isaiah in the New Testament*. London: T&T Clark, 2005.
———. "Paulus als Nutzer, Interpret und Leser des Jesajabuches." Pages 93–116 in *Die Bibel im Dialog*. Tübingen; Basel: Francke, 2005.
Willis, Timothy M. *Leviticus*. AOTC. Nashville: Abingdon, 2009.
Wintermute, O. S. "Jubilees." Pages 35–142 in *The Old Testament Pseudepigrapha Vol. 2*. Edited by James H. Charlesworth. 3rd ed. Peabody, MA: Hendrickson, 2013.
Witherington III, Ben. *1 and 2 Thessalonians: A Socio-Rhetorical Commentary*. Grand Rapids: Eerdmans, 2006.
———. *Conflict and Community in Corinth: A Socio-Rhetorical Commentary on 1 and 2 Corinthians*. Grand Rapids: Carlisle: Eerdmans; Paternoster, 1995.
Wolff, Christian. *Zweite Brief des Paulus an die Korinther*. THKNT 8. Berlin: Evangelische Verlagsanstalt, 1989.
Wright, N. T. *Paul and the Faithfulness of God*. COQG 4. London: SPCK, 2013.
Wright, Robert, ed. *Psalms of Solomon: A Critical Edition of the Greek Text*. JCTCRS 1. London: T&T Clark, 2007.
———. "Psalms of Solomon." Pages 639–70 in *The Old Testament Pseudepigrapha Vol. 2*. Edited by James H. Charlesworth. 3rd ed. Peabody, MA: Hendrickson, 2013.
Yinger, Kent L. *Paul, Judaism, and Judgement according to Deeds*. SNTSMS 105. Cambridge: Cambridge University Press, 1999.
Young, Frances M., and David Ford. *Meaning and Truth in 2 Corinthians*. BFT. London: SPCK, 1987.
Zerwick, Maximilian. *Biblical Greek: Illustrated by Examples*. Scripta Pontificii Instituti Biblici 114. Rome: Scripta Pontificii Instituti Biblici, 1963.
Ziegler, Joseph, ed. *Isaias*. 3rd ed. SVTG 14. Göttingen: Vandenhoeck & Ruprecht, 1983.

BIBLICAL CITATIONS INDEX

Exodus, 6:7, 83n
Leviticus, 78, 79
   26:1-2, 81
   26:11, 85
   26:12, 83
Deuteronomy, 10:12-13, 152
Isaiah
   49:4 LXX, 55
   50:4-11, 65
   50:10, 65n, 68
   50:10-11, 70
   50:10c, 74
   50:10d, 74
   51:1, 74
   51:2, 74
   51:6, 74
   51:7, 74
   51:15-16, 75
   51:17, 75
   52:1, 75
   52:11, 76
   65:22-23 LXX, 56
Jeremiah, 31:31-4, 91
Ezekiel
   36-37, 91
   37:23, 87
   37:26, 93
   37:26-28, 86
   37:27, 85
Romans
   2:16, 35
   3:18, 1n
   12:1-2, 33n
   14:10, 34
1 Corinthians
   2:3, 166
   10:12, 42
2 Corinthians
   2:17, 38
   2:19, 38
   5:9, 33
   5:10, 35n
   5:10-11, 139
   5:11, 30, 31n, 45
   6:1, 40, 139
   6:13, 139
   6:14, 139
   6:14-7:1, 23–24
   6:16b, 85
   6:16d, 85
   6:16de, 85
   7:1, 2, 85, 140, 151
   7:5, 163
   8:5, 48
   8:6, 146
   8:19, 49
   8:21, 49
   10:13, 49
   10:17, 50
   11:3, 166, 167
   11:17, 49
   12:19, 37
   12:20-1, 166, 167
   13:10, 49
Galatians, 3:3, 146
Philippians
   1:6, 146
   2:9-11, 51
   2:10-11, 52
   2:12, 166
Colossians, 4:3, 48
1 Thessalonians, 3:13, 146

GENERAL INDEX

Abraham, 65–66, 105, 107, 109
Adams, Sean A., 12–13
allusions, 15n, 16, 17n
allusive echo, 14–15
apostasy, 41–43
audience, 16–17
Aune, David Edward, 34–35

Beale, G. K., 54, 136–137, 159
Belial, 105–107, 123–125, 126, 128
believers, 10, 38–39, 148, 155. *See also*
        faithful; righteous; unbelievers
Betz, Hans Dieter, 141
Beuken, W.A.M., 69
Bieringer, Reimund, 132
Book of Jubilees, 20–21, 97, 102–111, 128,
      162, 168
    fear of God, 109–111
    judgment of God, 107–109
    similarities between 2 Cor 6:14–7:1
        and, 103–107
Bultmann, Rudolf Karl, 45

Cain, 126
Catena of Scripture
    Isaianic context, 57–63
        Isa 50:4–51:8, 64–67
        Isa 50:10–11, 67–74
        Isa 52:11, 74–77
    Lev 26:11–12, 77–84
    New Covenant, 84–93
        Ezekiel, 85–90, 104
        Jeremiah, 90–92
    semantic relationship between 2 Cor
        7:1 and, 26–30
Christ, 45, 46, 48, 49, 51. *See also* Jesus
cleansing, 143, 145, 149, 150, 157
combined citations, 12
command to separate, 157–159
commands. *See* double commands; doublets
        of promise-command/
        promise imperatives

composite citations, 11–14, 15, 16n, 77–78
condensed citations, 13n
conflated citations, 12
Corinthians
    2 Cor 4–6, Isaianic context of, 53–56
    2 Cor 5:10, judgment seat of Christ in, 45
    2 Cor 5:11, 30–33
        referent of the Lord, 44–53
    2 Cor 6:1, Paul's fear in, 40–44
    2 Cor 6:14–7:1
        command to separate, 157–159
        interpolation theories, 132–135
        past approaches, 138–139
        salvation-historical hermeneutic,
            136–138
        similarities between Book of
            Jubilees and, 103–107
        temple purity, 154–157
    2 Cor 7:1
        argument, 139–151
        cleansing, 143, 145, 149, 150
        completing holiness, 145–150
        defilement, 143–144, 145, 150
        fear of God, 1, 150–151
        flesh and spirit, 144
        immediate context, 23–30
        integrity, 131–139
        promises, 141–143
        semantic relationship between
            Catena of Scripture and,
            26–30
        and Testament of the Twelve
            Patriarchs, 127–128
    2 Cor 7:5–16, fear of God in, 163–166
    2 Cor 11:3 and 12:20–1, fear of God in,
        166–168
    Lord, 33–40
covenant context, 84–93
covenant formula, 82–84

Davila, James R., 113
day of the Lord, 52n

de Jonge, Marinus, 120, 121, 122, 126, 127
defilement, 143–144, 145, 150
deliverance, 61–63
Deuteronomistic literature, 7
Deuteronomy, 7, 151–152, 153
double (twofold) commandment, 121, 122, 123, 126, 127
double commands, 64, 75, 76
doublets of promise-command/promise imperatives, 24, 27–30
Dunn, James D.G., 33n, 35–36

Ehorn, Sean M., 12–13
ethics, 121–125
Exodus event, 83–84. *See also* second-Exodus redemption
Ezekiel, 85–91, 104
Ezra
    4 Ezra, 112–118, 128–129, 130
    6 Ezra, 113–114, 117, 129

faithful, 69–70, 71–72, 75, 76. *See also* believers; righteous
faithless, 69–70, 71–72. *See also* unbelievers; unrighteous
fear of God
    2 Corinthians, 1, 150–151
        argument of 2 Cor 7:1, 139–151
        fear of God in 5:11, 30–33
        fear of God in 7:5–16, 163–166
        fear of God in 11:3 and 12:20–1, 166–168
        immediate context of 2 Cor 7:1, 23–30
        integrity of 2 Cor 7:1, 131–139
        Isaianic context of 2 Cor 4–6, 53–56
        judgment seat of Christ in 2 Cor 5:10, 33–40, 45
        Paul's fear in 2 Cor 6:1, 40–44
        referent of the Lord in 2 Cor 5:11, 44–53
    Catena of Scripture
        Isaianic context, 57–63
            Isa 50:4–51:8, 64–67
            Isa 50:10–11, 67–74
            Isa 52:11, 74–77
            Lev 26:11–12, 77–84
            New Covenant, 84–93
            Ezekiel, 85–90
            Jeremiah, 90–92
    dual understanding, 4
    meaning in the New Testament (NT), 8–10
    meaning in the Old Testament (OT), 6–8
    Paul's eschatology, 151–159
    Second Temple Judaism, 18–19, 95–97, 128–130
        4 Ezra and 6 Ezra, 112–118, 128–130
        Book of Jubilees, 20–21, 97, 102–111, 128, 162, 168
        Psalms of Solomon, 97, 98–102, 128
        Testaments of the Twelve Patriarchs, 118–128, 129
fear of the Lord, 30–33, 38, 39, 45, 139
Fee, Gordon D., 44, 45
Fitzmyer, Joseph A., 134–135
flesh and spirit, 144
fulfilment, 1n
Furnish, Victor Paul, 45

garments, 66
Gignilliat, Mark, 17, 54–55
God as Lord, 45–53
God's deliverance, 61–63
God's judgment. *See* judgment of God
God's sanctuary, 79–80
God's servant, 54–56, 67n, 75
Gundry Volf, Judith M., 41, 43n
Guthrie, George H., 39–40

Hafemann, Scott J., 138, 159
Hayes, Elizabeth, 86
Hays, Richard B., 14–15
holiness, 75–76, 145–150, 155, 156
Hubbard, Moyer, 38
Hurtado, Larry W., 47, 47n

identity, 24–25, 26, 75
imperatives. *See* promise-imperative doublets
"in vain" language, 41–44
interpolation theories, 132–135
intertextual echo, 14–15
Isaianic context, 53–56, 57–63
    Isa 50:4–51:8, 64–67

Isa 50:10-11, 67-74
Isa 52:11, 74-77

Jeremiah, 90-92
Jerusalem, 75
Jesus, 46, 47, 47n, 51. *See also* Christ
judgment of God, 19, 20-21, 38, 44, 58-59, 67, 155
    4 Ezra, 114-117
    Book of Jubilees, 107-109
    Psalms of Solomon, 98-100
judgment seat of Christ, 33-40, 45
judgment seat of God, 34

Kee, H. C., 122
Koch, Dietrich-Alex, 12
Koole, Jan Leunis, 68

Leene, Henk, 89
Leviticus, 77-84
lexicography, 5-10
Lincicum, David, 151-152
Longenecker, Bruce W., 118
Lord
    day of, 52n
    fear of, 30-33, 38, 39, 45, 139. (*see also* fear of God)
    referent of, 44-53
Lyons, Michael A., 88

Macedonians, 48
Martin, Ralph P., 39, 50
Matsema, 106-107, 109-110
metalepsis. *See* allusive echo
methodology, 10-19
Milgrom, Jacob, 82
mixed citations, 12
Moyter, J. Alec, 76

Nestle-Aland, 11
new covenant, 84-93
New Testament (NT), 8-10
Noah, 107
Novum Testamentum Graece, 11

Old Testament (OT)
    meaning of the fear of God, 6-8
    referent of the Lord, 50-53
Oropeza, B. J., 41-43, 42n

Pálfy, Miklós, 6-7
Philo, 125n
Porter, Stanley E., 8-9
promise-imperative doublets, 24, 27-30
promises, 141-143
Psalms of Solomon, 97, 98-102, 128

Qumran writings, 101-102n, 123-124n, 135

redemption, 75
Rendtorff, Rolf, 18, 83
repentance, 62
righteous, 115-116, 118, 165. *See also* believers
Rosner, Brian, 152
Ruwe, Andreas, 79-80

salvation-historical hermeneutic, 136-138
salvation-history, 1n
sanctuary, 79-80
Sarah, 65-66
Sass, Gerhard, 148
Satan, 106
Scheuer, Blaženka, 62-63
Scott, James M., 137-138
Second Temple Judaism, 18-19, 95-97, 128-130
    4 Ezra and 6 Ezra, 112-118, 128-130
    Book of Jubilees, 20-21, 97, 102-111, 128, 162, 168
    fear of God, 109-111
    judgment of God, 107-109
    similarities between 2 Cor 6:14-7:1 and, 103-107
    Psalms of Solomon, 98-102, 128
    Testaments of the Twelve Patriarchs, 118-128, 129
    ethics and the fear of God, 121-125
    and fear of God in 2 Cor 7:1, 127-128
    Jewish and Christian backgrounds, 119-121
    Testament of Benjamin, 122, 125-127
second-Exodus redemption, 137-138
Segal, Michael, 105, 108n, 109
Seifrid, Mark A., 38

separate, command to, 157–159
servants. *See* God's servant
sexual immorality, 156
Shechem, 110
Silva, Moisés, 8
Stanley, Christopher D., 12, 16, 60, 60n
Starling, David I., 157
status quaestionis, 3–5

temple purity, 154–157
Testaments of the Twelve Patriarchs, 118–128, 129
   ethics and the fear of God, 121–125
   and fear of God in 2 Cor 7:1, 127–128
   Jewish and Christian backgrounds, 119–121
   Testament of Benjamin, 122, 125–127
   Testament of Naphtali, 121, 122
thesis outline, 20–21
thesis summary, 19

Thrall, Margaret E., 40
Thüsing, Wilhelm, 36–37
Toomann, William A., 16
transumption. *See* allusive echo
twofold commandment, 121, 122, 123, 126, 127

unbelievers, 10, 23, 139, 157, 158n. *See also* believers; faithless
unrighteous, 115–116, 118. *See also* faithless

VanderKam, James C., 108
vindication, 66
Vorlage(n), 59–60

Walker, William O. Jr., 135
Webb, J., 54
Webb, J. William, 85, 133–134, 137
wisdom literature, 7–8

Lightning Source UK Ltd.
Milton Keynes UK
UKHW022239081222
413461UK00016B/360